Heather— I hope this book provides some answers to your questions. It may cause drowsiness...

Scott Hadley

Co-Employment

Employer Liability Issues in
Third-Party Staffing Arrangements

Sixth Edition

Edward A. Lenz

T0204266

 American Staffing Association

277 S. Washington St., Suite 200
Alexandria, VA 22314-3675

This book is intended as information and not as legal advice. Readers requiring legal or other advice regarding the matters discussed in this book should consult with experienced legal counsel.

American Staffing Association
277 S. Washington St., Suite 200
Alexandria, VA 22314-3675
703-253-2020
703-253-2053 fax
americanstaffing.net

First edition 1992
Second edition 1994
Third edition 1997
Fourth Edition 2000
Fifth Edition 2003
ISBN: 978-0-9714306-1-7
Printed in the United States of America

Library of Congress Cataloging-in-Publication Data

Lenz, Edward A.
  Co-employment : employer liability issues in third-party staffing
  arrangements / Edward A. Lenz.—6th ed.
    p. cm.
  ISBN 978-0-9714306-1-7
1. Employment agencies—Law and legislation—United States. 2.
  Temporary help services—Law and legislation—United States. 3.
  Contract system (Labor)—United States. 4. Employers' liability—United
  States. 5. Third parties (Law)—United States. I. American Staffing
  Association. II. Title.

KF2042.E5L46 2007
344.7301'128—dc22
                                                2007005651

Contents

Acknowledgments

This book was first published in 1992 as a 14-page monograph and was the first, modest, attempt to examine co-employment across the multiple substantive law areas implicated in third-party employment relationships. In 1994, it was published in expanded form in an article in the *Labor Lawyer*, a publication of the American Bar Association section on labor and employment law. Its current size and scope is a reflection of the increased scrutiny by courts and regulators of the subject of co-employment.

Several distinguished private practitioners have contributed to this book over the years. Fred Oliphant, a partner in the employee benefits department of Miller & Chevalier, Chartered, has made material contributions to the discussion of employee benefits; John Irving, of counsel to Kirkland & Ellis LLP, represented the American Staffing Association in the *M.B. Sturgis* case and has advised on a variety of issues discussed in the book. Gerald Maatman, a partner with Seyfarth Shaw LLP, oversaw that firm's review and update of the entire book for the sixth edition. In addition, Stephen Dwyer, ASA deputy general counsel, and Ross Kiser, ASA legislative research coordinator, provided material assistance. ASA director of publications Luanne Crayton and editor Jennifer Silber oversaw all aspects of the book's production and design.

Edward A. Lenz
Alexandria, VA
Sept. 10, 2006

Preface

This book is intended to provide staffing professionals, human resource specialists, and business owners with a concise summary of the specialized legal principles and issues involved in third-party employment relationships. A general familiarity with the tax, benefits, labor, and employment law issues relating to employers is helpful but not essential. This book also is intended as an introduction to the subject and a starting point for further research for lawyers, regulators, and policy makers who may be unfamiliar with the legal issues relating to third-party employment or who do not regularly deal with such issues. All readers will find useful the appendixes, which contain many—sometimes hard-to-find—government publications, policy determinations, and rulings specifically addressing the relationships that are the subject of this book.

As third-party staffing relationships continue to assume an increasingly important role in the American economy, the legal principles relating to those arrangements continue to evolve. This new edition has been revised to reflect significant changes since publication of the fifth edition in 2003.

1

Introduction

In today's workplace, traditional employment relationships are changing. Flexibility is the watchword for both employers and employees. Companies are establishing smaller "core" work forces and supplementing them with part-time and temporary employees in a variety of alternative employment arrangements. Some businesses are outsourcing employer responsibilities under "professional employer" arrangements that often are confused with staffing services. This book examines the various arrangements and how they differ.

The growth of alternative staffing arrangements has raised complex issues regarding the legal relationships between staffing firms, the employees they supply, and the clients that use their services—including the potential liability of clients to the staffing firm's employees.

"Co-employment" is the term often used to refer to the relationship between staffing firms and their clients and to the legal issues that arise from that relationship. This book reviews some of the legal and operational implications of co-employment in a number of important areas such as civil rights, workers' compensation, labor relations, and employee benefits, and other areas affecting the terms and conditions of employment.

Throughout the book, "staffing services" is used as a generic term for a broad range of employment services, including temporary staffing, long-term staffing, placement and recruiting services, and managed services. More specific terms are used when needed for clarity or to distinguish among services in discussions of laws and regulations that may affect them uniquely.

It should be noted that courts and statutes generally do not use the term co-employment to describe the relationships discussed in this book. Among the terms used are "joint employers," "general and special" employers, and "primary and secondary" employers, depending on the subject matter. Although there are technical distinctions among these terms, most people in the staffing industry use co-employment; hence that term is used in this book as a nontechnical, shorthand way of referring to the various relationships and legal issues involved.

2

Staffing Services Defined

The best-known staffing service, temporary staffing, has existed since the 1920s and has experienced major growth in the past decade, both in volume and in the range of services provided. As changes in the work force have taken place, staffing firms have become more sophisticated in the services they provide, becoming partners with their clients to help them manage their human resource needs. The following are brief descriptions of the major staffing services discussed in this book.

Temporary and Contract Staffing

Firms that provide temporary and contract staffing services recruit, train, and test their employees and assign them to clients in a wide range of job categories and skill levels, from production and clerical employees to professional and high-tech employees.[1]

Role of Staffing Firms in Economy

Temporary and contract staffing firms play a vital role in the U.S. economy by providing employment flexibility for employees and businesses. The advantages of temporary work to individuals are widely recognized by employees, businesses, economists, and policy makers. Such work affords flexibility, training, and supplemental income for millions of individuals—and a bridge to permanent employment for those who are out of work, starting out, or changing jobs. A growing number of temporary employees are highly paid and highly skilled accounting, technical, computer, health care, legal, and other professional employees who choose temporary and contract work as a preferred employment option because of the flexibility, independence, and, in some cases, higher pay it allows.

The advantages of temporary work to businesses and the economy are no less significant. The use of temporary and contract staff gives businesses the

---

1. In this section, the term "contract" staffing services describes work performed by higher-skilled employees assigned by staffing firms, especially in the engineering and information technology areas. But "contract services" is sometimes used more broadly to include all types of services provided on an outsourced basis, such as building security, cleaning, landscaping, and cafeteria services. *See, e.g.,* Equal Employment Opportunity Commission Guidelines on Application of EEO Laws to Contingent Workers (Appendix H). The U.S. Bureau of Labor Statistics uses a similarly broad definition of "contract worker" in its analysis of contingent work. See Sharon R. Cohany, *Workers in Alternative Employment Arrangements,* MONTHLY LABOR REVIEW (Oct. 1996) p. 40. From the view of the staffing industry, such services are more accurately described as "managed services," which generally are distinguishable from temporary and contract services, as used in this section, primarily in that the customer does not directly supervise or control the work performed by the contract employees. *See* p. 14.

flexibility to adjust the size of their work force to meet business and economic exigencies quickly and at a predictable cost.[2] In testimony before the Senate Banking Committee in 2000, then-Federal Reserve Board chairman Alan Greenspan cited labor market flexibility as a key factor in innovation and growth of new technologies, resulting in more jobs.[3]

How Staffing Firms Operate

The American Staffing Association defines a "temporary staffing service" as

a service whose business consists primarily of recruiting and hiring its own employees and assigning them to other organizations to support or supplement their work forces; or to provide assistance in special work situations such as employee absences, skill shortages, and seasonal workloads; or to perform special assignments or projects, and that customarily attempts to reassign the employees to other clients when they finish each assignment.

As discussed in Chapter 4, variations of this definition have been adopted in a number of states to exempt temporary staffing services from laws designed to curb employee leasing abuses in the workers' compensation area.[4]

Staffing firms supply employees to every business sector in every job category, from general labor, industrial assembly, and production work to office support and technical, scientific, professional, and managerial positions. Staffing firm services include a wide range of critical human resource functions such as recruiting, skills assessment, skills training and upgrading, risk management, and payroll and benefits administration—allowing clients to concentrate on their core businesses.

Nature of Temporary Work

Temporary work generally is short-term, intermittent, highly variable—and often unpredictable. Many temporary employees work on short-term projects or assignments for multiple clients, often in the same weekly pay period. Some work on successive assignments for the same clients sometimes back-to-back, but often with a break in service between assignments that can vary from

---

2. The Conference Board, HR Executive Review: Contingent Employment (Vol. 3, No. 2, 1995); Peter F. Drucker, They're Not Employees, They're People, Harvard Business Review (2002).

3. U.S. Senate Committee on Banking, Housing, and Urban Affairs, Hearing on the Nomination of Alan Greenspan (Jan. 26, 2000) S. Hrg. 106–526 at p. 21; see also Greenspan, Global Economic Integration: Opportunities and Challenges (Aug. 25, 2000), Remarks at a Symposium Sponsored by the Federal Reserve Bank of Kansas City at pp. 2–3.

4. See, e.g., ARK. STAT. ANN. § 23-92-302; FLA. STAT. ANN. § 468.520; ME. REV. STAT. ANN. tit. 32, ch. 125 § 14051.

a few days to a few months. Clients often give staffing firms and their employees little or no notice that they are ending or extending an assignment.

Staffing firms typically provide their temporary job applicants with explicit notice that work is contingent and that clients have discretion to end assignments at any time. At the same time, staffing firms and their employees do not view the end of an assignment as the end of their relationship with the staffing firm since, in the normal course, the firms assign the employees to other assignments or start looking for other assignments for the employees.

How Temporary Employees Are Paid

Individuals seeking temporary work apply for jobs by completing an application process, either by visiting a staffing firm office or online. With the exception of so-called "day labor" operations (i.e., where work-seekers, usually general laborers, go to a central dispatching location and wait to be assigned to a job), temporary job applicants rarely are dispatched to an assignment from the staffing firm's premises. Instead, after successfully completing the application process, they leave the staffing firm's office and, depending on the availability of assignments, they may wait anywhere from a day to several weeks before being contacted by the staffing firm with an offer of work. Except for day laborers, who generally are transported back to the staffing firm's dispatching location at the end of the day to pick up their paychecks, temporary employees rarely have occasion to return to the staffing firm's premises.

When a staffing firm receives a client order for temporary help, it reviews its applicant database to determine which individual's skills and preferences best match the client's needs. The firm contacts the employee and describes the prospective assignment, the pay rate, and the expected length of assignment. If the individual accepts the assignment, he or she reports directly to work at the client's premises. Upon completion of the assignment—or, in the case of long-term assignments, at the completion of each week of work—the employee's work hours are recorded, verified by the client, and submitted to the staffing firm. The staffing firm uses the record of hours worked to generate employee paychecks and client invoices. Based on the time record, the staffing company pays the employee and bills the client for the services performed. The amount billed covers the employee's wages and benefits, unemployment insurance, and workers' compensation; the staffing firm's selling, general, and administrative expenses; and a profit element. The staffing company's obligation to pay its employees is not dependent on being paid by its clients.

Temporary employees usually are paid weekly by mail. Except for day laborers, who generally are paid daily and in person, payroll and billing are performed early the following week for the work of the prior week. Paychecks are normally mailed in the middle to latter part of the week following the week when the work was performed.

State Regulation of Temporary Staffing

Regulation of temporary and contract staffing services per se is relatively minimal. Three states—Massachusetts, New Jersey, and North Carolina—require temporary staffing firms to register prior to conducting business. Rhode Island imposes bonding and job-notice requirements. Six states—Arizona, Florida, Georgia, Illinois, New Mexico, and Texas—as well as several municipalities have laws governing the provision of unskilled industrial temporary labor, or "day labor." (See Appendix A.)

Part-Time and Temporary Work Distinguished

Temporary and part-time work are sometimes confused. There are two key differences. First, part-time employees always work less than a full-time workweek (i.e., less than 35 hours a week or the number of hours the employer considers to be full time). Second, part-time employees generally work a regular work schedule (e.g., four hours a day, five days a week, or eight hours a day Monday, Wednesday, and Friday). The schedule may be changed, but the employment relationship is an ongoing one and is not *inherently* limited in duration.

In contrast, temporary work generally is sporadic and intermittent and is not governed by a fixed or regular schedule. Temporary assignments are expected to end at some definite point in time, and the parties to the relationship know that at the outset. When temporary employees do work, however, they generally work full-time rather than part-time workweeks.

The second key difference between temporary and part-time work is that part-time employees generally are hired directly by the business for which the services are performed, whereas temporary employees generally are hired by firms that specialize in providing temporary staffing services and are then assigned to the clients of those firms. Of course, some businesses and government agencies hire their own temporary employees directly instead of using an outside firm.

Long-Term Staffing

Many staffing firms also supply employees to work on long-term, indefinite assignments. Employees are recruited, screened, and assigned in essentially the same manner as described previously in the case of temporary employees. Long-term staffing can involve just one or a few individuals, or it can involve a significant portion of the staff required to operate a specific client function on an ongoing basis.

As explained in Chapter 4, co-employment issues may arise under both temporary and long-term staffing arrangements to the extent that the client exercises supervision and control over the employees.

Employee Leasing (Professional Employer Organizations)

The term "employee leasing" is the subject of considerable confusion. It is sometimes used as a generic term to describe all forms of service arrangements involving the furnishing of labor. That is the broad sense in which it is used in the federal tax code. (See Leased Employee Rules in Chapter 4, p. 33.)

But employee leasing also is a distinct business service that does not involve supplying labor but rather offers a human resources outsourcing service in which the leasing firm assumes the legal and the administrative responsibilities of an employer for payroll, benefits, and other employer-related functions on behalf of all or substantially all of another firm's regular, full-time work force.[5]

Unlike staffing firms, employee leasing companies—or "professional employer organizations" (PEOs), as they are now called—do not recruit employees from the general labor market and assign them to their clients. Because they do not supply staff, they are not, strictly speaking, staffing services.

PEO arrangements appeal primarily to small and midsized employers that find it cost-effective to contract out their human resources functions rather than hire in-house staff to perform those functions. PEOs and their clients generally enter into written agreements in which the allocation of employer responsibilities between the PEO and the client are explicitly set forth. PEOs charge a service fee, generally based on a percentage of the client's total payroll costs.

PEOs are subject to significant regulation at the state level. Such regulation has taken two forms: state statutes requiring general licensing or registration of employee leasing organizations, and state regulations dealing specifically with workers' compensation and unemployment insurance. Services of leased employees for the purposes of health and pension benefits are also subject to special treatment under federal tax law. (See Leased Employee Rules in Chapter 4, p. 33.)

At this writing, 29 states have enacted licensing, registration, or other statutes that, among other things, impose financial disclosure and reporting

---

5.   *See* T. Joe Willey, THE BUSINESS OF EMPLOYEE LEASING (2nd ed., 1993).

requirements on employee leasing organizations. In many cases, the leasing industry itself has promoted these laws through the National Association of Professional Employer Organizations, which represents PEOs. States with employee leasing licensing or registration laws are Alabama, Arizona, Arkansas, Florida, Georgia, Idaho, Illinois, Indiana, Kentucky, Louisiana, Maine, Minnesota, Montana, Nevada, New Hampshire, New Jersey, New Mexico, New York, North Carolina, Ohio, Oklahoma, Oregon, Rhode Island, South Carolina, Tennessee, Texas, Utah, Vermont, and Virginia.

Rhode Island has a law requiring that the state division of taxation certify employee leasing companies as having complied with withholding requirements. Idaho has a law establishing guidelines for leasing firms but has no licensing requirement. Georgia has a statute recognizing employee leasing companies as employers and requires them to post a surety bond to cover payroll taxes. State code references to these provisions are presented in Appendix B.

The definition of employee leasing or a PEO under state laws varies, as do the provisions addressing how workers' compensation insurance and unemployment insurance will be provided. Arkansas and Florida, for example, provide that the leasing company is the employer for workers' compensation purposes. Other states, such as Texas, recognize the employee leasing company's employer status but require the client's experience modification to be used for a specified period of time. Utah's statute recognizes only the leasing company *client* as the employer for workers' compensation purposes. Because of these variations, each statute must be carefully reviewed to determine what rules apply in a given state.

As noted in the discussion of workers' compensation (see Special Rules for Employee Leasing Firms in Chapter 4, p. 26), several states also have adopted regulations to prevent so-called "mod-swapping" by requiring employee leasing firms to maintain separate workers' compensation policies for each client.

Tax Status of PEO Defined Contribution Plans

Federal legislation to clarify that PEOs that voluntarily apply for certified PEO status can assume responsibility for employment taxes and employee benefits has been considered for a number of years but has not been enacted.[6]

---

6. *See* Small Business Efficiency Act of 2006 S. 2913, 109th Cong. (2006). The legislation defines a PEO as an entity that enters into a service contract covering at least 85% of the client employees at a work site and pursuant to which it assumes responsibility—without regard to receipt or adequacy of payment from the client—for paying wages; reporting, withholding, and paying employment taxes; and paying any employee benefits required under the contract; on a shared basis with the client, the firing of workers and the recruiting and hiring of any new workers; and maintaining employee records. To become certified, a PEO must, among other things, satisfy IRS background requirements with respect to tax status, experience, business location, and financial condition; post a bond; and

After deferring action for several years, in the expectation that Congress might deal with the issue, the Internal Revenue Service issued Revenue Procedure 2002-21 to provide guidance to PEOs on the tax status of the defined-contribution retirement plans they maintain for employees covered under such arrangements. The guidance outlines the steps that PEOs can take to ensure that their 401(k) or other defined-contribution plan remains tax qualified.

The guidance was issued because of ongoing uncertainty about whether, under common-law principles, PEOs are employers of the employees covered under PEO 401(k) plans. Employer status is a critical issue because the Internal Revenue Code requires as one condition of tax qualification that retirement plans be maintained for the "exclusive benefit of employees."[7] If a PEO cannot establish that it employs the employees covered under its plan, the plan could lose its tax-qualified status, resulting in taxes and possible penalties to the PEO and the loss of tax benefits to the employees. The guidance establishes procedures that allow PEOs to avoid having a 401(k) or other defined-contribution retirement plan that covers work site employees disqualified for violating the exclusive benefit rule.

The IRS gives any PEO that has such a retirement plan the option of either converting it to a "multiple-employer" plan (under which each PEO client with employees covered by the plan must sign on as plan cosponsors if it wants its employees to stay in the plan) or terminating the plan according to the procedures specified in the guidance.

A PEO must decide which option to elect with respect to a defined contribution retirement plan, and notify its clients of its decision, within 120 days after the first day of the plan year beginning on or after Jan. 1, 2003, or, in the case of a calendar year plan, by May 2, 2003. Once an option is elected, the PEO generally must complete the steps required under that option by the last day of the first plan year beginning on or after Jan. 1, 2003, or, for a calendar year plan, by Dec. 31, 2003.

It should be noted that most laws and regulations enacted so far define "employee leasing" quite broadly. Potentially, such laws could be construed to cover non-PEO staffing arrangements involving employees on long-term, indefinite assignments. Although these laws generally have been narrowly construed, it is important to be aware of how and for what purpose employee leasing is defined in a particular jurisdiction.

---

meet certain independent financial review requirements on an ongoing basis. The bill stops short of declaring PEOs to be employers. In fact, it expressly disclaims any intent to resolve that basic issue, leaving PEOs' right to assume employer obligations, other than for federal employment tax and benefits purposes, subject to interpretation.

7. I.R.C. § 401(a)(2).

Payrolling

Many staffing firms offer a service sometimes referred to as "payrolling." Here, the client, not the staffing firm, recruits employees but asks the staffing firm to hire people and assign them to perform services for the client—for example, when the client has specialized needs and is in the best position to screen applicants for the required skills. Another form of payrolling involves individuals employed by the client whom the customer places on the payroll of the staffing firm. For example, an employee near retirement may be working on a project that is expected to continue beyond his or her scheduled retirement date. The employee can be payrolled until the project is completed without disrupting the normal retirement schedule.

Payrolling is distinguishable from employee leasing if the individuals are on temporary assignments or projects and the arrangement does not involve a substantial percentage of the client's total work force or the employees at a particular work site. But it may be considered employee leasing under the federal and state laws discussed above if the employees work on a long-term, ongoing basis.

Managed Services

Managed services, a form of outsourcing sometimes called facilities management, are services provided by an organization that has expertise in operating a specific client function. The firm contracts with the client not just to provide and supervise staff (as in temporary and long-term staffing), but to take full operational responsibility for performing the function—generally peripheral to the client's core business—on an ongoing basis. Examples include operating a mailroom or data processing center or supplying cafeteria, landscaping, guard, or maintenance and janitorial services. As discussed in Chapter 3, co-employment issues should be minimal under such arrangements because the client generally does not supervise or control the details of the work performed by the contractor's employees.

Managed services are distinguishable from PEO services in that PEOs do not assume operational responsibilities, and PEO clients retain day-to-day control over the work performed by employees.

Recruiting and Placement Services

Recruiting and placement services are services provided by employment agencies and executive recruiting firms that, for a fee, bring together potential employers (i.e., their clients) and job seekers for the purpose of establishing a regular, full-time employment relationship between the client and the job seeker. A significant number of states require employment agencies to be licensed.

Those laws and regulations are beyond the scope of this book. Because recruiting and placement firms do not involve employment by the recruiting and placement firm of the individuals who are placed, no co-employment issues arise.

Temporary-to-Hire

A growing staffing service, often called temporary-to-hire, combines elements of both temporary staffing and placement services. Because staffing firms have a high level of expertise in recruiting, screening, and training, many businesses are turning to them to help recruit and place individuals in full-time positions. Under these arrangements, the client asks the staffing firm to recruit individuals who may be interested in permanent employment and to assign them to the client for a trial period during which both the client and the potential employee can evaluate the relationship. The client often is given an opportunity to screen candidates before their assignment for a trial period. The U.S. Department of Labor has characterized the practice of first auditioning permanent employee candidates as temporary employees as the fastest-growing segment of the staffing industry.[8]

During the trial period, the staffing firm employs the individual in the same manner as in any other temporary assignment and pays all wages, benefits, and statutory insurance coverage. If the client and the temporary employee agree to enter into a full-time employment relationship, the individual and the staffing firm terminate their relationship. Termination may occur immediately after the client decides to hire the individual, in which case the client generally pays the staffing firm an additional fee as consideration for the successful placement. Alternatively, clients are often given the option of maintaining the individual on the staffing firm's payroll for a specified period of time after the hiring decision, at the end of which the client hires the individual at no additional fee. Unlike traditional employment agency and recruiting arrangements, in which applicants may or may not be charged a fee, temporary-to-hire arrangements do not involve charging individuals a fee.

With respect to the temporary employment component of these services, all of the co-employment issues discussed in this book may come into play. Indeed, to the extent the client becomes more intimately involved in the recruiting, screening, and wage-setting processes, it may increase the likelihood that the client will be considered a co-employer in cases in which issues of client control are deemed relevant. Ensuring that the staffing firm does not relinquish

---

8. *See* "Just-in-Time" Inventories and Labor: A Study of Two Industries, 1990–1998, Report on the American Workforce, U.S. Dept. of Labor (1999), p. 24. Washington, DC: U.S. Government Printing Office.

its status as an employer is especially important as the client's employer activities increase (see Chapter 5, p. 85). The addition of a recruiting and placement service component may also bring into play the laws and regulations that apply to employment agencies—requirements that do not apply to temporary staffing services standing alone.

Independent Contractors

The subject of independent contractors, in particular the legal rules for distinguishing them from employees, is beyond the scope of this book. These rules are complex and have led to confusion and uncertainty about how employees should be classified. The great majority of individuals assigned by staffing firms are classified by the staffing firms as employees. Most employees assigned under staffing arrangements perform their work under the supervision and control of either the staffing firm or the client, and the work performed generally is of a nature that does not require the employee to exercise a substantial degree of independent judgment. Hence, employees assigned by staffing firms generally can properly be classified only as employees under current law.

With the growth of the professional and technical segments of the staffing industry, however, it is not unusual to find staffing arrangements in which employees assigned in higher skill categories are classified as independent contractors. The federal tax code contains special provisions relating to the classification of technical services employees for income and employment-tax purposes. These rules are discussed in the section on Employment Taxes (Chapter 4, p. 27).

It is important to remember that the legal principles designed to distinguish between employees and independent contractors do not address the more difficult question from the perspective of the staffing industry: Assuming an employee should be classified as an employee, who is the employer—the staffing firm, the customer, or both? That is the basic question addressed in this book.

3

Co-Employment Defined

Simply defined, co-employment is a commercial relationship between two or more businesses in which each has actual or potential legal rights and obligations as an employer with respect to the same employee or group of employees.

Employers have myriad legal obligations to their employees. These include providing wages and benefits, paying and withholding employment taxes, providing workers' compensation insurance, complying with civil rights and labor laws, and maintaining a safe work environment. Employers also may have obligations to third parties under the legal principle of *respondeat superior* if employees' work-related activity causes harm to others.

The law imposes employer duties on an entity whenever the facts and circumstances establish a sufficient connection with a worker to warrant imposing a legal duty to the worker. Staffing firms and their clients often have enough contact with assigned employees that *each* will be viewed as an employer. The staffing company pays the employee, pays and withholds payroll taxes, provides workers' compensation coverage, has the right to hire and fire, hears and acts on complaints from the employee about working conditions, and so forth. Clients generally supervise and direct the employees' day-to-day work, control conditions at the work site, and determine the length of the assignment. Thus, in most staffing arrangements, co-employment is an *inherent* aspect of the relationship between the staffing firm and its clients.

The precedents discussed in Chapter 4 show that the liability arising from a co-employment relationship generally is not "joint and several," that is, one employer generally cannot be held vicariously liable for the wrongful acts or omissions of the other without regard to fault. Instead, each employer simply has whatever liability arises as a consequences of its own relationship with or actions toward employees. For example, a client can be held liable under the civil rights laws if it unlawfully discriminates against a staffing firm's employee. However, in one key area—workers' compensation—the client's co-employer status may *protect* it from liability.

4

Laws and Regulations

For the purposes of this book, the statutes and regulations dealing with co-employment, as well as related court cases, administrative rulings, and policy decisions, have been grouped into two broad categories: (1) compensation and benefits, and (2) employment practices. In general, liability for compensation and benefits is governed primarily by the operational relationship between the individual and the employer (e.g., the degree of direction and control over the employee, and the nature of any agreements). Liability for employment practices is governed both by the structure of the working relationship and by the employer's action or inaction as it affects the employee (e.g., unlawful discrimination and unsafe working conditions).

Compensation and Benefits

Workers' Compensation

The quintessential co-employment issue involves workers' compensation insurance. It has the longest legal pedigree and is by far the area most discussed by the courts. Ironically, it is also the one area in which clients may benefit from being a co-employer with their staffing firm because, in most states, that status protects them from tort liability for workplace injuries sustained by a staffing firm's employees.

General Employers and Special Employers

As every employer knows, state workers' compensation laws provide benefits on a no-fault basis to employees accidentally injured on the job. The basic premise of these laws is that, in return for such protection, employees are barred from suing their employer for damages. In other words, workers' compensation generally is the employee's *exclusive remedy* for workplace injuries.

Application of Exclusive Remedy Rule

In a long line of cases, courts in most jurisdictions have extended the exclusive remedy provisions of state workers' compensation laws to clients of temporary staffing firms. In reaching this conclusion, courts have applied the common-law "loaned" (or "borrowed") employee doctrine, under which the client is viewed as a special employer (the staffing firm being the general employer) of the loaned worker. At least 13 states have codified this principle in their state statutes.[9] (For a listing of court cases and statutes by state, see Appendix C.)

The key elements in establishing a client's special employer status are that the client supervises the individual's work; the assigned employee has consented to the arrangement, and the work is essentially that of the client. All three elements generally can be established in the typical staffing arrangement. Thus, the exclusive remedy defense is usually available to clients in suits brought against them by staffing firm employees for negligence in work site injury cases. The defense will not, however, protect a client that injures an employee intentionally. It also may not protect clients whose written contracts with staffing firms expressly disclaim any employment relationship with employees assigned to them[10] or clients with managed services arrangements (see Chapter 2, p. 14) in which they have no day-to-day control over workers' activities.

Some states have, in certain circumstances, allowed employees of a contractor to bring suit against a client for damages beyond the workers' compensation award.[11] In some cases, courts have distinguished contracts in which a contractor performs a specific function for a client from a temporary service that merely loans its employees to the client, holding that employees who are controlled by the client and perform its work are loaned employees who cannot sue the client for negligence.[12] Some courts have denied a temporary employee's claim against a client based on the negligence of the client's employee where the client's payment to the staffing firm included an amount for workers' compensation coverage.[13]

It should be noted that even in cases where the employee is allowed to sue the client, staffing firms still could protect the client through contractual indemnification provisions backed by adequate liability insurance coverage.

---

9. *See* ALA. CODE § 25-14-9; FLA. STAT. ANN. § 440.11(2); GA. CODE ANN. § 34-9-11; IDAHO CODE § 72-103; ME. REV. STAT. ANN. tit. 39-A §104; MONT. CODE ANN. § 39-8-207(8)(b) (applies to professional employer organizations only); N.D. CENT. CODE § 65-01-08(2); OR. REV. STAT. § 656.018(5)(b); CONSOL. LAWS OF N.Y. ANN. § 922; R.I. GEN. LAWS § 28-29-2(6); UTAH CODE ANN. § 34A-2-105; VA. CODE ANN. § 65.2-803.1; WIS. STAT. ANN. § 102.29(6).

10. *See, e.g.,* Parson v. Procter & Gamble, 514 N.W.2d 891 (Iowa 1994); Swanson v. White Consolidated Industries Inc., 77 F.3d 223 (8th Cir. 1996); cf. M.J. Daly Co. v. Varney, 695 S.W.2d 400 (Ky. 1985) (temporary employee expressly refused employment with client).

11. *See, e.g.,* Pate v. Marathon Steel Co., 777 P.2d 428 (Utah 1989); Runcorn v. Shearer Lumber Products Inc., 107 Idaho 389, 690 P.2d 324 (Idaho 1984); Card v. Curtis Prunty, No. 91946 (4th District, Idaho, Nov. 21, 1989). Cf., Koch Refining Co. v. Chapa, 11 S.W.3d 153 (Tex. 1999) (leasing firm employee assigned to contractor may not sue client/premises owner for workplace injuries when client did not have right to control worker); Hittel v. WOTCO, 996 P.2d 673 (Wyo. 2000) (staffing firm employee assigned to contractor may not sue client/premises owner for workplace injuries when client retained no right to control work site safety); Smith v. Wal-Mart Stores East, 2005 WL 2243355 (W.D.Ky. Sept. 14, 2005) (federal court said staffing firm worker assigned to cellular company's kiosk in department store can sue store for workplace injuries because cellular company was not a subcontractor of store).

12. Lines v. Idaho Forest Industries, 872 P.2d 725 (Idaho 1994).

13. Ghersi v. Salazar, 883 P.2d 1352 (Utah 1994); Walker v. U.S. General, 916 P.2d 903 (Utah 1996).

Client as Statutory Employer—Alternate Employer Endorsement

Some states hold clients directly liable to staffing company employees for the payment of workers' compensation benefits, even when the staffing company has expressly agreed to provide coverage. This requirement is based on strict application of the common-law rule that the employer that directs an employee's activities at the work site is the employer and therefore must be the employer for workers' compensation purposes.[14] In these states, staffing companies should ensure that their workers' compensation policies contain a temporary service contractor or alternate employer endorsement. These endorsements require the staffing firm's carrier to provide benefits directly to clients in the event that state law prevents payment of benefits to the employee. They also preclude the staffing firm's carrier from seeking reimbursement from the client's carrier.

Note that in states where the client is viewed as the sole employer for workers' compensation, the staffing company may be exposed to liability for negligence if sued by its own workers injured on the job because it cannot claim immunity as an employer.[15] But most states treat both clients and staffing companies as employers for workers' compensation purposes.[16]

Fellow Employee Rule

In addition to protecting employers from tort liability, most state workers' compensation statutes protect fellow employees from suing each other for job-related injuries. (See *6 Larson's Worker's Compensation Law*, Ch. 111.) For example, a temporary employee who negligently injures a client's employee on the job generally cannot be sued by the client's employee because the temporary worker is a special employee of the client and therefore a fellow employee of the client's employee. The question is whether the client's employee has any recourse against the staffing firm.

A number of courts have allowed a client employee to sue a staffing firm on the ground that there was no employment relationship between the staffing firm and the client's employee, and therefore the staffing firm is not immune from

---

14. *See, e.g.*, Virginia Polytechnic Institute and State Univ. v. Frye, 6 Va. App. 589, 371 S.E.2d 34 (Va. Ct. App. 1988); English v. Lehigh County Authority, 286 Pa. Super. 312, 428 A.2d 1343 (Pa. Super. Ct. 1981); JFC Temps Inc. v. Workmen's Compensation Appeal Board, 545 Pa. 149, 680 A.2d 862 (Pa. 1996); Shaw v. Thrift Drug, No. A98-5170, 1999 WL 994020 (E.D. Pa. Nov. 2, 1999); Kappas v. Andritz, 45 Pa. D. & C. 4th 288 (Pa. Com. Pl. March 17, 2000), *aff'd without op.* 769 A.2d 1215 (Pa. Super. 2000), *cert. denied* 566 Pa. 665, 782 A.2d 547 (Pa. 2001).

15. *See, e.g.*, Kappas, supra note 14.

16. *See, e.g.*, Wingfoot Enterprises v. Alvarado, 111 S.W.3d 134 (2003). For a complete discussion of dual employment issues in the area of workers' compensation insurance, *see* A. LARSON, 3 LARSON'S WORKERS' COMPENSATION LAW, § 67-68 (2001).

suit.[17] But to recover damages from the staffing firm in such cases, the client employee must show that the staffing firm is liable under the principle of *respondeat superior* (i.e., that the staffing firm had a right to control its temporary employee's activities at the work site or that the employee was performing work primarily for the staffing firm, not the client). This burden may be more difficult to meet in some states[18] than in others.[19] At least one court has held, however, that a staffing firm automatically enjoys the same immunity conferred on its employees and therefore cannot be sued by a client's employees.[20] In 1999, North Dakota codified protection for staffing firms against suits by employees of the client.[21]

Waivers of Client Liability

Courts in Arkansas and Massachusetts have upheld the validity of waivers executed by staffing firm workers in which the workers gave up their rights to sue any client for injuries covered by state workers' compensation laws.[22] In these states, a properly drafted and executed waiver may protect clients from liability for workplace injuries caused by negligence. Waivers may be viable in other states, and staffing firms should consult with legal counsel regarding their use.

Special Rules for Employee Leasing Firms

Specific state regulations may apply to employee leasing firms with respect to workers' compensation liability. In response to abuses involving employers transferring their employees to leasing company payrolls to avoid high experi-

---

17. *See, e.g.,* Marsh v. Tilley, 26 Cal. 3d 486, 606 P.2d 355, 162 Cal. Rptr. 320 (Cal. 1980); Kenyon v. Second Precinct Lounge, 177 Mich. App. 482, 442 N.W.2d 696 (Mich. Ct. App. 1989); Kunz v. Beneficial Temporaries, 921 P.2d 456 (Utah 1996); Morgan v. ABC Manufacturer, 710 So. 2d 1077 (La. 1998); Butts v. Express Personnel Services, 73 S.W.3d 825 (2002) (a Manpower employee injured by an Express Personnel employee was able to sue Express because no employment relationship existed between the two workers). *See* also, Warr v. QPS Companies Inc. 2206 WL 3783124 (Wisc. App.).

18. Kunz, *supra* note 17.

19. Cf. Bright v. Cargill, 251 Kan. 387, 837 P.2d 348 (Kan. 1992); Alvarado v. Ursua, No. B172601, 2005 WL 1125180 (Cal. App. 2 Dist. May 13, 2005). Not Reported in Cal.Rptr.3d. (California court of appeals held that staffing firm could be liable for injury caused by its temporary employee because it retained partial control over employee but dismissed claim because he was a fellow employee of the injured employee and therefore immune from liability under state law.) But employees of two different subcontractors may not be considered co-employees even if they share the same special employer. *See* Street v. Alpha Construction Services 143 P.3d (NM Ct. App. 2006) Cert. granted Sept. 21, 2006.

20. Parker v. Williams & Madjanik, 269 S.C. 662, 239 S.E.2d 487 (S.C. 1977).

21. N.D. CENT. CODE. § 65-01-08(2).

22. Horner v. Boston Edison Co., 45 Mass. App. Ct. 139, 695 N.E.2d 1093 (Mass. App. Ct.), *cert. denied,* 428 Mass. 1104 (Mass. 1998); Edgin v. Entergy Operations, 331 Ark. 162, 961 S.W.2d 724 (Ark. 1998). In Swisher v. Caterpillar Inc., 65 Pa. D. & C.4th 32 (Pa.Com.Pl. Dec 23, 2003), a Pennsylvania court relied on Horner and Edgin to find that a staffing firm worker who signed a waiver gave up his right to sue any client of the staffing firm, but an appellate court reversed without comment, Swisher v. Caterpillar, 888 A.2d 19 (Pa.Super. Sep 06, 2005) (TABLE, NO. 55 MDA 2004), and the Pennsylvania Supreme Court refused to hear the matter, Swisher v. Caterpillar Inc., 902 A.2d 1242 (Pa. Jun 30, 2006) (TABLE, NO. 869 MAL 2005).

ence modifications, the National Association of Insurance Commissioners and the National Council on Compensation Insurance have adopted model regulations that have been adopted in many states. Information on these regulations is available at the NCCI Web site, *ncci.com.*

Employers considering participation in an employee leasing arrangement should check with their state workers' compensation department to determine how such an arrangement will be treated for workers' compensation purposes. Most employee-leasing licensing and registration laws provide that a leasing firm and its clients are protected from injury suits by the workers' compensation exclusive remedy rule.

Unemployment Insurance

Staffing firms are generally recognized as the employer for unemployment insurance purposes. In Arizona, clients of temporary staffing firms can be held jointly liable as co-employers for any unpaid unemployment insurance premiums. Rhode Island holds clients jointly liable for certain employment taxes if they use the services of a staffing firm that is not certified with the state tax department.[23]

Thirty-six states have special unemployment insurance rules for employee leasing organizations (see Appendix B). Some provisions expressly recognize the employer status of employee leasing companies (professional employer organizations, or PEOs) and temporary staffing firms for unemployment insurance purposes,[24] which means that claims filed by leased employees will be charged to PEOs or staffing firms, not their clients. In some states (e.g., Delaware, Illinois, Kentucky, Mississippi), the rules expressly *deny* employer status to employee leasing firms.

In Minnesota, Missouri, and Nebraska, clients of employee leasing firms can be held jointly liable as co-employers for any unpaid unemployment insurance premiums.[25] Clients in these states can protect themselves by dealing with reputable, financially sound firms—good advice when using any outside service. (For state statutes and administrative code references to these provisions, see Appendix B.)

Employment Taxes

Liability for employment taxes is one area in which staffing firms have generally been viewed as the *sole* employer, even in cases where clients direct the employees' activities at the work site, provided they are viewed as controlling the payment of wages.

---

23. R.I. GEN. LAWS § 44-30-71.4.

24. *See, e.g.,* ALA. CODE § 25-14-9; ARIZ. REV. STAT. ANN. § 23-614; CAL. UNEMP. INS. CODE § 606.5; N.D. CODE § 52-04-24; UTAH CODE ANN. § 35A-4-202.

25. *See* MO. REV. STAT. § 288.032; MINN. STAT. § 268.065; NEB. REV. STAT. § 48-648.

As employers, staffing firms pay their employees' wages and all employment taxes. They pay the employer's share of Social Security (Federal Insurance Contributions Act—FICA) and federal unemployment taxes (Federal Unemployment Tax Act—FUTA). When they are viewed as the common law employer or the party controlling the payment of wages, staffing firms have been expressly recognized by the courts and by the Internal Revenue Service as employers for employment-tax purposes.[26] Moreover, clients generally should not be held liable as co-employers, even if staffing firms default on their obligation to withhold taxes. But some courts, in considering client arrangements with a PEO or staff leasing firm, have questioned the client's ability to avoid liability if the tax withholdings are not paid by such firms.[27]

A case supporting the exclusive liability of staffing firms for employment taxes is *General Motors Corporation v. United States*.[28] GM contracted with a technical services staffing firm to supply it with design engineers. Neither GM nor the staffing firm paid employment taxes for the staffing firm's workers. The IRS assessed both firms for the taxes owed. GM paid under protest and filed suit for a refund. In its motion for summary judgment, GM argued that it had no obligation to withhold taxes because it did "not have control of the payment of the wages" within the meaning of section 3401(d) of the IRS code. The IRS replied that GM controlled the workers on the job and that the staffing firm was no more than a "disbursing agent." Citing the Supreme Court's decision in *Otte v. United States*,[29] the U.S. District Court for the Eastern District of Michigan held that "the responsibility for withholding employment taxes is directed toward the person who pays the workers *and not the person who has control over the workers' duties*" (emphasis added). The court found no evidence that GM was responsible for making payments to the staffing firm's employees, and that its only responsibility "was to make payments to [the staffing firm] pursuant to services rendered under the contract." Although the court found that the staffing firm's responsibilities to the workers were much more than those of a "disbursing agent," whether GM or the staffing firm controlled the workers at the job site was deemed irrelevant.

---

26. *See, e.g.*, General Motors Corp. v. United States, 91-1 U.S. Tax Cas. (CCH) ¶ 50,032 (E.D. Mich. Dec. 20, 1990); *In re* Critical Care Support Services Inc., 138 Bankr. 378 (Bankr. E.D.N.Y. 1992); Rev. Rul. 75-41, 1975-1 C.B. 323.

27. *See* United States v. Garami dba Tidy Maid, 184 Bankr. 834 (M.D. Fla. 1995) (client of employee leasing firm held liable for employment taxes where leasing firm held to be performing mere "administrative acts" and client provided no proof of payment of taxes by leasing firm); *See also In re* Earthmovers Inc., 199 Bankr. 62 (Bankr. M.D. Fla. 1996).

28. General Motors Corp., *supra* note 26.

29. Otte v. United States, 419 U.S. 43, 50 (1974).

Independent Contractor Issues

Staffing firms that send their employees out as "independent contractors" to avoid paying employment taxes and workers' compensation and unemployment insurance expose themselves, and possibly their clients, to liability if the workers assigned do not meet IRS or U.S. Department of Labor definitions of independent contractors.[30]

Over the years, the IRS and the Social Security Administration have compiled a list of 20 factors used in court decisions to determine worker status for federal employment tax purposes. (See Revenue Ruling 87-41, 1987-1 C.B. 296 in Appendix D). According to the IRS, the 20-factor test is an analytical tool, not the legal test for determining worker status. The legal test is whether there is a right to direct and control the means and details of the work.

In 1978, Congress enacted section 530 of the Revenue Act of 1978, which provides "safe harbor" protection to taxpayers that classify employees as independent contractors for employment tax purposes, even if they cannot meet the 20-factor common-law worker classification test, provided there is a reasonable basis for such treatment and the taxpayers meet certain consistency and reporting requirements. A reasonable basis for treating an employee as an independent contractor exists if the taxpayer reasonably relies on published rulings or judicial precedent, past IRS audits of the taxpayer, longstanding practice of a significant segment of the industry, or some other reasonable basis.

The Small Business Job Protection Act of 1996 modified the section 530 safe harbor rules. Some of the changes make it easier for taxpayers to defend their classification of workers as independent contractors. Some, however, make it harder.

For example, one provision that makes it easier for employers to defend their classification of workers shifts the legal burden of proof to the IRS if the taxpayer establishes a *prima facie* case—based on published rulings or cases, a prior IRS audit, or industry practice—that it was reasonable not to treat a worker as an employee. Furthermore, a worker no longer has to first be determined to be an employee under the 20-factor common-law test before section 530 can be applied. In addition, the industry-practice safe harbor rules were liberalized by providing that the taxpayer's classification practice need not be followed by more than 25% of the industry. A lower percentage may suffice, although the act does not specify it. Moreover, the industry practice need not have been in effect before 1978, as required under the old rule.

---

30. *See, e.g.,* TAX ADMINISTRATION, U.S. GENERAL ACCOUNTING OFFICE, INFORMATION RETURNS CAN BE USED TO IDENTIFY EMPLOYERS WHO MISCLASSIFY WORKERS, GAO/GGD-89-107, at 14 (Sept. 1989); Brock v. Superior Care, 840 F.2d 1054 (2d Cir. 1988).

However, the 1996 law makes it harder for employers to claim protection under the "past audit" safe harbor. Employers seeking to rely on audits after 1996 now have to show that the past audit specifically included an examination (without a resulting assessment) of whether the worker (or a person holding a substantially similar position) should have been treated as an employee or an independent contractor for employment tax purposes.

Application of Section 530 to Technical Services

Section 1706 of the 1986 Tax Reform Act provides that section 530 does not apply to staffing firms that provide the services of an "engineer, designer, drafter, computer programmer, systems analyst, or other similarly skilled worker engaged in a similar line of work."[31] Under this exception, individuals who are retained by firms and who provide technical services will be classified for income and employment tax purposes as employees or independent contractors under the common-law test, without regard to the safe harbor provisions of section 530.

IRS Classification Guidelines

At the same time that Congress enacted the section 530 changes, the IRS issued new guidelines to its audit staff on the issue of worker classification. In a July 15, 1996, memo, IRS commissioner Margaret Miner Richardson pledged that in future training of auditors, the IRS would "assure that both businesses and workers, whether under the withholding rules or under the rules governing the self-employed, pay the proper amount of taxes." In other words, there should be no bias in favor of either employee or independent contractor status. Rather, she wrote, "The examiner has a responsibility to the taxpayer and to the government to determine the correct tax liability and to maintain a fair and impartial attitude in all matters relating to the examination."

Although legislation has been introduced in recent years to modify the criteria used to classify workers for employment tax purposes, the IRS audit training manual continues to rely on the traditional common-law standard, which focuses on the right to direct and control the worker. However, the agency's guidelines make clear that the 20 factors are not the only relevant factors. According to the guidelines, "Every piece of information that helps determine the extent to which the business retains the right to control the worker is important." The guidelines distill the 20 factors into three major evidentiary categories: behavioral control, financial control, and the relationship of the parties.

---

31. GENERAL EXPLANATION OF THE TAX REFORM ACT OF 1986 (H.R. 3838, 99th Cong. P.L. 99-514) Joint Committee on Taxation (May 4, 1987), p. 1341.

Wage and Hour Issues

The federal Fair Labor Standards Act establishes minimum wage, overtime, equal pay, and child labor requirements for most employers. The act applies to any business on which a worker is dependent as a matter of "economic reality."

The courts have established a five-part economic reality test for determining the existence of an employment relationship under the act. The five parts are the degree of control exercised by the service recipient over the worker, the worker's opportunities for profit or loss and his or her investment in the business, the degree of skill and independent initiative required to perform the work, the permanence or duration of the working relationship, and the extent to which the work is an integral part of the employer's business.[32]

In addition, DOL regulations expressly impose joint employment obligations in specified circumstances. For example, if an employee is employed jointly by two or more employers during a workweek, all of the employee's work during the week is considered one employment, and all employers are responsible for compliance with the wage and hour provisions for the period worked for each employer.[33]

In a 1968 opinion letter, DOL applied these regulations in a case involving temporary staffing (see Appendix E). DOL made two key points. First, temporary staffing companies, not their clients, have primary responsibility for keeping records of hours worked and for paying the proper amount of overtime. At the same time, however, the department held that temporary employees assigned to work for various clients are "typically" employed jointly by the temporary staffing company and its clients—and clients may be held jointly responsible for overtime and minimum wage obligations. In the case of overtime, a client is jointly liable with the temporary staffing firm for the payment of overtime only if the temporary employee worked more than 40 hours in the week for that client.[34] If the staffing firm exercises no control over the employees (i.e., has no right to hire or fire, set pay, or determine assignments) and is simply a payroll agent, the client may be considered the employer for FLSA purposes.[35]

---

32. Brock, *supra* note 30, at 1058. For a more recent discussion of the economic reality test as applied in the Second Circuit, see Zheng v. Liberty Apparel Co. 355 F.3d 61 (2003).

33. 29 C.F.R. § 791.2.

34. Department of Labor Opinion Letter No. 874, Oct. 1, 1968. *See, e.g.*, Barfield v. New York City Health and Hospitals Corp., 432 F.Supp.2d 390 (S.D.N.Y. 2006). Of course, temporary employees are not always jointly employed by the client. *Pfohl v. Farmers Insurance Group*, 2004 WL 554834 (C.D.Ca. 2004) (court held that an insurance company exercised no control over the job activities of a worker assigned by a staffing firm as a claims adjuster and therefore had no obligation to pay overtime to the worker).

35. Catani v. Chiodi, No. CIV. 00-1559 (DWF/RLE), 2001 WL 920025 (D. Minn. Aug. 13, 2001) (the staffing firm had no authority to fire, schedule, or give raises to the workers, nor did it train, supervise, or discipline them).

Health and Pension Benefits

No area of co-employment has created greater confusion than the issue of benefits. The most frequently asked question is, Does the client have to provide benefits to a staffing firm's employee after the employee has worked a specified number of hours for the client? The answer is no. (A quick-reference guide to the most frequently asked questions in this area is included in Appendix F.)

Except for a few states and one municipality that currently require employers to provide health coverage (Hawaii, Massachusetts, San Francisco, and Vermont), employers are not required to provide health or pension benefits to their employees or to anyone else's employees. So what motivates questions like the above? Generally, the answer is section 414(n) of the Internal Revenue Code, which deals with leased employees. Congress passed section 414(n) in 1982 as part of that year's Tax Equity and Fiscal Responsibility Act. To understand how the rules relating to leased employees work, it is essential to understand the tax policy behind the so-called "coverage tests."

Coverage Tests

Federal tax law does not require employers to provide their employees with benefits such as pensions and health insurance. However, it does provide incentives designed to encourage employers to offer benefits to certain rank-and-file employees. For example, businesses may deduct the cost of the benefits, which generally are not included as taxable income to employees. To qualify for favorable tax treatment, however, plans must cover employees fairly (i.e., they cannot discriminate in favor of higher-paid employees).[36]

To ensure that employer-provided retirement plans do not discriminate in favor of higher-paid employees, the law establishes coverage tests that require plans to cover a minimum percentage of lower-paid employees.[37] To determine if they pass the tests, employers have to count their employees and make a number of calculations. Plans that pass the tests and meet other requirements qualify for the tax benefits described in the previous paragraph (hence, the term "qualified" plan). Because serious adverse tax consequences can result if a plan fails the coverage tests, staffing firms and their clients should seek profes-

---

36. Note that in the case of stock purchase plans (section 423 plans) such as those involved in the Microsoft lawsuit (see discussion beginning on p. 38, *infra*), employers may not be able to exclude individuals deemed to be their common-law employees. This is because the IRS rules applicable to those plans require virtually all employees to be covered. As a result, many employers that provide such benefits use *nonqualified* stock purchase plans, which are not subject to nondiscrimination rules.

37. I.R.C. § 410 (b).

sional tax advice concerning the specific application of the tests to their benefit plans.

Beginning with plan years after Dec. 31, 1988, the 1986 Tax Reform Act imposed much stricter coverage tests for retirement plans. Under the act's amendments, one of two tests must be met: A plan must cover (1) a percentage of rank-and-file employees equal to at least 70% of the percentage of higher-paid employees benefited, or (2) a nondiscriminatory classification of employees based on objective standards *and* provide lower-paid employees an average benefit that is at least 70% of the average benefit provided to higher-paid employees.

Since the new coverage tests became effective, employers can no longer simply cover a nondiscriminatory classification of employees (e.g., full-time salaried employees). Staffing firms, for example, must now apply more stringent tests that require counting their temporary employees. This makes it virtually impossible for them to maintain their plans' tax-qualified status because the relatively large numbers of temporary employees excluded from the plans practically guarantee that the plans will fail the tests. Consequently, many staffing firms have been forced to terminate their qualified retirement plans.

The new coverage tests apply to retirement plans but not to other kinds of benefit plans, such as self-insured group health plans and group life insurance. (Insured health plans are not subject to any nondiscrimination coverage tests.) Self-insured health plans and group life insurance plans remain subject to pre-1986 coverage tests, which permit employers to provide benefits to nondiscriminatory classifications of workers (e.g., home office staff or employees assigned to particular clients). It is not entirely clear, though, to what extent the determination of what is a nondiscriminatory classification is affected by the new objective standards applicable to retirement plans. Insured health plans are not subject to any nondiscrimination coverage tests, either pre-1986 or post-1986.[38]

Leased Employee Rules

As noted above, the tax code requires employers to satisfy applicable coverage tests by taking into account workers who are their common-law employees. When applying the coverage tests, the tax code also requires employers to include in their head count certain employees, who are not their common-law employees, supplied by third-party contractors. These rules, sometimes referred

---

38. It should be noted that staffing firms generally cannot include in their plans workers who are not their common-law employees.

to as the "leased employee rules," are set forth in section 414(n) of the code, which applies to tax years after Dec. 31, 1983.

Section 414(n) was prompted by an abuse in which certain small professional groups fired their entire staffs, transferred them to the payroll of leasing organizations, and then set up rich pension plans for themselves, thus circumventing the coverage tests. Section 414(n) dealt with these leasing arrangements by requiring employers to treat certain outside employees as leased employees who must be counted along with their own employees when applying the coverage tests. (For the full text of section 414(n), see Appendix F.) As the following definition indicates, section 414(n) is very broad. Employees supplied by many traditional service providers, including long-term employees supplied by staffing firms, may have to be counted as leased employees, even though clients do not use them to replace full-time employees or to circumvent the coverage tests.

Definition of Leased Employee

Section 414(n) defines a leased employee as any person furnishing services to a recipient if the following conditions are met:

- The person must perform services under an agreement between the recipient employer and the leasing organization.
- The person must perform services under the primary direction and control of the recipient.
- The person must perform services on a substantially full-time basis for a one-year period. Under IRS guidance, this test is met if one of the following conditions is met during a 12-month period: The employee performs at least 1,500 hours of service for the client (or related entities), or the employee performs a number of hours of service for the client (or related entities) that is equal to at least 75% of the average number of hours customarily worked by the client's own employees performing similar services.

The "substantially full-time" test under section 414(n) is different from the "year of service" test under the Employee Retirement Income Security Act, which uses a 1,000-hour standard for participation, benefit accrual, and vesting. Erisa and section 414(n) have different purposes and requirements. Erisa sets forth rules for an employer's benefit plans, but they apply only to the employer's own employees. Section 414(n) applies to an employer's use of outside employees.

Control Test

The "primary direction and control test" of section 414(n), enacted as part of the Small Business Job Protection Act of 1996, replaced a test under prior law that looked to whether services performed by employees for a recipient were of a type historically performed by employees in the recipient's field of business. This test was widely criticized as being too broad in its application. The control test significantly narrows the scope of the leased employee rules.

Effective Jan. 1, 1997, clients do not have to count third-party employees as potential leased employees when their work is directed and controlled primarily by a staffing firm and not the client. Whether an individual performs services under the primary direction or control of the client depends on the facts and circumstances. Relevant factors include whether the client has the right to direct where, when, and how the employee performs services; whether the client has the right to direct that services be performed by a specific person; whether the client supervises the worker; and whether the employee must perform services in an order set by the client.

The legislative history of the control test indicates that professionals (e.g., attorneys, accountants, actuaries, doctors, computer programmers, systems analysts, and engineers) are not considered leased employees if they regularly use their own judgment and discretion on matters of importance in the performance of their services and are guided by professional, legal, or industry standards. They do not have to be counted by the client, even though the staffing firm does not closely supervise them on a continuing basis and even though the client requires their services to be performed on site and in accordance with client-determined timetables and techniques.

The control test may benefit clients using professional services and managed services arrangements, in which the actual day-to-day direction and control of employees at the work site is in the hands of the staffing firm. Office and clerical staffing services could also be exempt, but clients claiming exemption from the head-counting rules will have to satisfy a heavy burden of proof on the issue of control because the legislative history provides that clerical and similar support staff generally are considered to be subject to the client's primary direction or control and would be leased employees if the other requirements of section 414(n) are met.[39]

---

39. *See* Small Business Job Protection Act of 1996, H.R. REP. No. 104-737, Aug. 1, 1996, p. 260.

Benefit Plans Affected by the Leased Employee Rules

Section 414(n) leased employee rules come into play when applying coverage tests to retirement, life insurance, and cafeteria plans and when determining whether group health plans are subject to the Consolidated Omnibus Budget Reconciliation Act and certain Medicare coordination-of-benefit rules. But section 414(n) rules do not currently apply to the coverage tests relating to group health plans.

Record-Keeping Exemption

The Tax Reform Act directed the Treasury Department to issue regulations to minimize employer record-keeping under section 414(n).[40] According to the legislative history of this provision, Congress contemplated that employers do not have to maintain records of outside employees for coverage testing purposes unless the total number of such individuals performing 1,500 hours or more of service exceeds 5% of the employer's total lower-paid work force. To take advantage of this exemption, a client's benefit plans must not be top heavy under IRS rules and must specifically exclude leased employees.[41]

Safe Harbor Plans

Employees will not be treated as leased employees for pension plan purposes if they participate in a safe harbor pension plan provided by the leasing organization that meets the following conditions:

- The leasing organization must contribute at least 10% of the employee's compensation to the plan.
- The employee must be 100% vested in the contribution.
- In general, *all* leasing organization employees who provide services to clients must participate in the plan without any waiting period. This provision prevents a leasing organization from providing safe harbor plans that cover only the employees assigned to certain clients.

If, for any plan year, leased employees constitute more than 20% of an employer's nonhighly compensated work force, all of the leased employees furnished to the recipient will have to be counted, notwithstanding the existence of a safe harbor plan. Of course, a safe harbor pension plan does not relieve recip-

---

40. *See* I.R.C. § 414(o).

41. For a full explanation of this exemption, *see* I.R.C. section 414(o) and the accompanying conference committee explanation at H.R. REP. No. 99-841 (Vol. II, Sept. 18, 1986), pp. 496–497.

ients of the obligation to count leased employees for any other benefit plan subject to coverage testing. Few, if any, safe harbor plans exist.

Coverage Testing of Leased Employees— Consequences of Failing the Tests

Generally, under the record-keeping exemption described above, if an employer's use of outside employees working 1,500 hours or more is 5% or more of its lower-paid work force, it will have to maintain records, and those employees meeting the definition of "leased employee" will have to be counted as leased employees for coverage testing purposes.[42] Outside employees generally must be counted after working 1,500 hours or more in a year, assuming the client uses a 40-hour workweek as full time. Plans that continue to satisfy the coverage tests after leased employees are counted will remain qualified. However, plans that fail the tests will lose some or all of their tax benefits, depending on the type of plan.

For example, if a retirement plan fails the coverage tests, the employer stands to lose its tax deduction for all contributions made to the plan. Higher-paid employees will be immediately taxed on the value of their vested plan benefits, and the income of the retirement trust will become taxable. Consequently, clients should keep careful track of any outside employees working 1,500 hours or more to ensure that their retirement plans do not fail the coverage tests. Clients without tax-favored benefit plans need not be concerned with the leased employee rules.

Credit for Benefits Provided by Leasing Organization

Even if a client must count a staffing firm employee for coverage testing purposes, the client is entitled to a credit to the extent that the employee receives benefits from the staffing firm. The law states that "contributions or benefits provided by the leasing organization that are attributable to services performed by the recipient shall be treated as provided by the recipient."[43] Hence, if the benefits provided by the staffing firm are fully comparable to those provided by the client, the client may be entitled to full credit under the coverage tests. Comparability must be determined case by case, and certain technical requirements be satisfied. The mere fact that a staffing firm covers its assigned employees under a benefit plan does not exempt the client from having to take leased employees into account when applying the coverage tests.

---

42. Under the legislative history describing the record-keeping exception, the employer would also be required to count any individual who provides satisfactory evidence of entitlement to treatment as a leased employee. *See* note 41, *supra*.

43. I.R.C. § 414(n)(1)(B).

Any plan covering staffing firm employees must meet the IRS's 50-employee rule, which requires that plans cover at least 50 employees or 40% of the employer's total work force, whichever is less.[44] In the case of a staffing firm plan, this means that, assuming a staffing firm has more than 200 employees (including all of its temporary employees), at least 50 employees must be covered under any plan established for those assigned to a particular client. As a result of changes enacted as part of the Small Business Job Protection Act of 1996, this 50-employee requirement does not apply to defined-contribution plans, such as profit-sharing and 401(k) plans, effective for plan years beginning in 1997.

In addition, of course, any plan established for temporary employees must satisfy the coverage tests, which will not be a problem if the plans maintained by the staffing firm do not cover highly compensated employees and only cover common-law employees of the staffing firm.

Prior Service Credit for Employees Hired by Client

Employees who perform services for a client through a staffing firm and are later hired directly by the client are entitled to credit under the client's pension plan for hours of service performed for the client as an employee of the staffing firm. Section 414(n)(4)(B) requires a client to take into account, for the purpose of determining an employee's years of service under Erisa, "any period for which such employee would have been a leased employee but for the requirements of subparagraph 2(B)" (i.e., the 1,500-hour test). This requirement may have the effect of accelerating the entry and vesting of the hired employee in the client's plan.

Section 414(n) requires only that leased employees be treated as employees for the purpose of including them in the client's head count for coverage testing purposes. They are not required to be treated as participants in the client's benefit plans.[45] Indeed, leased employees may be excluded as a class from participating in the client's plan.[46] However, as the following discussion illustrates, it is critically important to use clear and unambiguous language.

The Microsoft Case

Section 414(n) simply requires businesses to count certain longer-term leased employees for coverage testing purposes. The *Vizcaino v. Microsoft Corp.*

---

44. I.R.C. § 401(a)(26).

45. *See* Notice 84-11 Internal Revenue Bulletin No. 1984-29, July 16, 1984, which states in Q&A 14: *"Q–14. Must a leased employee participate in the plan? A–14. No. Section 414(n)(1)(A) requires only that a leased employee be treated as an employee; it does not require that a leased employee be a participant in the recipient's qualified plan."* (*See* Appendix F.)

46. *Id.* Q&A 15–16.

case, however, raised the specter that staffing firm employees may be considered a client's common-law employees under certain circumstances and thus become eligible for the client's benefit plans.

In 1993, a group of former Microsoft freelancers, whom the IRS said should have been classified by Microsoft as employees, sued the company for benefits under its 401(k) and stock purchase plans. The class of workers suing for benefits involved two groups: (1) those who worked directly for Microsoft from 1987 to 1990 as independent contractors, and (2) those who were employed by staffing firms after the IRS reclassified the workers as Microsoft employees for tax purposes in 1990.

Microsoft challenged the workers' claims on the basis that their work agreements and the company's benefit-plan language excluded them from coverage. The U.S. District Court for the Western District of Washington denied the workers' claims, but the U.S. Court of Appeals for the Ninth Circuit ultimately sided with the employees.

The court ruled that Microsoft was bound by the wording of its stock purchase plan, which referred to a provision of the tax code requiring all common-law employees to receive benefits for a plan to qualify for preferential tax treatment. That reference, the court ruled, created a legal obligation to provide benefits to any common-law employee, which a client cannot avoid merely because a staffing firm can establish that it is also an employer.[47] In an earlier ruling, the Ninth Circuit found that Microsoft had conceded the employees' common-law status, and thus the company would not be permitted to reopen that issue,[48] although the court did allow Microsoft to challenge particular employees' claims if it could prove special circumstances rendering the employees ineligible. But Microsoft elected to settle the case, agreeing to pay almost $97 million in damages relating to the company's stock purchase plan.

In the wake of the *Microsoft* case, several lawsuits have been filed against private-sector corporations and state government agencies seeking benefits. Most of the private-sector cases have been won all or in part based on plan exclusions.[49]

---

47. Vizcaino v. U.S. Dist. for Western Div. of Wash., 173 F.3d 713 (9th Cir. 1999), *as amended by, In re* Vizcaino, 184 F.3d 1070 (9th Cir. 1999).

48. Vizcaino v. Microsoft Corp., 97 F.3d 1187 (9th Cir. 1996).

49. Bronk v. Mountain States Telephone & Telegraph 140 F.3rd 1335 (10th Cir. 1998); Wolf v. Coca Cola Co., 200 F.3d 1337 (11th Cir. 2000); Moxley v. Texaco (unpublished opinion) 2001 WL 840363 (C.D. Cal. 2001); Montesano v. Xerox Corp. Retirement Income Guarantee Plan, 256 F.3d 86 (2d Cir. 2001); MacLachlan v. ExxonMobil Corp. 350 F.3d 472 (5th Cir. 2003); Edes v. Verizon Communications Inc. 417 F.3d 133 (1st Cir. 2005); Central Pennsylvania Teamsters Pension Fund v. Power Packaging Inc., No. 04-2867, 2005 WL 2522163 (3rd Cir. Oct. 12, 2005); Curry v. CTB McGraw-Hill LLC, reported in F.Supp.2d, 2006 WL 228951 N.D.Cal. (2006); Martin v. Public Service Electric and Gas Co. Inc., 2006 WL 3491063 (D. NJ).

One case involved a trial court ruling that the assigned workers were not the client's common-law employees.[50] Other cases involved claims that were dismissed based on statutes of limitations, not on the merits.[51] And some were settled.[52] All of the public-sector defendants have lost or settled.[53] A class-action suit filed in 2005 against Hewlett Packard was still pending at the time this edition went to print.[54]

Because the law generally does not require employers to provide benefits or mandate that all employees be covered, businesses can take steps to reduce the likelihood that such claims will be successful.

Operational Steps—Avoiding Control

Ironically, the *Microsoft* case itself provides guidance on how staffing firm clients can avoid being considered the employer of staffing firm employees claiming benefits under client plans. *Microsoft* and other cases have relied on criteria for determining employer status set forth by the U.S. Supreme Court in the case of *Nationwide Mutual Insurance Co. v. Darden.*[55]

Clients can structure their relationships with staffing firms and assigned workers to avoid some of the contacts that might imply an employee-employer relationship. Although day-to-day supervision of workers by the client may be unavoidable in most cases, other factors can be controlled. For example, the client can control who recruits and trains the worker, the length of the worker's assignment, the right to assign the worker to other projects, and the client's influence on the relationship between the worker and the staffing firm. Other factors would also be relevant in making this determination.

A 1999 federal district court decision in California, *Burrey v. Pacific Gas & Electric*, recognized the substantial employer responsibilities of the staffing firm and held that it, not the client, was the employer for benefits purposes despite the client's substantial day-to-day involvement with the workers.[56]

---

50. Burrey v. Pacific Gas & Electric, (unpublished order) No. C-95-4638 DLJ (N.D.C.A. May 12, 1999).

51. Berry v. Allstate Insurance Co., 252 F.Supp.2d 336 (E.D.Tex. 2003), aff'd 84 Fed.Appx. 442 (5th Cir. 2004); Schultz v. Texaco Inc., 127 F.Supp.2d 443 (S.D.N.Y. 2001); Edes v. Verizon Communications Inc., 417 F.3d 133 (1st Cir. 2005) (E.D.Tex. 2003).

52. Casey v. Atlantic Richfield Co., 2000 WL 657397 (C.D.CA.) Reversed and remanded 21 Fed.Appx. 727 (9th Cir. 2001, not published in Federal Reporter); Mascari v. San Diego Gas and Electric Co., No. 97-CV1652K(JFS) (S.D.Cal., filed Sept. 10, 1997); Thomas v. SmithKline Beecham, 297 F.Supp.2d 773 (E.D.Pa.,2003).

53. Clark v. King County, No. 95-2-29890-7SEA (Wash. Super. Ct. King County); Jordan. v. City of Bellevue, No. 98-2-21515-1SEA (Wash.Super.Ct. King County); Metropolitan Water District of Southern California v. Los Angeles Superior Court, 84 P.3d 966, (Cal. 2004).

54. Miller v. Hewlett-Packard Co., No. 1:05-CV-00111-BLW (D.Id., filed March 21, 2005).

55. Nationwide Mutual Insurance Co. v. Darden, 503 U.S. 318 (1992).

56. Burrey v. Pacific Gas & Electric, see note 50 supra.

As other courts address these issues, it may become clearer how these factors are to be weighed. The *Microsoft* ruling is, of course, limited to the Ninth Circuit, leaving other courts free to decide the same issues differently. However the rules evolve, clients are well advised to place stricter limits on their involvement with staffing firm employees, consistent with operational necessity, to mitigate the risk of benefits liability.

Benefit Plan Exclusions Must Be Clear and Unequivocal

Another way for clients to avoid benefits liability is to draft their plans to clearly and explicitly exclude staffing firm employees, even if they are determined to be the client's common-law employees. The Ninth Circuit in the *Microsoft* case itself explicitly held that Microsoft had the legal right to exclude the workers who were claiming benefits and could have done so if it had drafted its plan more explicitly. As previously noted, this right has been recognized by a number of federal courts that have considered the issue.[57] Hence, clients should carefully review their benefit plan documents to ensure that they are properly drafted.

Further support for the ability of staffing firm clients to protect themselves through exclusionary plan language can be found in a technical advice memorandum issued by the IRS national office and unofficially published in 2000.[58] (See Appendix G.)

The memorandum involved a taxpayer seeking an IRS plan determination. The plan excluded from coverage individuals not on the client's payroll, even if the individuals were subsequently reclassified as common-law employees. The IRS upheld the exclusion. Use of language similar to that used by the taxpayer in the memorandum would therefore appear to offer protection.

---

57. *See, e.g.,* Abraham v. Exxon Corp., 85 F.3d 1126 (5th Cir. 1996); Trombetta v. Cragin Federal Bank for Savings Employee Stock Ownership Plan, 102 F.3d 1435 (7th Cir. 1996); Clark v. E.I. Dupont De Nemours & Co. Inc., 105 F.3d 646 (Table—unpub'd. op.) (4th Cir. Jan. 9, 1997), *cert. denied* 520 U.S. 1259 (1997); Bronk v. Mountain States Telephone & Telegraph, note 49 *supra*; Wolf v. Coca Cola Co., note 49 *supra*; Casey v. Atlantic Richfield Co., note 52 *supra*; Montesano v. Xerox Corp., note 49 *supra*; Moxley v. Texaco, note 47A *supra*; Berry v. Allstate Insurance Co., No. 1-98-CV1758, 2003 WL 1350374 (E.D. Tex. March 18, 2003). Cf. National Shopmen Pension Fund v. Burtman Iron Works, 148 F. Supp.2d 60 (D.D.C. 2001) (staffing firm clients had to make contributions to a joint labor–management pension fund on behalf of the staffing firm employees because a collective bargaining agreement required contributions to be made on behalf of "all full-time production and maintenance employees" and did not distinguish or exclude staffing firm employees). One federal district court has decided that workers found to be the common-law employees of an employer are entitled to benefits under the employer's plan even if the plan expressly excludes the workers. Renda v. Adam Meldrum & Anderson Co. 806 F. Supp. 1071 (W.D. N.Y. 1992). However, most Erisa experts believe that this is not a correct view of the law.

58. U.S. Internal Revenue Service *Technical Advice Memorandum* (Section 410—Minimum Participation Standards) (Release Date: July 28, 1999) (Doc 2000-14434) Department: Official Announcements, Notices, and News Releases; Other IRS Documents; *Reclassified Workers Can Be Excluded by Retirement Plan Language.* Tax Analysts Tax Notes Today (May 24, 2000), 2000 TNT 101-45.

Keeping in mind that any plan language should be discussed with legal counsel, the following template language may be suggested to clients for the purpose of excluding staffing firm workers from participation in the client's Erisa plan: [59]

"The Plan includes any employee of [Client] who is paid in U.S. currency, but shall not include

1. An individual whose services are used by [Client] pursuant to an employment agreement or personal services agreement if such agreement provides that such individual shall not be eligible to participate in [Client's] Plan
2. Individuals who are not paid directly by [Client] or an affiliate of [Client]
3. Individuals who are not on [Client's] payroll
4. Individuals who are 'leased employees' within the meaning of § 414(n) or (o) of the Internal Revenue Code
5. Individuals whom [Client] does not treat as its employees for federal income tax withholding or employment tax purposes"

Employee Contracts and Waivers

In addition to careful plan drafting, it may be possible for clients to achieve additional protection from benefits liability through carefully drafted employee agreements or waivers. One of the many court proceedings in the *Microsoft* case discussed the issue of waivers.

Beginning in July 1998, Microsoft required temporary workers whose annual contracts were up for renewal to sign an agreement acknowledging that they were employees of the staffing firm, not Microsoft, and waiving any claim to compensation or benefits from Microsoft. The district court, upon learning of the new agreements, objected to the following provision:

> ...[e]ven if a court or government agency determines that Temporary Personnel and Microsoft have had a common law employer-employee relationship at any time, Temporary Personnel will still be bound by this Agreement and will not be entitled to receive from Microsoft or have Microsoft provide on his/her behalf any different or additional pay, or any benefits, insurance coverage, tax payments or withholding, or compensation of any kind.

---

59. Clients will need to be careful in how any exclusion is framed. Exclusions viewed as "service related" (e.g., exclusions for "part-time," "seasonal," or "temporary" employees) may run afoul of the IRS and Erisa minimum service requirements, as opposed to exclusions that are job-related (e.g., exclusions for substitute workers or workers who are not on the employer's payroll). See Feb. 14, 2006, IRS Quality Assurance Bulletin posted on the ASA Web site, *americanstaffing.net*. Click on Legal & Government Affairs, then Issue Papers, then scroll down to "Assignment Limits and Customer Concerns About Benefits Liability: Issues and Answers."

Microsoft argued that the waiver pertained only to work performed after the date of the agreement, and that it was not intended to affect workers involved in the pending litigation who had performed services before the agreement. The court disagreed that the waiver was limited in this manner.

In response to the court's concerns, Microsoft agreed to revise the workers' agreement to provide the following:

> *Regardless of how the legal status of Worker may be characterized—as an employee of Temporary Agency, an employee of Microsoft, an independent contractor, or otherwise—Worker acknowledges and agrees that Microsoft will not provide to Worker or on Worker's behalf any compensation, insurance or benefits, including without limitation....* [The agreement then lists Microsoft's insurance and benefits plans.]

In a separate provision, workers, regardless of their legal status, were also asked to waive any right to any claim for benefits or other compensation from Microsoft. Microsoft explained to the court that the revised waivers would apply only to new temporary workers, would not affect claims for benefits relating to any services they provided before signing the agreement, and would not affect claims for benefits if a court found the waiver invalid. The revised waiver provides the following:

> *I have read carefully this entire agreement including this highlighted provision, and I have had sufficient time to consider my waiver of any entitlement or claim to compensation, insurance, and benefits from Microsoft. This waiver does not affect any claim worker might have for any type of compensation, insurance, or benefits from Microsoft attributable to services provided by worker prior to the date of this agreement or attributable to services provided at any time if this waiver were ever found to be ineffective or otherwise invalid by any court of competent jurisdiction.*

Microsoft also agreed to take corrective measures regarding workers who had signed the original waiver. Without expressly ruling on the validity of the revised agreement, the judge conceded that it "goes a long way toward satisfying the court's earlier expressed concern."[60]

---

60. Vizcaino v. Microsoft Corp., Hughes v. Microsoft Corp., Nos. C-93-178 and C-98-1646, (W.D. Wash.) transcript of proceedings Jan. 26, 1999, Judge John C. Coughenour, at p. 15, lines 5–9. Hughes v. Microsoft Corp., Nos. C-93-178 and C-98-1646, (W.D. Wash.) transcript of proceedings Jan. 26, 1999, Judge John C. Coughenour, at p. 15, lines 5–9.

Even though the court did not expressly decide the effectiveness of the new Microsoft waiver, its action suggests that voluntary and specific waivers executed at the outset of an employment relationship may be valid.

A 1998 decision by the 10th U.S. Circuit Court of Appeals[61] supports the conclusion that clients can protect themselves through carefully worded agreements with employees. In that case, newspaper carriers who worked as independent contractors sued the company, claiming that they were common-law employees entitled to company benefits. The carriers had signed agreements acknowledging their status as independent contractors and agreed that they were not entitled to benefits under the company's plans. The court rejected the carriers' claims, holding that the agreements signed before the start of their work determined their right to benefits. The court ruled that the issue was one of contract rather than waiver (which involves forgoing a right that already exists) and that the carriers were not entitled to benefits.[62]

Some benefits experts believe that temporary employee waivers are not enforceable unless they are consistent with and expressly sanctioned by the client's benefit plan, suggesting that any waiver language should be tailored to particular client situations. Because of the complexity of the issues, staffing firms and their clients should consult with expert legal counsel about plan-drafting issues and any agreements with workers relating to benefits eligibility.

Do Time Limits on Worker Assignments Offer Protection?

To protect against "retro-benefits" claims following the Microsoft litigation, clients increasingly began to adopt policies limiting the length of assignment of staffing firm workers. Some of these policies seem to be based on the erroneous belief that, after working for a certain period of time, such employees are automatically eligible for coverage under client benefits plans or even entitled to be hired into regular full-time positions with the client.

But length of assignment is not the sole issue in determining the employment status of workers supplied by staffing firms. For tax and benefits purposes, it is but one of many factors under the common-law control test. Assignment limits may even carry some risk if the client has not clearly excluded staffing firm workers from its plan because they might be construed as an effort to deny benefits by preventing workers from reaching the hours needed for plan participation. Clients could face charges of violating Erisa, which protects employees from such employer action.

---

61. Capital Cities/ABC Inc. v. Ratcliff, 141 F. 3d 1405 (10th Cir. 1998).

62. Cf. Laniok v. Brainerd, 935 F. 2d 1360 (2d Cir. 1991).

Because assignment limits can cause economic harm to workers whose assignments are terminated prematurely and can disrupt client business operations, clients should examine their time limits policies to ensure that they are necessary and are not based on misinformation. For example, it is important to understand that while Erisa sets rules for employer benefit plans, it does not require employers to offer benefits and does not dictate what level of benefits must be provided—and that federal tax law, while it requires that plans satisfy certain coverage and nondiscrimination rules as a condition of receiving favorable tax treatment, does not require employers to offer benefits or to cover all employees in their plans. As previously noted (See Coverage Tests), a company generally can exclude up to 30% of its rank-and-file employees under a pension, profit-sharing, or 401(k) plan without endangering the plan's tax-advantaged status. This "slack" is why clients generally can exclude staffing firm workers from their benefit plans without jeopardizing their tax status.

Nevertheless, some clients, relying on the Erisa "year of service" rule, terminate the staffing firm's workers before they reach 1,000 hours in the erroneous belief that all individuals who work at least 1,000 hours in a year are entitled to participate in the client's retirement plan. This is unnecessary because the year of service rule does not apply to nonemployees or to employees who have been expressly excluded from the plan under a proper exclusion provision.

Other clients' assignment limit policies are based on the federal tax code provisions dealing with "leased employees," IRS Code section 414(n). Again, those provisions do not require clients to provide benefits to leased employees—in fact, leased employees can and should be excluded from client plans. The rules require only that leased employees be included in a client's head count for discrimination testing purposes. This is not a problem unless the client has so many leased employees (and other excluded employees) that they exceed the "slack" in the client's plan discussed earlier, which could affect the plan's tax qualification. Staffing firms can help manage this for clients by keeping track of the number of leased employees to ensure that the slack is not exceeded.

Family and Medical Leave

Covered Employers

The most recent federal law to address the issue of co-employment is the Family and Medical Leave Act of 1993. The FMLA applies to employers with at least 50 employees per day for 20 or more weeks in the current or preceding calendar year. Such employers must provide up to 12 weeks of unpaid family and medical leave in any 12-month period to employees who meet eligibility requirements. Employer obligations include maintaining health insurance benefits during the leave period and, except for certain key employees, restoring employees to the same or equivalent position upon return from leave.

Eligible Employees

To be eligible for leave, employees of a covered employer must satisfy three tests: (1) they must have been employed by the employer for at least 12 months (not necessarily consecutively), (2) they must have worked at least 1,250 hours during the 12-month period immediately preceding the beginning of leave, and (3) they must have been employed at a work site with 50 or more employees.

Primary and Secondary Employers

DOL regulations address the potential co-employer obligations of staffing firms (specifically temporary staffing and employee leasing firms) and their clients under the FMLA. Under these rules, clients using temporary or leased employees may have to include those employees in their own head count in determining whether they are subject to the FMLA.[63]

Although the rules state that in determining whether a joint employment relationship exists "the entire relationship is to be viewed in its totality," the rules go on to provide that a temporary staffing or employee leasing firm and its clients will ordinarily be deemed joint employers.[64] If a co-employment relationship is found to exist, both the staffing firm and the client must count the temporary or leased employees in determining whether the employer is covered under the FMLA and whether the employee is eligible for benefits.[65] For example, if a client has 40 regular, full-time workers and is a co-employer of 15 workers assigned by a temporary staffing or employee leasing firm for 20 or more weeks in the current or preceding calendar year, the client is covered by the FMLA because it will be deemed to have 50 or more employees.

However, the rules make clear that only the primary employer is responsible for giving required notices to its employees, providing leave, and maintaining health benefits during leave. Factors considered in determining who is the primary employer include the authority or responsibility to hire and fire, assign or place the employee, make payroll, and provide employment benefits. The rules

---

63. 29 C.F.R. § 825.106.

64. 29 C.F.R. § 825.106(b).

65. 29 C.F.R. § 825.106(d).

state that temporary staffing companies and employee leasing firms are generally primary employers.[66]

Clients do have some obligations, similar to those generally found in the civil rights laws, as secondary employers under the rules. Regardless of whether they are covered by the FMLA, secondary employers must comply with the rules' "prohibited acts" provisions with respect to temporary or leased employees. Prohibited acts include interfering with an employee's attempt to exercise rights under the FMLA and discharging or discriminating against an employee for opposing a practice that the FMLA makes unlawful.[67]

It should be noted that because a business must employ 50 or more employees a day for 20 or more weeks in the current or preceding calendar year before it is subject to the FMLA,[68] it is possible for a client with fewer than 50 employees to limit its use of temporary employees to peak or seasonal workloads and not subject itself to the FMLA. But regular, ongoing use of such services could cause a business to come under the law if it causes its daily head count to reach or exceed 50 for at least 20 weeks in a calendar year.

Duty to Restore Temporary Employee Returning From Leave

The final regulations address the specific obligations of staffing firms and their clients to restore a temporary or leased employee to the same or equivalent position on his or her return from leave. Under the rules, the primary employer (i.e., the staffing firm) has primary responsibility for restoring the employee.

However, the client also has obligations. The final rules provide that if the client is using staffing firm services in the same or equivalent position at the time the employee returns from leave, the staffing firm must reinstate the employee immediately, even if this means removing another employee from the job.[69] Moreover, the rules expressly provide that, in such cases, the client must accept the returning employee.[70]

If, however, a client for legitimate business reasons discontinues the services of the staffing firm or the services performed by the employee who took leave and no equivalent jobs are available with the same client, then the staffing firm must try to find an equivalent position with another client. If no equivalent job

---

66. 29 C.F.R. § 825.106(c).

67. 29 C.F.R. § 825.106(e).

68. 29 C.F.R. § 825.105(e).

69. 29 C.F.R. § 825.106(e).

70. *Id.*

is available, the returning employee is given priority consideration for other assignments for which he or she is qualified.[71]

The final regulations' commentary suggests that the head-of-the-line approach can be used only if the returning employee typically experienced waiting periods between temporary assignments.[72] However, the issue is not whether an individual actually has to wait. Because the FMLA rules also expressly state that the FMLA does not give employees any greater rights than what their employment agreement otherwise would have entitled them to,[73] it seems reasonable to conclude that it is the understanding between the staffing firm and the employee that there could be waiting periods—not the employee's actual experience—that should be relevant in applying the head-of-the-line principle.

Application of 75-Mile Rule to Staffing Firms

Under the regulations, an employee is not eligible for leave unless the employer employs 50 or more employees within 75 miles of the employee's work site. In the case of temporary employees, the rules specify that the work site is the temporary staffing office from which employees are assigned, not the client's places of business. Thus, all employees assigned from a temporary staffing office—even if a client work site is more than 75 miles from the office—are included in the head count for the purpose of determining the eligibility of both temporary and full-time staff employees.[74] To avoid undue hardship to small temporary staffing offices, the staffing industry had urged that staffing firms be allowed to exclude their temporary employees in determining the eligibility of their full-time staffs. DOL declined to adopt such a two-tiered counting test. In meetings with industry representatives, DOL officials said that there was no practical way to apply such a test only to staffing firms because other businesses also assign employees from central offices to work at remote client locations and that it would create significant administrative problems.

---

71. *60 Fed. Reg.* at 2214.

72. *See id.*

73. 29 C.F.R. § 825.216.

74. 29 C.F.R. § 825.111(a)(3). Note that the U.S. Court of Appeals for the 10th Circuit has held that DOL's regulation requiring the 75-mile rule to be measured from the staffing firm's office does not apply when the employee is assigned to a permanent, fixed work site. In such cases, the court held that the 75 miles should be measured from that work site, not the staffing firm's office. Harbert v. Healthcare Services Group Inc., 391 F.3d 1140 (10th Cir. 2004).

Employment Practices

Equal Employment Opportunity Laws

Liability of Clients

Staffing arrangements cannot be used to shield companies from compliance with the equal employment opportunity (EEO) laws. The remedial purpose of Title VII of the Civil Rights Act of 1964 is so broad that every party to a staffing arrangement may be liable for discriminatory acts against staffing firm employees as long as the party controls some substantial aspect of their compensation, terms, conditions, or privileges of employment. Liability may even extend to acts committed by persons with whom the party has no employment relationship.

For example, in the 1984 landmark case of *Amarnare v. Merrill Lynch*, a federal court in New York held a client of a temporary staffing firm to be a co-employer in a suit brought by a temporary employee under Title VII.[75] The employee alleged that the client discharged her from her assignment and refused to hire her on a permanent basis because of her sex, race, and national origin. The client moved to dismiss the case, arguing that it had no employer-employee relationship with her. The employee asserted that the client was an employer because it "controlled her work hours, workplace, and work assignments; hired, trained, and assigned her; and ultimately discharged her."

The court agreed that there was a sufficient employer-employee relationship to support a Title VII claim against the client. It found that the employee "was subject to the direction of [the client] in her work assignments, hours of service, and other usual aspects of an employer relationship." This finding permitted an inference that she was an employee of both the temporary staffing firm and the client during the period of the assignment. In passing, the court also noted that the client could be liable under Title VII even if it were not an employer because Title VII allows suits against persons "who are neither actual nor potential direct employers of particular complainants, but who control access to such employment and who deny access by reference to invidious criteria."

Although the client in the *Amarnare* case was ultimately found not to have discriminated, the case established that clients can be held accountable if they unlawfully discriminate against a staffing company's employees.

---

75. Amarnare v. Merrill Lynch, 611 F. Supp. 344 (S.D.N.Y. 1984), *aff'd*, 770 F.2d 157 (2d Cir. 1985). While most of the case law on employment relationships under the EEO laws involves claims brought under Title VII of the Civil Rights Act of 1964, which bans employment discrimination on the basis of race, color, religion, sex, and national origin, these legal standards are applicable to all the EEO laws.

In another case, *Magnuson v. Peak Technical Services*,[76] a federal court in Virginia held that staffing firm Peak; its client Volkswagen of America; Volkswagen's Fairfax, VA, dealership; and the dealership's general manager could all be employers under Title VII and potentially liable for the sexual harassment of Peak's employee by the general manager. The court ruled that both Peak and Volkswagen of America could be liable for the general manager's acts, even though he was not employed by them, if "(i) they knew of the harassment; and (ii) failed to take any corrective action to remedy the situation."[77]

Some federal courts have required a common-law employment relationship between a client and a temporary employee in order to hold the client liable under the EEO laws[78] and have rejected claims in which the client exercises too little control to be an employer.[79]

Most state courts have interpreted state human rights laws broadly to protect workers against client discrimination, even in cases in which the parties to the staffing arrangement entered into a written contract that expressly provided that temporary employees assigned to the client were not the client's employees.[80]

Liability of Staffing Firms

Staffing firms, of course, also may have EEO liability. The court in the *Amarnare* case expressly held that the temporary employee was employed by

---

76. Magnuson v. Peak Technical Services, 808 F. Supp. 500 (E.D. Va. 1992). King v. Chrysler Corp., 812 F. Supp. 151 (E.D. Mo. 1993) (court held client could be liable for sexual harassment of third party employee under Title VII even though it did not employ the victim).

77. *Id.* at 513. *See also* Williams v. Grimes Aerospace Co., 988 F. Supp. 925 (D.S.C. 1997) (the staffing firm was not liable if it did not know about the client's alleged discriminatory conduct); Mullis v. Mechanics & Farmers Bank, 994 F. Supp. 680 (M.D.N.C. 1997) (the staffing firm could be liable because it knew of the client's alleged harassment but failed to take action for six to eight weeks); Neal v. Manpower International Inc., No. 3:00-CV-277/LAC, 2001 WL 1923127 (N.D. Fla. Sept. 17, 2001) (a staffing firm could not be held liable for sexual harassment by a client's employee since the firm was not informed about the harassment).

78. *See* Beaulieu v. Northrop Grumman Corp., 161 F. Supp.2d 1135 (D. Haw. 2000), *aff'd* 23 Fed. Appx. 811 (9th Cir. 2001); Callicutt v. Pepsi Bottling Group, Inc., No. CIV. 00-95DWFAJB, 2002 WL 992757 (D. Minn. May 13, 2002); Freeman v. State of Kansas, 128 F. Supp.2d 1311 (D. Kan. 2001), *aff'd* 22 Fed. Appx. 967 (10th Cir. 2001); Hunt v. State of Missouri, Department of Corrections, 297 F.3d 735 (8th Cir. 2002); Lyles v. Alamo Rent-A-Car Inc., No. CIV. H-00-786, 2001 WL 135844 (D. Md. Feb. 14, 2001); Richardson v. Century Products Inc., 163 F. Supp.2d 771 (N.D. Ohio 2001). Cf. Dunn v. Uniroyal Chemical Co., 192 F. Supp.2d 557 (M.D. La. 2001) (because the client did not exercise complete control over the worker—the staffing firm paid the worker and could reassign her at any time, and there was no employment contract between the worker and the client—no employment relationship existed between the worker and the client).

79. *See* Redd v. Summers, 232 F.3d 933 (D.C. Cir. 2000) (the staffing firm was responsible for hiring, training, and supervising all the workers while the client only inspected the staffing firm's services and exercised little control); West v. MCI Worldcom Inc., 205 F. Supp.2d 531 (E.D. Va. 2002) (the client did not exercise supervisory control over the worker's tasks nor did it evaluate her performance, coach her, train her, provide her with administrative support, or pay directly for her services). Allen v. Tyco Electronics Corp., 294 F.Supp.2d 768 (M.D.N.C. 2003) (staffing firm on-site coordinator was responsible for answering employee's work questions and client did not have power to hire, fire, pay, or control duties); Reith v. TXU Corp., 2006 WL 887413 (E.D. Tex. April 4, 2006) (applying economics realities test, court found that the staffing firm, not the client, retained the right to hire and fire the plaintiff, transfer him, and pay his wages and employment taxes).

80. *See*, e.g., Rodriquez v. Chemical Bank, No. 117827/95 (Sup. Ct. N.Y., June 11, 1996).

both the temporary staffing firm and the client.[81] However, some federal courts have found it unnecessary to decide whether the staffing firm was an employer under Title VII when the firm acted promptly to correct the alleged discriminatory conduct against an assigned employee.[82]

But in several cases courts have held that staffing firms were not employers for EEO purposes. For example, in *Williams v. Caruso*,[83] a federal court in Delaware concluded that a staffing firm could not be held liable as an employer for a hostile environment at a client's work site because the staffing firm did not control the details of the work at the site. The court concluded instead that the staffing firm was an employment agency—and as such could potentially be held liable for a retaliatory discharge. However, because the staffing firm took prompt action when it learned of the alleged hostile environment, the court rejected the worker's claim.

EEOC Guidance on Contingent Workers

In contrast to the courts, the Equal Employment Opportunity Commission has shown no ambivalence regarding the employer status of staffing firms and their clients for EEO purposes. The agency's views on the subject are set forth in EEOC Enforcement Guidance on the Application of EEO Laws to Contingent Workers Placed by Temporary Employment Agencies and Other Staffing Firms, issued in 1997 (see Appendix H) and in agency opinions.[84]

The guidance applies to temporary staffing firms, contract firms, long-term staffing arrangements, and PEO services. A contract firm is defined as one that takes on "full operational responsibility for performing an ongoing service and supervises its workers at the client's work site." This definition essentially corresponds to industry definitions of managed services or outsourcing.

The guidance confirms the long-held view of the American Staffing Association that, in the great majority of circumstances, staffing firm workers

---

81. *Compare* Atchley v. Nordham Group, 180 F.3d 1143 (10th Cir. 1999) (holding that the client of a staffing firm, not the staffing firm, was the employer of an assigned worker for Title VII purposes when the client controlled "every aspect" of employment).

82. *See* Caldwell v. ServiceMaster Corp., 966 F. Supp. 33 (D.D.C. 1997); Riesgo v. Heidelberg Harris Inc., 36 F. Supp. 2d 53 (D.N.H. 1997).

83. Williams v. Caruso, 966 F. Supp. 287 (D. Del. 1997). *See also* Kellam v. Snelling Personnel Services, 866 F. Supp. 812 (D. Del. 1994), *aff'd without op.* 63 F.3d 162 (3d Cir. 1995); Watson v. Adecco Employment Services, No. 6:01-CV-1268-ORL-31J, 2003 WL 1357539 (M.D. Fla., March 6, 2003); Blagg v. Technology Group Inc., 303 F.Supp.2d 1181 (D.Colo. 2004). (The court concluded that the clients and not the staffing firms controlled the job functions of the workers.)

84. *See* Baker v. Harvey, No. 01A45313, 2006 WL 755933 (EEOC March 16, 2006).

are employees, not independent contractors. It sets forth a nonexhaustive list of 16 factors to be used in making this determination, with no one factor being decisive. The guidance specifically rejects the reasoning of courts in several cases that held that temporary workers are not staffing-firm employees. It states that the courts "placed undue emphasis on daily supervision of job tasks and underestimated the significance of other factors indicating an employment relationship."

The EEOC guidance says that the staffing firm, the client, or both could be employers and be held liable for unlawful discriminatory conduct. If both have the right to control a worker under the factors test, and each has the statutory minimum number of employees (under rules spelled out in the guidance), they are covered as joint employers. In contrast, clients of a contract firm are not joint employers if the contract firm furnishes the job equipment and has the exclusive right, through on-site managers, to control the details of the work, make or change assignments, and terminate workers.

Staffing firms that lease employees in an arrangement in which a client puts its employees on the staffing firm's payroll solely to transfer the responsibility of administering wages and insurance benefits would not be an employer under the guidance. But if a staffing firm has a right to exercise control over the worker, it would be an employer. Hence, PEOs would be employers if they have the authority to hire and fire workers independent of the client. Staffing firms engaged in pure payrolling services probably would not be employers, although they still may have liability even though they are not employers.

Staffing firms that are not employers may still be liable for discrimination because the EEOC views the antidiscrimination laws as not only prohibiting an employer from discriminating against its own employees, but also prohibiting it "from interfering with an individual's employment opportunities with another employer."

Where the combined discriminatory actions of a staffing firm and its client harm the worker, both are jointly and severally liable for back pay, front (i.e., prospective) pay, and compensatory damages, the guidance says. This means that employees can collect the full amount from either the staffing firm or the client. Neither the employee nor the EEOC has any obligation to pursue a claim against both the staffing firm and the client, and neither the staffing firm nor the client, if sued, has a right to bring the other into the proceeding or any right to contribution from the other. In contrast, punitive damages can only be assessed individually against each party on the basis of its respective degree of malicious or reckless conduct.

Head Count Issues Under Title VII

Title VII of the Civil Rights Act defines "employer" for the purposes of the Act as one that employs 15 or more employees (42 USC §2000e[b]). The question sometimes arises whether and under what circumstances temporary employees assigned to a client by a staffing firm must be included in the head count of both the staffing firm and the client to determine whether each employer has met the 15-employee head count requirement. It is a complex question, and federal courts do not agree on the answer. For an excellent overview of the criteria courts have applied in determining when the employees of two or more employers should be aggregated in determining whether statutory head count requirements have been satisfied under Title VII and other laws, see *Arculeo v. On-Site Sales & Marketing LLC*, 425 F.3d 193 (2d Cir. 2005).

Affirmative Action, EEO-1 Reporting, And Other Record-Keeping Issues

The purpose of affirmative action programs is not to address specific acts of discrimination against particular individuals but to take positive steps to ensure that all individuals belonging to those groups are given an opportunity to "catch up" to make up for past discrimination against them as a class.

Federal law requires certain federal contractors and subcontractors to comply with rules intended to proactively benefit specific classes of employees (i.e., minorities, women, veterans, and the disabled). What are the obligations of staffing firms under these rules, and do clients have any responsibility to the staffing firm's employees? This section addresses those questions in two areas. One involves the rules covering minorities and women under executive order 11246. The other involves the job-listing requirements under the Vietnam Era Veterans' Readjustment Assistance Act of 1974.

Affirmative Action Policy Under Executive Order 11246

President Johnson established the federal government's affirmative action policy regarding minorities in 1965 with executive order 11246. The policy is enforced under regulations issued by the DOL Office of Federal Contract Compliance Programs. The order and regulations apply to federal contractors with 50 or more employees and contracts of $50,000 or more and to certain subcontractors.

A threshold question is how the 50-employee head count test applies to staffing firms. Although there is no known ruling involving the staffing industry, it is possible that courts would apply the head count test similar to the way such tests are applied to determine coverage under other civil rights laws. For example, Title VII and the federal Age Discrimination in Employment Act apply head count tests (15 and 20 employees, respectively) using a 20-week rule. Under those laws, if an employer employs the requisite number of employees in 20 or more calendar weeks in the current or preceding calendar year, the employer is subject to the law. If a 20-week rule were applied to the 50-employee test under executive order 11246, a staffing firm whose weekly head count (including employees assigned to clients) was at least 50 in 20 or more calendar weeks in a year would be subject to the executive order, assuming it had federal contracts or subcontracts over the specified dollar amount.

If a staffing firm is subject to the executive order, and is therefore required to have an affirmative action plan, the next question is whether all of its employees must be included in plan. The American Staffing Association has historically asserted that only a staffing firm's full-time employees, not its temporary employees, must be included in the plan. This was because the affirmative action plan rules were singularly ill suited for a temporary work force and because the guidelines issued by the EEOC, in recognition of that fact, created an express exemption for temporary employees from the record-keeping and reporting rules businesses were required to follow in developing their affirmative action plans.

In 1965, the EEOC (a separate federal agency independent of DOL and the Office of Federal Contract Compliance Programs) proposed record-keeping and reporting rules requiring employers to identify employees based on their minority status. These rules require all private employers with 100 or more employees (including employers with fewer than 100 if they are owned or affiliated with another company and the entire enterprise employs 100 or more) to file an EEO-1 report showing all full-time and part-time employees by race, ethnicity, and gender. Federal contractors with 50 or more employees and federal business worth $50,000 or more also must file.

When the rules were first proposed in 1965, the American Staffing Association voiced concern about the impact on temporary staffing firms. The association pointed out that it would be impossible to visually determine the minority status of thousands of employees who work for customers at remote locations in unpredictable, short-term tenures. Moreover, the association was concerned that if temporary staffing firms had to record the racial status of their workers, they would run afoul of state antidiscrimination laws because the information potentially could be used in making assignments—a classic catch-22. The EEOC eventually acknowledged these problems and expressly excluded temporary workers from its record-keeping and reporting requirements. The exclusion is set forth in the instructions to employers for completing the EEO-1 report (see Appendix J). The instructions, which are jointly issued by the EEOC and OFCCP, state that the following persons are excluded from the definition of employee:

> *[P]ersons who are hired on a casual basis for a specified period of time, or for the duration of a specified job, and work on remote or scattered sites or locations where it is not practical or feasible for the employer to make a visual survey of the work force…persons temporarily employed…who are obtained through a hiring hall or other referral arrangement through an employee contractor or agent…or persons (EXCEPT leased employees[85]) on the payroll of an employment agency[86] who are referred by such agency for work to be performed on the premises of another employer under that employer's direction and control.*

The affirmative action rules issued by DOL under executive order 11246 expressly referred to the EEO-1 report as the basis for developing and monitoring employer affirmative action plans.[87] Because the report that DOL directed employers to use expressly excludes temporary employees, the American Staffing Association believed that it was reasonable to conclude that DOL did not intend to require such employees to be included in staffing company affirmative action plans. Moreover, the association believed that the exclusion extends to clients' plans as well because the EEO-1 instructions exclude persons "obtained…through an employee contractor."[88]

The staffing industry took this position for almost 30 years, and while some regional OFFCP offices disagreed, no steps were taken to formally challenge the industry's view. Nor did DOL take any position on the matter until Nov. 13, 2000, when—in an overview of the scope of final OFCCP regulations—it assert-

---

85. The exception for leased employees applies to "a permanent employee provided by an employment agency for a fee to an outside company *for which the employment agency handles all personnel tasks including payroll, staffing, benefit payments, and compliance reporting*" (emphasis added)—a clear reference to the services provided by professional employer organizations (PEOs). Employees employed under such arrangements must be reported on the EEO–1 form.

86. The EEOC uses employment agency to refer not just to permanent placement firms but generically to all forms of employment services, including temporary staffing firms.

87. *See, e.g.,* 41 C.F.R. § 60-2.11 and 60-3.4B.

88. It might be asked why this reasoning would not exclude temporary employees in applying the 50-employee head count test for determining whether a federal contractor is subject to the executive order. Although that argument has never been tested to the author's knowledge, a court might hold that there is a difference between excluding certain workers from an employer's affirmative action plan because it is not practical or feasible to include them, and holding that they are not employees for the purpose of determining whether the firm is subject to the executive order at all. Hence, although the EEO-1 rules applicable to private employers exclude temporary employees for both head count and reporting purposes, the head count exclusion might not extend to federal contractors under the executive order.

ed, almost in passing, that temporary employees should be included in affirmative action plans. Responding to a comment on the proposed rules,[89] DOL stated, "the term 'employees' is broad enough to include part-time, temporary, and full-time employees." This view, DOL said, did not "signal any change in OFCCP's requirement for reporting [such employees] in written [affirmative action plans] now or in the future."[90] Since issuing that brief statement, DOL has issued no further statement on the matter or issued any guidance as to how the affirmative action plan rules should be applied to temporary employees.

OFCCP Internet Applicant Rules

In fall 2005, the OFCCP issued special rules pertaining to "Internet applicants" that require certain federal contractors and subcontractors to collect and maintain résumés as well as data on applicants' sex, race, and ethnic data, when job seekers and employers use the Internet to find jobs and fill positions.[91] The American Staffing Association believes that the exclusion of temporary employees for EEO-1 reporting purposes provides a basis for asserting that the OFCCP Internet applicant rules do not apply to temporary employees.

Exemption for "Recruitment Practices" Under EEOC and Department of Labor Rules

The EEOC has not adopted any specific requirement that employers must make or keep personnel or employment records—only that such records that are kept must be preserved for one year from the date of the making of the record or the personnel action involved, whichever occurs later (29 CFR § 1602. 14). In 1978, the EEOC and DOL issued "Uniform Guidelines on Employee Selection Procedures," which specify which records employers should maintain to determine whether their employment selection procedures have a disparate impact on minorities and other protected groups. The guidelines also prescribe methods for validating procedures that are found to have a disparate impact.[92]

---

89. The proposed rules, issued on May 4, 2000, made no mention of the issue of coverage of temporary employees.

90. 65 Fed.Reg. 68024 (Nov. 13, 2000). No view was expressed as to whether temporary employees assigned by staffing firms should be considered the employees of the staffing firm or the client for affirmative action plan purposes.

91. 70 Fed. Reg. 58946, Oct. 7, 2005.

92. The Uniform Guidelines on Employee Selection Procedures can be found at 29 CFR part 1607 (EEOC) and 41 CFR part 60-3 (DOL). The courts have held that the guidelines are not legally binding, and no court has ever applied the record-keeping requirements to temporary employees.

In 2004, the EEOC and DOL published questions and answers to clarify the application of the guidelines to Internet recruitment practices.[93] Question 95 asks whether Internet recruitment, like traditional recruitment, is exempt from uniform guideline requirements. The answer given is as follows:

> *As a business practice, recruitment involves identifying and attracting potential recruits to apply for jobs. Under [the guidelines], recruitment practices are not considered…to be selection procedures,[94] and the [guidelines'] requirements geared to monitoring selection procedures do not apply.*

Based on these guidelines, the American Staffing Association believes that staffing firms that identify and attract recruits for direct hire by clients are engaged in "recruitment practices" as defined above and should be exempt from requirements to maintain applicant flow data under both the uniform guidelines and the OFCCP regulations pertaining to Internet applicants. Moreover, ASA believes that the exemption for recruitment practices applies not only to direct placements, but also to those made through "temporary-to-hire" arrangements; however, the exemption may have little practical application if clients require staffing firms to provide EEO information.

Client Requests for Race and Ethnic Data

The American Staffing Association believes that the EEOC and OFCCP record-keeping and affirmative action rules, including the Internet applicant rules, are not applicable to temporary employees, and that staffing firms engaged in recruitment practices may be exempt from the requirement to maintain applicant flow data. At the same time, ASA and its members remain firmly committed to ensuring that temporary employees are recruited, assigned, and employed on a nondiscriminatory basis and to assisting clients in meeting their EEO obligations.

In particular, the association recognizes that clients increasingly use staffing firms to recruit employees for hire, either through direct placements or through "temporary-to-hire" arrangements, and that clients may request sex, race, and ethnic information regarding such candidates pursuant to EEOC or OFCCP requests for applicant flow data. ASA encourages staffing firms to comply with lawful client requests for such information when possible.

---

93. 69 Fed. Reg. 10152 (March 4, 2004) at 10155.

94. 41 CFR § 60-3.2C.

But providing such data may present challenges. For example, temporary job applicants generally do not apply for assignments with specific clients, and identifying individual employees among the hundreds, or even thousands, of applicants who were considered for assignment to a particular client may be a complex and costly undertaking. Even if this task is accomplished, the results may be misleading because of vagaries in the process of assigning temporary workers. For example, qualified candidates are often assigned primarily because they happen to be available when called, with scant regard to other selection criteria. Nevertheless, staffing firms should work with their clients to develop a reasonable process for obtaining the desired information.

Employer Obligations to Military Reservists and National Guard Members

Given America's continuing military involvement overseas, U.S. armed forces have in recent years made greater use of military reservists and National Guard members. When these men and women return from active duty, civilian employers must be prepared to face the legal issues concerning their re-employment rights. For staffing firms, these issues prompt three common questions:

What are staffing firms' re-employment obligations to their internal staff?

What are the obligations to reinstate temporary workers with the clients to which they previously were assigned?

To what extent must a returning temporary worker receive preferential treatment for future assignments with clients?

Uniformed Services Employment and Re-Employment Rights Act

The Uniformed Services Employment and Re-employment Rights Act (38 U.S.C. § 4301 et seq.) protects any employee who must be absent from civilian employment because of active-duty military service when all of the following apply:

The employee provides advance notice to the civilian employer.

The cumulative length of the employee's military absence does not exceed five years.

The employee returns to work within the period prescribed by law or submits a timely application for re-employment.

The character of the employee's service does not disqualify him or her from re-employment.

Internal Employees—Seniority and Position Upon Return

After military service, an employee's re-employment rights and seniority are governed by the "escalator principle." The Supreme Court has stated that the returning employee "does not step back on the seniority escalator at the point he stepped off. The employee steps back on at the precise point he would have occupied had he kept his position continuously." Thus, a staffing firm's returning internal employees suffer no loss of seniority because they have served on active duty.

When an employee returns after being absent for 90 days or fewer, the employee is entitled to the position he or she would have attained had the absence not occurred (the "escalator" position), provided the employee is qualified to perform the duties of that position. If, despite the staffing firm's reasonable efforts, the returning employee is not qualified to perform a higher-skilled position, the employee may be reassigned to the position held when the absence started.

For absences exceeding 90 days, the returning employee must be assigned to either the "escalator" position or a position with equivalent seniority, status, and pay, assuming the employee is qualified to perform the duties of the position. If the returning employee is unqualified despite the staffing firm's reasonable efforts, the employee must be assigned to his or her former position or a position with equivalent seniority, status, and pay. If the returning employee is unqualified for that position, the firm must try to reassign the employee to an alternative position of lesser status and pay, with full seniority.

Hardship Exception

USERRA provides that there may be no obligation to re-employ an individual if the employer's circumstances have changed such that re-employment is impossible or unreasonable, or re-employment would create an undue hardship for the employer.

Whether re-employment is required will depend on the specific facts and circumstances. For example, re-employment may not be required if the employee's position has been eliminated during his or her absence. There is no requirement to re-establish a position that is no longer needed.

However, the returning employee may be entitled to re-employment if other positions exist that involve his or her former duties. The veteran may also be entitled to re-employment in a position to which he or she would have advanced or been transferred if employment had continued without interruption. And the veteran may be entitled to re-employment in a position of equivalent seniority, status, and pay. Thus, re-employment cannot necessarily be refused if equivalent positions exist for which the veteran is qualified or could be qualified after reasonable training.

Reinstatement With Clients

USERRA contains a broad definition of the term "employer," which potentially encompasses both staffing firms and their clients as joint employers of temporary workers.

The statute is silent, however, about the obligations of employers in joint employment situations. While the law is not clear, the FMLA may provide useful guidance. It provides that, in joint employment situations, the primary employer (the staffing firm) has an obligation to restore to employment an employee returning from leave. The secondary employer (the client) also may be required to accept the returning employee, depending on the facts.

However, USERRA's re-employment provisions do not apply if the employment at issue was "for a brief, nonrecurrent period and there [was] no reasonable expectation that such employment [would] continue indefinitely or for a significant period" (38 U.S.C. § 4312[d][1][C]). Whether a temporary worker is entitled to re-employment with the client he or she was previously assigned to, therefore, will depend on the nature of the former assignment. If the assignment was reasonably expected to be continuous and for an indefinite period, re-employment with the client would likely be required.

Casual and nonrecurrent assignments, however, would not likely implicate USERRA's reinstatement requirements. For example, an extra clerk hired during the holiday rush or a substitute employee hired during the absence of a regular employee on a year's leave would not likely be entitled to re-employment with a staffing firm's client (see *Martin v. Roosevelt Hospital*, 426 F.2d 155 [2nd Cir. 1970]). Similarly, a temporary worker placed with a client to perform a particular task, such as a defined piece of research, that was completed during military service would not be entitled to re-employment with the client if the client does not regularly employ people for such tasks.

Depending on the facts, a worker occupying a temporary-to-hire position might be entitled to re-employment by the client under USERRA. While there do not appear to be any cases addressing such a situation, the law provides that employees on probationary status are entitled to re-employment if they reasonably anticipated that, on completion of the probationary period, he would receive regular employee status.

Priority Consideration for Future Assignments

Because USERRA does not provide guidance about joint employment situations in general, it is unclear whether staffing firms are under any obligation to provide returning veterans with priority consideration for future assignments.

However, in view of USERRA's strong protections for returning veterans, embodied in the escalator principle, an argument can be made that priority consideration is required.

Under the FMLA, when individuals returning from medical leave cannot be reinstated with the client they were previously assigned to, the staffing firm must give them priority consideration or place them at the "head of the line" for possible assignments with other clients for which they are qualified. Staffing firms wishing to take a conservative approach may wish to adopt a similar approach under USERRA.

Job Listing Requirements Under the Vietnam Era Veterans' Readjustment Assistance Act

In recent years, a number of staffing firms have been advised by their state employment services office that they have mandatory job listing obligations under the Vietnam Era Veterans' Readjustment Assistance Act. The issue is whether and under what circumstances those obligations apply to staffing firms and their clients.

The act requires each federal contractor or subcontractor having contracts or transactions of $25,000 or more in a year to list all employment openings with the local office of their state employment service.[95] Openings include temporary jobs lasting more than three days. However, regulations issued under the act expressly provide that there is no obligation to list positions that will be filled from within the contractor's organization, including openings filled from regularly established "recall" lists.[96]

All staffing firms that assign employees to customers maintain a database of qualified employees who have been previously screened and hired. When a client order is received, the firm selects from this inventory an employee who best fits the client's requirements. When the assignment is completed, the employee may be immediately reassigned to another job or, if one is not immediately available, returned to the firm's active list for recall when another assignment becomes available. Staffing firms have taken the position that client orders filled in this manner are filled from within their own organization within the meaning of the regulations and therefore do not have to be listed with the employment service.

In contrast to filling jobs from within, staffing firms sometimes place classified advertisements for the purpose of filling a specific client's requirements that cannot

---

95. 41 C.F.R. § 60-250.5(a)2.

96. *Id.* at (a)(6)(i) and (iii).

be met from the firm's existing list or to replenish its own inventory of qualified employees in various job categories. Jobs published in such ads could be construed as openings to which the listing requirements apply, provided they are expected to last more than three days. Assuming the listing requirements would apply in such cases, it would appear reasonable to conclude that a staffing firm could comply by providing a copy of the ad to the local employment service in a timely manner.

In regard to the client's obligation, it also would appear reasonable to conclude that a client that decides to contract out a particular job or function to an outside labor supply firm has created an employment opening within the meaning of the act. However, the opening is arguably not with the client but with the supplier (e.g., a staffing firm) that has contracted to provide the labor and that directly hires the worker.

Americans With Disabilities Act

There has been very little case law on the application of the Americans With Disabilities Act (ADA),[97] which became effective for most employers in 1992, to staffing firms. However, in December 2000, citing a study that suggests employment with staffing firms can provide a "critical means for people with disabilities to move from unemployment to competitive permanent employment," the EEOC issued specific enforcement guidance on how the ADA applies to staffing firms and their clients (Appendix I). The new guidance addressed ADA issues not covered in the EEOC's 1997 general enforcement guidance (Appendix H) on contingent workers. It covers three main areas: disability-related inquiries and medical examinations; reasonable accommodation and undue hardship; and qualification standards, employment tests, and other selection criteria.

When Medical Questions May Be Asked

One important practical concern staffing firms have in complying with the ADA is the issue of when temporary job applicants may be asked disability-related questions or be required to submit to medical examinations. The law generally prohibits employers from making such inquiries before making an "offer of employment." The question is, when is a staffing firm considered to have offered employment to a temporary job applicant?

Before the guidance was issued, the staffing industry operated on the assumption that, for ADA purposes, job offers were made when applicants completed the initial hiring process and were deemed qualified for assignments. This prac-

---

97. 42 U.S.C. §§ 12101 to 12213.

tice was based on an agreement between a large national staffing firm and the EEOC that provided that the staffing firm could request medical information even though no assignments had been offered.

However, the EEOC now says that staffing firms cannot ask for medical information until a worker is actually offered an assignment. Citing Congress's concern that individuals should know whether they have been denied employment because of a medical condition, the EEOC says that job applicants cannot reasonably make that determination before a job offer is made. According to the EEOC, only after a job offer is made and medical information is disclosed can job applicants have a reasonable basis for attributing any subsequent withdrawal of the offer to the disclosure of that information.

Exceptions to the Rule

The American Staffing Association had preliminary discussions with EEOC officials about the guidance. The association expressed concern that restricting medical questions until after an assignment is offered could make it difficult, if not impossible, for staffing firms to make ADA-required accommodations in a timely manner. The EEOC provided exceptions in the guidance to mitigate any hardship.

The EEOC acknowledges that temporary jobs may become available on short notice and last for only brief periods of time. So the guidance expressly provides that if a reasonable accommodation cannot be provided quickly enough for a worker to begin or complete an assignment in a timely manner, the EEOC will consider that an "undue hardship" and relieve the staffing firm of its obligation to accommodate the worker.

The guidelines also say that if a worker cannot provide required medical information before an assignment is scheduled to begin, the staffing firm may revoke the offer of employment and assign another employee.

Finally, the guidelines make clear that when job applicants have obvious disabilities or when they voluntarily disclose that they have disabilities or that they need accommodations, staffing firms may, during the initial interview, ask what reasonable accommodations they may need to perform the types of jobs they are seeking, even though no assignments have been offered.

Clients Are Co-Employers

The guidance confirmed a long-standing American Staffing Association position that staffing firm clients generally have a joint obligation with the staffing firm for ADA compliance. This obligation includes sharing the cost of providing reasonable accommodations to workers with disabilities. When it is unclear what accommodation should be provided, the EEOC says that staffing firms and their clients "should engage in an informal, interactive process with the worker" to determine the employee's needs.

Undue Hardship

The ADA has always relieved employers from making accommodations if doing so would impose an "undue hardship." One example cited in the new guidance is an accommodation that would involve a "significant expense for both the staffing firm and the client," even if their resources are combined. In such a case, both would incur an undue hardship. "Significant" is not defined and must be determined on the facts and circumstances of each case. Staffing firms and clients can also show undue hardship if the cost of the accommodation would be significant to one of them, and it has made a good-faith but unsuccessful effort to get the other to contribute.

Labor–Management Relations

In the area of labor relations, the key to determining co-employment is whether the client is substantially involved in determining the terms and conditions of employment of the staffing firm's employees. In such cases, clients may have joint employer obligations with respect to a staffing firm's employees.

Inclusion of Staffing Firm Employees in Client Bargaining Units

Going back as far as 1970, the National Labor Relations Board and at least one federal court have held that temporary employees employed by staffing firms may be included in client bargaining units where there is a sufficient "community of interest" between a staffing firm's employees and the client.[98]

But an equally long line of NLRB cases, beginning with the *Greenhoot* case in 1973, have held that even where the requisite community of interest can be shown, the employees of one joint employer cannot be forced into the bargaining unit of the other joint employer without the consent of both employers.[99]

Greenhoot involved a building management firm, Greenhoot, which had contracted to supply maintenance workers to 14 separate office buildings. The NLRB held that the workers were jointly employed by Greenhoot and the 14

---

98. *See* Manpower Inc. of Shelby County, 164 N.L.R.B. 287 (1967); Add-a-Man, No. 7-RC-9639 (N.L.R.B. Jan. 26, 1970) (unpublished opinion); Continental Winding Co. and Kelly Services, 305 N.L.R.B. 122 (1991); N.L.R.B. v. Western Temporary Services, 821 F.2d 1258 (7th Cir. 1987) (temporary help firm and its client both exercised substantial control over the employees, and both were involved in determining the essential terms and conditions of employment).

99. Greenhoot Inc., 205 N.L.R.B. 250 (1973).

separate building owner clients. The NLRB ruled that the union's petition for a bargaining unit consisting of the employees working at all 14 buildings was a multiemployer unit that, under federal labor law, required the consent of each of the employers.

In rejecting the unit, the board held the following:

> *[T]here is no legal basis for establishing a multiemployer unit absent a show-ing that the several employers have expressly conferred on a joint bargaining agent the power to bind them in negotiations or that they have by an estab-lished course of conduct unequivocally manifested a desire to be bound in future collective bargaining by group rather than individual action.*[100]

Seventeen years later, the board applied the *Greenhoot* ruling in the *Lee Hospital* case.[101] Unlike *Greenhoot*, *Lee Hospital* involved only one client, the hospital. The employees in question were nurse anesthetists jointly employed by the hospital and an anesthesiologist group. The NLRB held that the jointly employed nurses could not be included in a bargaining unit with the hospital's other professionals without the consent of both employers.

In 2000 the NLRB, in the *M.B. Sturgis* and *Jeffboat* cases, overturned *Lee Hospital*, saying that it had misapplied *Greenhoot*.[102] In *Sturgis*, the NLRB held that as long as all of the workers in a bargaining unit are employed, solely or jointly, by a single client, it is not a multiemployer unit and the consent requirement does not apply, even if the unit includes employees of multiple suppliers.

Board member J. Robert Brame III dissented, arguing that the facts in *Lee Hospital* were not materially different from the *Greenhoot* case so as to justify abandoning the consent requirement. Brame said that staffing firms and their clients, even if they are joint employers, still retain their separate employer status, and, therefore, any bargaining unit composed of the employees of both employers is still a multiemployer bargaining unit that legally requires the consent of both employers.

Brame predicted that the decision would lead to controversy and confusion as the employers strove to protect their differing interests. Subsequent NLRB cases construing *Sturgis*—involving complex, and contentious questions regarding

---

100. *Id* at 251.

101. Lee Hospital, 300 N.L.R.B. 947 (1990).

102. M.B. Sturgis Inc., 331 N.L.R.B. No. 173 (2000).

application of the "community of interest" standard and the allocation of bargaining responsibilities among multiple employers—showed that Brame's concerns were not unfounded.[103]

But in 2004, in *H.S. Care LLC dba Oakwood Care Center*, the NLRB overruled its decision in *Sturgis*.[104] Citing the decades of precedent beginning with the *Greenhoot* case, the board in a 3–2 decision said that allowing such units to be formed without consent results in a "bifurcation of bargaining…[that] hampers the give-and-take process of negotiation between a union and an employer, and places the employers in the position of negotiating with one another as well as with the union."[105]

Overall, the *Sturgis* decision had minimal impact on the staffing industry. While no formal study has been conducted to determine how many temporary employees employed by staffing firms actually belong to a union, the number is probably small. Also small is the pool of temporary employees who would even potentially be eligible for union membership. Anecdotal evidence suggests that as little as 5% of temporary employees employed by staffing firms work at union work sites, mostly on short assignments—not especially fertile ground for recruiting new union members.

Crediting Prior Service When Temporary Workers Are Hired by Clients

Even if a temporary worker is not included in a joint bargaining unit, he or she may be entitled to benefits under a collective bargaining agreement covering the client's employees if the client directly hires the temporary employee following completion of a temporary assignment. At least one labor arbitrator has held that the temporary employee may be entitled to back pay to make up any difference between what he or she was earning as a temporary employee and the wage rate specified for that work classification in the client's collective bargaining agreement.[106]

---

103. Professional Facilities Management Inc., 332 N.L.R.B. 40 (Sept. 26, 2000); J.E. Higgins Lumber Co., 332 N.L.R.B. 109 (Oct. 31, 2000); Lodgian Inc., 332 N.L.R.B. 128 (Nov. 14, 2000); Interstate Warehousing of Ohio, 333 N.L.R.B. 83 (March 27, 2001); Outokumpu Copper Franklin Inc., 334 N.L.R.B. 39 (June 6, 2001) Engineered Storage Products Co., 334 N.L.R.B. 138 (Aug. 10, 2001); Kaiser Foundation Hospitals, 337 N.L.R.B. 165 (2002); Trumbull Memorial Hospital and Western Reserve Personnel, 338 N.L.R.B. 132 (April 3, 2003).

104. H.S. Care LLC. dba Oakwood Care Center, 343 N.L.R.B. No. 76 (2004).

105. *Id*, slip op. p. 5.

106. Metz Baking Co., 100 LA 671 (March 9, 1993).

Liability for Unfair Labor Practices

'Salts'

A unique twist on the theme of co-employment involves the use by unions of "salts," individuals employed and paid by unions to apply for work with a nonunion employer for the express purpose of organizing the employer's work force. The U.S. Supreme Court held in *NLRB v. Town & Country Electric* that salts are "employees" within the meaning of the National Labor Relations Act and therefore cannot be rejected or dismissed from employment solely on the basis of their union activities.[107]

The case involved a nonunion electrical contractor in Minnesota. The contractor retained the services of an employment agency to recruit electricians. The agency rejected 10 of 11 union applicants, and the contractor fired the one union employee it had hired. The NLRB held that the contractor and its employment agency committed an unfair labor practice by discriminating against the workers on the basis of their union membership.

The narrow issue decided by the Supreme Court was whether the workers were employees of the electrical contractor within the meaning of the National Labor Relations Act, which protects employees from unfair labor practices. The contractor argued that as employees of the union, the workers could not also be its employees and therefore were not protected. However, the Supreme Court held that the workers were employees of both the union and the contractor (i.e., the union and the contractor were co-employers) and therefore were protected against discrimination by the contractor.

Although nothing in the court's ruling prohibits an employer from rejecting unqualified applicants or from disciplining or dismissing workers who perform poorly or who engage in unlawful conduct, staffing firms and their clients should exercise care not to discriminate against applicants or employees on the basis of union membership. However, the NLRB has upheld an employer's refusal to hire applicants who were also full-time employees of a union on the basis of the employer's policy against moonlighting.[108]

In another case involving salts, a federal court of appeals ruled that votes cast by union salts hired by a construction staffing firm should be counted in a

---

107. N.L.R.B. v. Town & Country Electric, 516 U.S. 85 (1995).

108. Little Rock Electrical Contractors and IBEW Local 480, 327 N.L.R.B. 166 (1999). *See also* Contractors' Labor Pool v. N.L.R.B. No. 01-1393 (D.C. Cir. 2003), in which the court held that a construction staffing firm did not violate the National Labor Relations Act by refusing to hire workers whose prior wages were 30% higher or lower than the staffing firm's going rate. The court said the policy was designed to minimize employees' quitting for pay reasons and found no intent to discriminate against union members.

representation election involving all the firm's plumbers in the Boston area.[109] The salts gave the union the edge in the election. The court ruled that the salts shared a sufficient community of interest with the firm's other assigned workers to be included in the same bargaining unit.

The staffing firm argued that the salts did not have the same interests as the firm's other employees because they accepted employment solely to organize the work force and would likely leave employment once this task was accomplished. The court, however, found no evidence that the workers lacked the same interest in employment as the other workers. The union organizers did not receive compensation from the union for their activities and did not, in the court's opinion, appear solely motivated by their desire to organize the work force. The court noted that the salts did not resign after the election but instead were laid off by the staffing firm. It also found no evidence that they would have refused subsequent employment with the staffing firm if they had not found other jobs before the staffing firm had a chance to recall them.

Staffing Firm Liability for Unfair Labor Practices of Client

The NLRB established, in the 1993 case of *Capital EMI Music*, that a staffing firm will not be held liable for a client's unfair labor practice unless it knew or should have known that the client acted against the employee for unlawful reasons and acquiesced in the unlawful action by failing to protest it or exercise any contractual right it might have had to resist it.[110] In that case, the client terminated an assigned worker because of his union activities, and the staffing firm removed the worker without knowledge of those activities. The NLRB rejected an administrative law judge's ruling that the staffing firm was vicariously liable for the unlawful acts of its client solely because of their co-employer relationship.

The NLRB subsequently applied the principle established in *Capital EMI Music* in a 2000 case, *SOS Staffing Services*.[111] The board found the staffing firm guilty of an unfair labor practice for failing to protest its client's actions. The client unlawfully terminated a temporary worker's assignment because the worker engaged in protected union activity. The board said the staffing firm was obligated to register its protest with the client, even though the staffing firm did not learn of the client's action until three weeks after the employee had been terminated.

---

109. TradeSource Inc. v. N.L.R.B., 17 Fed. Appx. 159, 168 L.R.R.M. (BNA) 2799 (4th Cir. Aug. 28, 2001).

110. Capitol EMI Music Inc., 311 N.L.R.B. 997 (1993).

111. SOS Staffing Services Inc., 331 N.L.R.B. 97 (2000).

Similarly, in *Action Temporary Employment* in 2001, temporary workers struck to protest their staffing firm's practice of asking applicants about their union membership. The board found that the workers had unconditionally offered to return to work and that the client had engaged in an unfair labor practice by refusing to reinstate them. The board held that the staffing firm had not only engaged in an unfair labor practice in its own right by asking job applicants about their union membership but also was jointly liable for the client's unfair labor practice because it took no action to determine why the client refused to reinstate two workers.[112]

As in the past, changes in the composition of the NLRB could result in changes in the law on these and other issues.

Work Site Safety

The federal Occupational Safety and Health Act and state workplace safety laws require employers to maintain safe and healthy workplaces. The issue of who is primarily responsible for ensuring the safety of staffing firm employees at the work site—the staffing firm or the client—was unclear during the early 1970s, and staffing companies were sometimes cited for safety violations.

A clear policy began to emerge in 1977 in an administrative agency decision. Manpower Inc. was cited as solely responsible for the safety violations that led to the death of one of its temporary employees; its client was not cited at all. After reviewing the facts, an administrative law judge with the Occupational Safety and Health Review Commission ruled that although Manpower was an employer under common law because it had the right to hire and fire the employees, it was not the responsible employer. Because the focus of the act is prevention, the judge held that the government must first look to the employer that created the hazard and supervised the workers. It would be "unconscionable," he said, to require temporary staffing firms to satisfy the safety requirements of each and every work situation.[113]

Since this decision, OSHA offices have been advised that when temporary or other leased employees are used, the party in direct control of the workplace and the actions of the employees should be cited (usually, the work site, or uti-

---

112. Action Temporary Employment, 337 N.L.R.B. 39 (2001); Mingo Logan Coal Co. v. N.L.R.B, 67 Fed.Appx. 178 (4th Cir. 2003); Dunkin' Donuts Mid-Atlantic Distribution Center v. NLRB, 363 F.3d 437 (D.C. Cir. 2004) (federal appeals court upheld NLRB decision that staffing firm and client were joint employers and thus both were responsible for unfair labor practices committed against the workers).

113. Secretary of Labor v. Manpower Temporary Services Inc., 1977 WL 6891 (OSHRC), 1977-78 O.S.H.D. (CCH) 21,542.

lizing, employer).[114] Under these determinations, a temporary staffing company generally will be cited only if necessary to correct the violation, or if it knew or should have known of an unsafe condition. The OSHA Field Inspection Manual states in its definition of an employee:

> *Whether or not exposed persons are employees of an employer depends on several factors, the most important of which is who controls the manner in which the employees perform their assigned work. The question of who pays these employees may not be the determining factor.*[115]

Under OSHA's rules for recording and reporting occupational injuries and illnesses, clients are also required to maintain records of illnesses and injuries of temporary employees if the temporary workers are subject to the client's supervision, which generally will be the case.[116] This long-standing OSHA policy was formally adopted in regulations in 2001.[117] The purpose is to ensure timely and accurate record-keeping by the employer in the best position to obtain the information and to assist OSHA in identifying high-hazard employers. Clients also are required to cover temporary employees under OSHA's 1986 Hazard Communication Standard, which requires employers to notify employees of hazardous substances in the workplace.[118]

Some staffing firms reportedly have told clients that they can relieve the clients of the obligation to maintain records of illnesses and injuries of temporary employees by providing "supervisory" staffing firm employees at the client's work site. Such arrangements should be carefully scrutinized. According to OSHA, day-to-day supervision means supervision of the "details, means, methods, and processes by which the work is to be accomplished" (see Appendix K). Staffing firms typically do not provide such detailed supervision, and providing a few supervisory employees is unlikely to meet that test.

---

114. *See, e.g.*, Memorandum to regional administrators from Richard P. Wilson, deputy director, federal compliance and state programs, OSHA, Department of Labor (July 5, 1977). This position was reaffirmed in a Feb. 28, 1985, memorandum from John B. Miles Jr., then OSHA's director, directorate of field operations.

115. OCCUPATIONAL SAFETY AND HEALTH ADMINISTRATION, *U.S. Department of Labor, Field Inspection Manual.* CPL 2.103 at Chapter III, Inspection Documentation; paragraph. C, Violations; subparagraph b, Employee Exposure (1994).

116. 29 C.F.R. § 1904.31(b)(2).

117. 29 C.F.R. § 1904.31 (2003). However, an exemption for staffing firm offices from record-keeping requirements was removed. Firms with more than 10 employees are now required to keep occupational injury and illness records of their corporate and branch in-office employees.

118. OCCUPATIONAL SAFETY AND HEALTH ADMINISTRATION, *U.S. Department of Labor,* OSHA Standard Interpretations, Hazard Communication Standard, Employers' responsibilities towards temporary employees, Feb. 3, 1994, Letter from Roger Clark, director, OSHA Directorate of Compliance Programs. (See Appendix K for the text of the interpretation.)

The utilizing employer principle also is generally recognized under state law. North Carolina, for example, has codified the principle in amendments to its occupational safety statutes,[119] and New Mexico has incorporated a similar provision into its workers' compensation regulations.[120] These provisions require clients to include in their work site safety programs staffing firm employees whose work they supervise and control.

Although clients have primary responsibility for maintaining safe work sites, staffing firms have a responsibility to take reasonable steps to determine conditions at the work site, provide generic safety information, and advise employees as to how they can obtain more specific information at the work site to protect themselves from hazards they are likely to face on the job. Staffing firms can be penalized for failing to inquire about the conditions at the work site and to take adequate steps to ensure that their employees are properly informed of any hazards and how to protect themselves.[121]

California is a notable departure from the general view that the client is the primary employer for work site safety. The state occupational safety and health board has held that staffing firms are the primary employer and must not only inspect the work site but provide adequate safety training.[122] In addition, California provides that every employer in a staffing arrangement is required to report injuries to the California OSHA, and that staffing firms may not delegate this duty to clients.[123]

Wrongful Discharge

Wrongful discharge refers to a situation in which an employer's common-law right to terminate an employee at will is limited, either because of an agreement not to terminate the employee except for cause or because of a public policy exception (e.g., termination for refusal to engage in illegal activity).

Strictly speaking, a client cannot fire temporary employees. It can only ask that they be removed from the assignment. Only the staffing company has the

---

119. N.C. GEN. STAT. §§ 95-251(a)(2), 95-252(b).

120. THE WORKER'S COMPENSATION HANDBOOK FOR NEW MEXICO, BOOKLET DI, ANNUAL SAFETY INSPECTIONS (reprinted 1999) at p. 9, incorporated by reference at 11 N.M.A.C. § 4.2.9.1.2.

121. See, e.g., Friday Temporary Services, (unpub'd order) No. OSHANC 93-2651 (N.C. OSHA Review Board, April 9, 1996); Secretary of Labor v. Froedtert Memorial Lutheran Hospital Inc., OSHRC, No. 97-1839 (Jan. 16, 2004) (Milwaukee hospital violated the OSHA by failing to provide temporary housekeeping workers with hepatitis B vaccines and training regarding bloodborne pathogens).

122. Manpower Inc., No. 98-R4D5-4158, 2001 WL 575154 (Calif. OSHA Appeals Board, May 14, 2001); Sully-Miller Contracting Co. v. California Occupational Safety and Health Appeals Board, 138 Cal.App.4th 684, 41 Cal.Rptr.3d 742 (2006).

123. Labor Ready Inc., No. 99-R3D3-3350, 2001 WL 575152 (Calif. OSHA Appeals Board, May 11, 2001).

right to hire and fire and employees removed from an assignment at the client's request may be reassigned to another client. Temporary employees generally understand (and certainly should be made to understand) that even if the assignment purports to be for a specified period, the client always has a right to terminate the assignment for any lawful reason.

Special problems may exist in PEO arrangements where most or all of the client's entire work force are covered under the arrangement and work on a long-term, indefinite basis. In such cases, it is especially important to make sure that the right to hire, fire, and reassign is carefully spelled out in the agreement between the employee leasing firm and the client and that the employees are clearly informed.

Even if a client were held to be an employer for the purpose of a wrongful discharge claim based on the removal of the employee from a staffing assignment, the client could protect themselves from claims that the employees could be removed only for cause by ensuring that it does not make representations to such employees (e.g., in employee handbooks or orientations) that could be construed as limiting its common-law right to terminate an employee at will.

For example, a California appeals court ruled in an unpublished opinion that a temporary employee was not unlawfully discharged by the client.[124] The worker had been on assignment with the client for two and one-half years under a series of contracts with the staffing firm. He claimed that he had an implied-in-fact contract of employment with the client that entitled him to be discharged only for good cause, in accordance with the client's employee policy manual. The court rejected his claim, finding that no contract existed. It noted that even if the worker were an employee of the client, he did not have a contract and would only be an at-will employee, whose employment was terminable for any legal reason at any time.

Immigration and I-9 Verification

In 1986 Congress passed the Immigration Reform and Control Act, making it unlawful for an employer to hire any person not authorized to work in the U.S. To prove that only authorized persons have been hired, all employers must complete a Form I-9, attesting that they have verified each individual's right to work. Employees must establish their identity and work authorization by showing certain documents described in regulations.

---

124. Maikish v. Pacific Gas and Electric Co., (unpub'd op.) 2d. Civ. No. B098600 (Cal. App. 2d. June 5, 1997); *see also* Hankins v. Adecco Services of Ohio, No. 17-01-13, 2001 WL 1475801 (Ohio Ct. App. Nov. 20, 2001) (the employee knew that assignments were temporary and nothing in the client's work program manual guaranteed a permanent job with the client).

Regulations issued under the act make clear that clients using contract services do not have any obligation to verify the employment status of the contractor's employees. The regulations provide that "in the case of an independent contractor or contract labor or services, the term 'employer' shall mean the independent contractor or contractor and not the person or entity using the contract labor."[125] Accordingly, clients have no obligation to verify the employment status of a staffing firm's employees.[126]

Because the staffing firm is responsible for performing the I-9 verification and for maintaining the records relating to this requirement, it is also the staffing firm's responsibility to ensure that the information obtained from a job applicant about national origin is not used in a discriminatory manner.

Privacy Protection

Health Information Privacy Rules Under HIPAA

The Health Insurance Portability and Accountability Act of 1996 required the establishment of privacy rules that apply to organizations in the health care industry and set a compliance date of April 14, 2003, for most covered entities.[127]

In general, the privacy rules govern the use and disclosure of "protected health information" in the hands of health care organizations. Service providers that contract with health care organizations services involving the use or disclosure of protected health information are considered "business associates" under the rules and must contractually agree to protect the information in the same ways as their health care clients. Such "business associate contracts" must be in writing and must contain certain privacy provisions as specified in the rules. Members of the health care organization's "work force" are not considered business associates.

In a typical relationship between a staffing firm and a client—in which the staffing firm assigns its temporary employees to provide services at the client's premises under the client's supervision—arguably neither the staffing firm nor its employees should be treated as business associates because in such circumstances the temporary employees should be treated as members of the client's work force. Other arrangements—for example, where services are to be per-

---

125. 8 C.F.R. § 274a.1(g).

126. *See* IMMIGRATION AND NATURALIZATION SERVICE, U.S. DEPARTMENT OF JUSTICE, HANDBOOK FOR EMPLOYERS M-274 (Rev. 11/21/91) at 3, 12.

127. 42 U.S.C. § 1320d–1329d-8.

formed off-site or under the staffing firm's direct control—might result in a different outcome.

If the staffing firm and its employees are not treated as business associates, a client is not required to include privacy provisions in its contract with the staffing firm.

Definition of 'Business Associate'

The HIPAA privacy rules define a business associate as any person who performs or assists in performing a function or activity involving the use or disclosure of individually identifiable health information (i.e., protected health information) on behalf of the covered entity.[128] Under this broad definition, a staffing firm could be a business associate of a client health care organization if the assigned employees use or disclose protected health information. In such cases, the staffing firm would have to enter into a business associate contract with the client containing the required privacy provisions.

Argument for Not Treating Staffing Firms or Their Temporary Employees as Business Associates

The HIPAA privacy rules appear to provide two bases for arguing that staffing firms and their temporary employees are not business associates of their clients, at least in the typical case where the temporary employees provide services on the client's premises under the client's supervision.

First, since the definition of business associate excludes individuals who act "in the capacity of a member of the work force" of a covered entity, temporary employees will not be treated as business associates if they can be characterized as members of the client's work force. "Work force" is defined as employees, volunteers, trainees, and other persons who perform work under the *direct control* of a covered entity, whether or not they are paid by that entity.[129] While the rules do not define "direct control," where the individual works might be a significant factor.[130]

---

128. *See* 45 C.F.R. 160.103.

129. *Id.*

130. A person may be treated as a work force member "if the assigned work station of persons under contract is on the covered entity's premises and such persons perform a substantial proportion of their activities at that location." 65 Fed. Reg. 82480 (Dec. 28, 2000). *See also* 65 Fed. Reg. 82643 (Dec. 28, 2000) (employee of contractor such as a software vendor who works on-site may be treated as work force member); 65 Fed. Reg. 82645 (Dec. 28, 2000) (volunteers who work off-site and need protected health information should be treated as business associates rather than as work force members).

The focus on location makes practical sense, given that the purpose of the business associate contract is to protect protected health information when it leaves the control of the covered entity. If an individual works with such information on the premises of the covered entity, the information arguably has not left the covered entity's control in a way that requires the protection of a business associate contract. By contrast, if the service provider is using protected health information off-site, there is arguably a greater need for such protection.

Because a staffing firm's temporary employees typically work at the client's premises and the parties would not contemplate protected health information leaving the client's premises and control of the covered customer, temporary employees generally should be treated as under the client's direct control and, therefore, as members of the client's work force rather than its business associates.

Second, even if temporary employees, for some reason, are not treated as actual members of the client's work force, they still should not be treated as the client's business associates because they are "acting in the capacity" of work force members. Staffing firms typically assign their employees to perform, on a temporary basis, functions similar to those performed by the client's regular employees and, in that sense, they "act in the capacity" of the client's work force.

Under either of the above arguments, staffing firms generally should not be required to enter into business associate contracts with the covered clients to which they send temporary employees.

Who Decides Whether a Staffing Firm Is a Business Associate?

The HIPAA privacy rules appear to indicate that the covered entity, not the potential business associate, decides how individuals are to be treated, and that the decision is more of a choice than a mandate.[131] Therefore, covered entities are likely to view it as their decision to make. Covered staffing firm clients—because of "co-employment" or other concerns—might be motivated to treat temporary employees as business associates rather than as members of their work force.

The following arguments might be helpful in persuading clients that it is not only appropriate but advantageous to treat the employees as members of the client's work force.

---

131. *See* 65 Fed. Reg. 82480 (Dec. 28, 2000) (the covered entity may choose to treat individuals who work on its premises as work force members or business associates).

- The definition of "work force" clearly includes individuals (e.g., volunteers) who are not common-law employees, so characterizing temporary employees as work force members for HIPAA purposes would not create "co-employment" issues under other laws.

- By treating temporary employees as work force members and providing them the proper training, the client would be better able protect its protected health information than would the staffing firm.

- Although the preamble to the regulations indicates the covered entity can elect how to treat certain service providers, that choice is not reflected in the actual regulatory language. Because any reasonable reading of the actual regulatory language is likely to result in on-site temporary employees being categorized as work force members, a covered client might want to treat them as such from the beginning to protect itself.

- Treating temporary employees as members of the client's work force obviates the need for the client to include business-associate privacy provisions in its contract with the staffing firm.

- Treating temporary employees as members of the client's work force avoids having to include irrelevant and potentially burdensome privacy provisions in its contract with the staffing firm. Many of HIPAA's privacy provisions contemplate that protected health information is held in the possession of the business associate, that is, the staffing firm. For example, one provision requires a business associate to agree that it will provide access rights to protected health information in its possession.[132] Other provisions require the business associate to agree to permit amendment and accounting rights, make its books and records available to the Secretary of Health and Human Services for audit purposes, and destroy or return all information in its possession at the end of the contract.[133] Where the staffing firm itself holds no protected health information, it does not seem reasonable to include such provisions in its contract.

Financial Information Privacy Rules (Gramm-Leach-Bliley)

The Financial Services Modernization Act of 1999, also known as the Gramm-Leach-Bliley Act (GLB), established rules for financial services institutions that took effect in November 2000, with full compliance required by July 1, 2001. New regulations issued May 23, 2002, imposed additional requirements that were phased in over the following two years.

---

132. 45 C.F.R. 164.504(e)(2)(ii)(E).

133. 45 C.F.R. 164.504(e)(2)(ii)(F), (G), (H), and (I).

Under GLB, financial services institutions are required to take certain steps to protect the privacy of nonpublic consumer financial information. The question is whether, when a staffing firm provides temporary employees to a client covered by GLB, the client must include special GLB privacy provisions in their contracts with staffing firms. The American Staffing Association believes that regulations issued by the Federal Trade Commission require financial institutions to include special GLB provisions in their contracts with staffing firms to safeguard consumer information. Prior to the issuance of the most recent regulations, the association believed that special contract language was required only in limited circumstances.

Several other federal agencies have issued implementing privacy regulations for the industries they regulate.[134] In addition, the GLB left it to the states to issue GLB-related privacy and safeguard regulations for insurance companies.[135] This book deals only with the Federal Trade Commission rules.

There are two commission regulations that potentially impose obligations on financial institutions to include special language in their contracts with third-party service providers. Both rules are discussed below.

Federal Trade Commission Privacy Rules

The FTC issued regulations May 24, 2000, which are generally referred to as the "privacy rules." The privacy rules regulate financial institutions and their disclosure of "nonpublic personal information" to "nonaffiliated third parties."[136] In general, the rules permit disclosures to be made to temporary employees in the following circumstances.

▪ The temporary employee is treated as a joint employee of the client. The privacy rules exclude from the definition of "nonaffiliated third party" persons who are "employed jointly" by the financial services institution and another company. Hence, if a temporary employee assigned by a staffing firm is treated as jointly employed by the client, the privacy rules would not apply. In such cases, even though the staffing firm would remain a nonaffiliated third party, a confidentiality agreement would appear not to

---

134. Office of Comptroller of the Currency; Board of Governors of the Federal Reserve System; Federal Deposit Insurance Corporation; Office of Thrift Supervision; National Credit Union Administration; Secretary of the Treasury; Securities and Exchange Commission.

135. The National Association of Insurance Commissioners issued a model regulation for implementing GLB, which some states have adopted. Other states have adopted different privacy regulations. Significantly, the NAIC's model rule states that compliance with the HIPAA privacy regulations—i.e., for health insurers—constitutes compliance with GLB's privacy requirements.

136. Codified at 16 C.F.R. part 313.

be necessary if the financial services institution discloses information only to the temporary employees and not to the staffing firm.[137]

▪ The financial institution gives notice of the disclosures to its consumers/customers and provides them with the opportunity to "opt out"—and they do in fact opt out.[138]

▪ If the financial institution has a confidentiality agreement with the service provider limiting the use and reuse of protected information, this obviates any opt-out requirement.[139] If the service provider refuses to enter into a confidentiality agreement, the financial institution must provide its consumers/customers with the opportunity to opt out.

▪ The disclosures are made to "effect, administer, or enforce a transaction that a consumer requests or authorizes."[140] Such disclosures are excluded from the privacy rules, eliminating the need for a confidentiality agreement or opt out. It seems likely that this exception applies to the types of activities that financial institutions assign to temporary staff, but staffing firms should review the circumstances on a case-by-case basis.

Federal Trade Commission Safeguard Rules

The most recent regulations under GLB, issued in May 2002, create a new set of "Standards for Safeguarding Customer Information."[141] These "safeguard rules" apply in addition to the "privacy rules." They establish standards for financial institutions for protecting customer information and also require them to ensure by contract that all service providers undertake appropriate safeguards to protect customer information. Whereas the privacy rules focus on prohibiting the disclosure and reuse of private information, the safeguard rules establish the administrative, technical, and physical safeguards that financial institutions must take to ensure the security of records and to protect them from unauthorized access.

The safeguard rules require financial institutions to "[r]equire [their] service providers by contract to implement and maintain" safeguards for customer infor-

---

137. ASA has not sought to determine whether or under what circumstances temporary employees would be considered "joint employees" of a client under the Federal Trade Commission privacy rules. Accordingly, staffing firms that assign employees to perform services that do not fall within the section 313.14 exception discussed above may want to pursue this issue further.

138. Note that the FTC privacy rules differ in this respect from the HIPAA privacy rules. Whereas the HIPAA rules generally prohibit disclosure unless the individual gives permission, the FTC privacy rules generally permit disclosure unless permission is withdrawn.

139. *See* 16 C.F.R. § 313.13.

140. 16 C.F.R. § 313.14.

141. 16 C.F.R. § 314.3.

mation. The preamble to the rules makes clear that such a contract is required even if a contract is not required under the privacy rules:

> *[T]he Commission has determined that the Rule should apply to all service providers, even those that the Privacy Rule does not require to enter into agreements concerning reuse and redisclosure of the relevant information. Although the Privacy Rule allows certain service providers to receive information without entering into confidentiality agreements, these confidentiality provisions do not address the range of security issues that are contemplated by the Safeguards Rule.*"[142]

Who Is the Service Provider Under the Safeguard Rules— The Staffing Firm, the Temporary Employee, or Both?

The safeguard rules broadly define "service provider" as "any person or entity that receives, maintains, processes, or otherwise is permitted access to customer information through its provision of services directly to a financial institution."[143] Staffing firms might argue that the temporary employee is the "service provider" because the staffing firms never directly "receive, maintain, process, or otherwise are permitted access" to the private information.[144] The counterargument is that the staffing firm, as the entity directly paid by the financial institution for services rendered, is "deemed" to be in receipt of the information. Given that the safeguard rules do not contain any of the exceptions that are recognized in the privacy rules and are intended to broadly apply to "all" service providers that receive protected customer information, it seems likely that they would apply to *both* staffing firms and their temporary employees.

Even assuming that they, not their employees, are the service providers, staffing firms may be able to minimize their exposure by limiting the GLB language in their contracts. That language need not be onerous. The preamble to the final safeguard rules states that "financial institutions are well positioned to develop and implement appropriate contracts with their service providers...that do not impose undue or conflicting burdens."[145] Staffing firms should accept

---

142. 16 C.F.R. § 314.3.

143. 16 C.F.R. § 314.2(d).

144. It may be possible to argue that neither the privacy rules nor the safeguard rules should apply to a staffing firm when it can be shown that the staffing firm does not direct or control the work of its assigned employee and that protected information was given only to the employee. In such cases, it might be argued, it would be unreasonable to impute to the staffing firm any improper disclosure of the information by the employee. However, asserting this argument may have adverse implications with respect to a staffing firm's employer status vis-à-vis its workers in other areas of the law.

145. *Id.* at 36490.

language that is appropriately tailored to their business (i.e., providing temporary staff) and to the risk of inappropriate disclosure of information protected
by the GLB rules.

Background and Reference Checks Under the Fair Credit Reporting Act

Employers, including staffing firms, that use credit bureaus or other firms that
specialize in employee background checks are subject to notice and disclosure requirements under the federal Fair Credit Reporting Act.[146] The FCRA also imposes
requirements on staffing firms that provide clients with information obtained from a
job applicant's former employer as part of a routine reference check.

Consumer Reports Obtained From Third Parties

The FCRA governs an employer's use of two types of reports, "consumer
reports" and "investigative consumer reports," for making employment-related
decisions. A consumer report is any communication received from a "consumer
reporting agency" bearing on a person's credit worthiness, credit standing, character, general reputation, personal characteristics, or mode of living.[147] An "investigative consumer report" is a consumer report that contains similar information
obtained through personal interviews as well as written records.[148] A consumer
reporting agency is a person or entity that regularly engages in the practice of
collecting such information and providing it to third parties for a fee.[149]

When a staffing firm obtains a consumer report from a consumer reporting
agency, it must

■ Before obtaining the report, clearly advise the job applicant in a stand-
alone written statement that such a report might be obtained.

■ Receive written authorization from the job applicant to obtain the report.

■ Certify to the consumer reporting agency that it has followed the above
steps and will not use the information unlawfully.

■ Before taking any adverse action based on the report, give a copy of the
report to the job applicant along with a summary of the consumer's rights
(summary available from the consumer reporting agency) and wait a reasonable period after furnishing this information to take any action.

---

146. *See* 15 U.S.C. § 1681 *et seq.*

147. 15 U.S.C. § 1681a(d).

148. 15 U.S.C. § 1681a(e).

149. 15 U.S.C. § 1681a(f).

■ After taking adverse action, notify the job applicant of the action taken; provide the name, address, and telephone number of the consumer reporting agency that furnished the report; advise the individual of his or her right to dispute the accuracy of the report with the agency; inform the individual that the agency did not make the adverse decision and cannot explain it; and inform the individual that he or she has the right to obtain a free copy of the report from the consumer reporting agency within 60 days.[150] If a staffing firm obtains an "investigative consumer report," it must comply with additional disclosure requirements provided in the FRCA.[151]

Routine Reference Checking—Communications of Information to Clients

The FRCRA rules on consumer reports do not apply to information obtained by staffing firms from a job applicant's former employers as part of a routine reference check. This is because former employers generally do not regularly collect and furnish such information for a fee and therefore are not considered to be "consumer reporting agencies."[152] Staffing firms that wish to communicate the results of a reference check to clients may take advantage of simplified disclosure rules that apply to firms that regularly procure employees for employers or procure job opportunities for people.[153] Those rules require

■ Prior consent (oral or written) from the candidate to make the reference check.

■ Prior consent from the candidate to communicate that information to the prospective employer.

■ Written confirmation by the candidate of any oral consent within three business days.

■ Written notification to the candidate of the candidate's right to request the "nature and substance" of any information in the candidate's file at the time the information is requested.

■ Written disclosure to the candidate of the nature and substance of all information in the file (sources need not be disclosed) within five days of a request.[154]

---

150. 15 U.S.C. §§ 1681b, 1681g, 1681m.

151. *See* 15 U.S.C. §§ 1681d, 1681g.

152. *See* 15 U.S.C. § 1681a(f).

153. *See* 15 U.S.C. § 1861a(o).

154. 15 U.S.C. § 1681a(o).

Note that many states have enacted laws regarding background reports that limit an employer's right to make employment decisions based on a consumer report. Those laws must also be observed, provided they do not conflict with the FCRA.

Maintaining the Staffing Company's Employer Status

Being an employer involves more than merely administering payroll.

Even if a staffing firm pays employees' wages, pays employment taxes, and provides required insurance coverage (i.e., workers' compensation and unemployment insurance), there may be some risk, if nothing more is done, that a court could hold that the staffing firm is a mere payrolling agent and not an employer at all. Staffing firms providing temporary-to-hire, long-term staffing services, and professional employer organization arrangements should be especially alert to the need to assume and maintain an active role in decisions that affect the terms and conditions of employment.

Temporary-to-hire arrangements may pose risks if the client assumes a pervasive role in the employment relationship from the outset of the arrangement and the staffing firm's role is nominal. Long-term, open-ended staffing assignments plus negligible contact with an employee also increase the chance that the employee could be held to be solely the client's employee.

In PEO arrangements, employees generally are the client's employees to begin with, and their day-to-day working relationships and job functions remain essentially unchanged under the arrangement. Hence, failure of the PEO to assume an active employer role could lead to the conclusion that nothing has really changed and that the client retains sole legal responsibility for the employees.[155]

Staffing firms have been held not to be the employer in cases involving liability for sexual harassment (temporary employees were held not to be staffing firms' employees for the purpose of the rule requiring employers to have at least

---

155. *See, e.g.,* Black v. Employee Solutions, 725 N.E.2d 138 (Ind. App. 2000) (employee leasing firm with no right of control over leased employees was not their employer for wage payment purposes); Cf. United States v. Garami dba Tidy Maid, 184 Bankr. 834 (Bankr. M.D. Fla. 1995) (employee leasing firm client was held liable in absence of proof that leasing firm paid taxes).

15 employees to be subject to Title VII),[156] when determining whether temporary employees are employees of the client for the purpose of including them in the client's collective bargaining unit (temporary staffing firm was held to be mere payroll agent),[157] and when determining who is liable for overtime pay.[158] Fortunately, steps can be taken to avoid these outcomes under current legal principles, provided that both parties clearly understand what is at stake and take affirmative steps to ensure that the staffing company is actively involved as an employer.

For example, in addition to issuing paychecks, collecting and remitting all tax and other required withholdings, and providing required insurance coverage, the staffing firm should ensure that it has the right, *and exercises the right*, to take the following actions with respect to the employees it supplies:

1. Interview, test, hire, and fire.
2. Assign and reassign.
3. Set pay rates and benefits.
4. Negotiate with clients the nature, hours, duration, working conditions, and other aspects of all assignments.
5. Maintain general supervisory responsibilities. (A staffing company does not have to be on-site to supervise but could call in, check on employees, handle complaints, administer discipline, etc.)
6. Evaluate performance and provide counseling.
7. Maintain employee records.

Even if the client has a say in some of these areas, the staffing firm's employer status should be recognized legally as long as it also is involved in them.

The question sometimes is asked whether a staffing company can reinforce its employer status by placing a full-time supervisor at the client's work site to provide day-to-day supervision and control over employees' work. Providing full on-site supervision and control over the work performed by the staffing firm's employees will reinforce the staffing firm's employer status and may even help clients avoid some co-employer obligations, although, as discussed in this book, some obligations (e.g., civil rights) may exist even if the client is not an employer. However, merely providing nominal supervision, for example, by arbitrarily designating one of the employees assigned as the supervisor, will not negate the client's co-employer status.

---

156. Kellam v. Snelling Personnel Services, 866 F.Supp 812 (D. Del. 1994), *aff'd without op.* 63 F.3d 162 (3d Cir. 1995); Williams v. Caruso, 966 F. Supp. 287 (D. Del. 1997).

157. Walker Manufacturing (United Paperworkers International Union), (unpub'd op.) No. 25-RC-9373 (N.L.R.B. Jul. 28, 1995).

158. Catani v. Chiodi, No. CIV. 00-1559 (DWF/RLE), 2001 WL 920025 (D. Minn. Aug. 13, 2001).

Moreover, as discussed previously, elimination of the client's co-employer status may have a downside. If placement of supervisors is held to have completely negated the client's co-employer status, it could expose the client to negligence suits by the staffing company's employees in work-related injury cases because the client will no longer be able to invoke the exclusive remedy provisions of state workers' compensation laws.

6

The Future of Staffing Services

In the old high-volume enterprise, fixed costs such as factories, equip-ment, warehouses, and large payrolls were necessary in order to achieve control and predictability. In the high-value enterprise, they are an unnec-essary burden. Here, all that really counts is rapid problem identifying and problem solving.... Everything else...can be obtained as needed. Office space, factories, and warehouses can be rented; standard equip-ment can be leased; standard components can be bought...secretaries, routine data processors, bookkeepers, and routine production workers can be hired temporarily.

—*Robert B. Reich, former U.S. Secretary of Labor*[159]

159. Robert B. Reich, THE WORK OF NATIONS, 90–91 (1991).

As the dynamic changes taking place in the American workplace continue, it is reasonable to expect that businesses will increasingly rely on staffing services as part of their overall human resources management strategies. As those services evolve in response to these work force changes, the legal environment may also change. Court rulings such as Vizcaino v. Microsoft show that staffing firm clients may, under certain circumstances, have an obligation to provide benefits to assigned employees. But those rulings also show that clients generally can avoid such liability by limiting its contacts with workers supplied by outside contractors and by careful benefit plan drafting and design.

Aggressive proposals to regulate the industry—for example, by mandating that temporary workers receive pay and benefits comparable to clients' regular employees, limiting how long temporary workers may be used, and shifting staffing firm employer responsibilities to the clients—have thus far not been adopted. This may be because policy makers have come to recognize that the flexible jobs provided by staffing firms have significantly helped workers and the economy. Another reason, as this book has shown, is that the rights of employees working under staffing arrangements are already substantially protected under existing federal and state labor and employment laws.

With common sense and a high degree of sensitivity to the existing legal rights of these employees by both staffing firms and their clients, significant new regulation is unlikely to be necessary.

Appendixes

State Laws That Regulate Temporary Staffing Firms

Table A1.

States That Regulate All Staffing Firms

State	*Statute Citation*
Massachusetts *Registration*	MASS. GEN. LAWS ANN. § 140-46B, "Employment Agencies"
New Jersey *Registration*	N.J. STAT. ANN. § 56:8-1.1, "Consumer Fraud Act"
North Carolina *Registration*	N.C. GEN. STAT. § 95-47.14, "Regulation of Private Personnel Services"
Rhode Island *Bonding and job description notice requirements*	R.I. GEN. LAWS ANN. § 5-7-3, "Employment Agencies" (bonding requirements law; § 28-6.10-1 to 28-6.10-4, "Temporary Employee Protection Act" (job description notice requirements law)

Table A2.

States That Regulate Day Labor Staffing Firms

State Citation	Scope	Statute
Arizona *No license or registration requirement; clarifies responsibilities of labor pools*	"Day labor" means unskilled labor. The law excludes "employment of a professional or clerical nature" from the definition of day labor"	ARIZ. REV. STAT. § 23-551 to 23-553, "Day Labor"
Florida *No license or registration requirement; clarifies responsibilities of labor pools*	The law applies only to firms that specialize in unskilled labor and where workers assemble before being dispatched to customers.	FLA. STAT. ANN. § 31.448.20 to 31.448.25, "Labor Pool Act"
Georgia *No license or registration requirement; clarifies responsibilities of labor pools*	The law applies only to firms that send workers on assignments of casual labor. "Casual labor" means work that does not require a professional or occupational license, a high school diploma, vocational education, proficiency in a type of machinery, or training before the assignment that exceeds one hour. "Labor pool" does not include a firm that requires advanced applications, job interviews, and references.	GA. CODE ANN. § 34-10-1 to 34-10-6, "Labor Pools"

Table A2.

States That Regulate Day Labor Staffing Firms *(continued)*

State Citation	Scope	Statute
Illinois *Registration*	"Day labor" means unskilled labor. The law excludes "employment of a professional or clerical nature" from the definition of day labor. Firms are also required to post notices describing wages, available transportation, work details, and attire and equipment costs.	820 Ill. Comp. STAT. § 175/1 TO 175/99, "Day Labor Services Act"
New Mexico *No license or registration requirement*	Clarifies wage responsibilities of day labor firms and provides for check-cashing fees. "Day labor" means unskilled labor. The law exempts temporary services employment agencies where advanced applications, a screening process, and job interviews are required.	N.M. STAT. ANN. § 50-15-1 to 50-15-7, "Day Laborer Act"
Texas *License requirement*	The law applies only to firms that specialize in unskilled labor and where workers assemble before being dispatched to customers.	TEX. LABOR CODE ANN. § 92.001 to 92.031, "Temporary Common Worker Employers"

Some cities have laws that impose license requirements and/or location restrictions on labor service staffing firms. These include the following:

Akron, OH	Chicago, IL	Elgin, IL
Englewood, CO	Kansas City, MO	Littleton, CO

B

State Laws That Regulate Employee Leasing Services

Table B1.

States With Licensing or Registration Requirements for Employee Leasing Companies

State	Statute Citation
Alabama	ALA. CODE § 25-14-1 to 25-14-11, "Alabama Professional Employer Registration Act"
Arizona	AZ. REV. STAT. ANN. § 23-561 to 23-576, "Professional Employer Organizations"
Arkansas	ARK. STAT. ANN. § 23-92-301 TO 23-92-315, "Arkansas Employee Leasing Act"
Florida	FLA. STAT. ANN. § 468.520 TO 468.535, "Employee Leasing Companies"
Georgia	GA. CODE ANN. § 34-7-6, "Professional Employer Organizations" *Note: Employer recognition law; no licensing requirement*
Idaho	IDAHO CODE § 44-2401 TO 44-2407, "Idaho Professional Employer" *Note: Establishes guidelines; no licensing requirement*
Illinois	215 ILL. COMP. STAT. 113/1-99, "Employee Leasing Company Act"
Indiana	IN. CODE 27-16-1-1 to 27-16-10-3, "Professional Employer Organizations"
Kentucky *Registration only*	KY. REV. STAT. ANN. § 342.615, "Registration of Employee Leasing Companies"

Table B1.

States With Licensing or Registration Requirements for Employee Leasing Companies (continued)

State	Statute Citation
Louisiana *Registration only*	LA. REV. STAT. ANN. § 22: 1131 TO 22: 1139, "Louisiana Professional Employer Act" (insurance law); § 23:1761 to 23: 1768, "Professional Employer Organizations"*(labor and workers' compensation law)*
Maine	ME. REV. STAT. TIT. 32, § 14051 TO 14058, "Employee Leasing Companies"
Minnesota	MINN. STAT. § 79.255, "Compensation Insurance" *Note: Registration is a prerequisite to obtaining workers' compensation insurance.*
Montana	MONT. CODE ANN. § 39-8-101 TO 39-8-403, "Professional Employer Organizations and Groups Licensing"
Nevada	NEV. REV. STAT. § 616.254 TO 616. 2547, "Employee Leasing Companies"
New Hampshire	N.H. REV. STAT. ANN. § 277-B:1 TO 277-B:18, "Employee Leasing Companies"
New Jersey *Registration only*	N.J. STAT. ANN. § 34:8-67 to 34:8-77, "Leasing Companies"
New Mexico	N.M. STAT. ANN. § 60-13A-1 to 60-13A-14, "Employee Leasing"
New York	N.Y. LABOR CODE ART. 31, "New York Professional Employer Act"

Table B1.

States With Licensing or Registration Requirements for Employee Leasing Companies (continued)

State	Statute Citation
North Carolina *Registration only*	N.C. GEN. STAT. § 58-89-1 to 58-89-30, "North Carolina Professional Employer Organization Act"
Ohio	OH. REV. CODE ANN. 4125.01 to 4125.99, "Professional Employer Organizations"
Oklahoma *Registration only*	OKLA. STAT. TIT. 40, § 600.1 to 600.8, "Oklahoma Professional Employer Organization Recognition and Registration Act"
Oregon *Registration only*	OR. REV. STAT. § 656.850 to 656.855, "Worker Leasing Companies"
Rhode Island *Registration only*	R.I. GEN. LAWS § 5-75-1 TO 5-75-11, "Professional Employer Organizations Act of 2004"; R.I. GEN. LAWS § 44-30-71.4, "Personal Income Tax" *Note: The state tax division must certify that the company has complied with withholding obligations.*
South Carolina	S.C. CODE ANN. § 40-68-10 to 40-68-180, "Regulation of Staff Leasing Services"
Tennessee	TENN. CODE ANN. § 62-43-101 to 62-43-120, "Employee Leasing"
Texas	TEX. REV. CIV. STAT. ANN. ART. 9104, "Staff Leasing Services Act"

Table B1.

States With Licensing or Registration Requirements for Employee Leasing Companies (continued)

State	Statute Citation
Utah	UTAH CODE ANN. § 58-59-101 to 58-59-503, "Employee Leasing Company Licensing Act"
Vermont	VT. STAT. ANN. TIT. 21, § 12-1031 to 12-1043, "Employee Leasing Companies"
Virginia *Registration only*	VA. CODE ANN. § 65.2-803.1, "Requirements for Registration as Professional Employer Organizations"

Table B2.

States With Special Workers' Compensation Laws Applicable to Employee Leasing Services

State	Law Citation
	The citations for Washington and West Virginia are to the state administrative codes; the other citations are to the state statutes.
Arkansas	ARK. CODE ANN. § 23-92-315
Florida	FLA. STAT. ANN. § 468.529
Idaho	IDAHO CODE § 72-103
Illinois	215 ILL. COMP. STAT. ANN. § 113/30
Kentucky	KY. REV. STAT. ANN. § 342.615
Louisiana	LA. REV. STAT. ANN. § 1210.56
Maine	ME. REV. STAT. ANN. tit. 25, § 2385-E
Massachusetts	MASS. ANN. LAWS CH. 152, § 14A
Minnesota	MINN. STAT. ANN. § 268.163
Missouri	MO. REV. STAT. § 287.282
Montana	MONT. CODE ANN. § 39-8-403
Nevada	NEV. REV. STAT. § 616.254 TO 616. 2547
New Hampshire	N.H. REV. STAT. ANN. § 277-B:10
New Jersey	N.J. STAT. ANN. § 34:8-67 TO 34:8-77

Table B2.

States With Special Workers' Compensation Laws Applicable to Employee Leasing Services (continued)

State	Law Citation
New Mexico	N.M. STAT. ANN. § 59A-2-9.1
New York	N.Y. LAB. LAW ART. 31, § 922
North Dakota	N.D. CENT. CODE § 65-08.1-01
Oklahoma	OKLA. STAT. TIT. 40, § 600.7
Oregon	OR. REV. STAT. § 656.855, 737.270
Rhode Island	R.I. GEN. LAWS § 28-47-1
South Carolina	S.C. CODE ANN. § 40-68-75
Tennessee	TENN. CODE ANN. § 62-43-113
Texas	TEX. LAB. CODE ANN. § 91.006
Utah	UTAH CODE ANN. § 34A-2-103
Vermont	VT. STAT. ANN. TIT. 21, § 1037
Virginia	VA. CODE ANN. § 65.2-803.1
Washington	WASH. ADMIN. CODE § 296-17-87301
West Virginia	W. VA. CODE ST. R. TIT. 85, § 31-1 through 31-11

Table B2.

States With Special Workers' Compensation Laws
Applicable to Employee Leasing Services (continued)

The following states have adopted modified versions of the National Council on Compensation Insurance model workers' compensation rules as part of their internal state agency manuals but not as part of their administrative codes: Alabama, Arkansas, Connecticut, the District of Columbia, Florida, Indiana, Iowa, Kansas, Kentucky, Maryland, Massachusetts, Mississippi, New Hampshire, New Mexico, North Carolina, Rhode Island, South Carolina, South Dakota, Tennessee, and Vermont. California, Maine, Nevada, and New York have similar rules.

Table B3.

States With Special Unemployment Insurance Laws Applicable to Employee Leasing Services

State	Statute Citation
	Citations for Massachusetts, Ohio, and Washington are to the state administrative code; the citation for Kentucky is to a letter by the state unemployment insurance agency.
Alabama	ALA. CODE § 25-14-9
Arizona	ARIZ. REV. STAT. ANN. § 23-614
Arkansas	ARK. STAT. ANN. § 11-10-717
California	CAL. UNEMP. INS. CODE § 606.5
Colorado	COLO. REV. STAT. § 8-70-114
Delaware	DEL. CODE ANN. § 3302(8)(J)
Florida	FLA. STAT. § 443.036
Georgia	GA. CODE ANN. § 34-8-32
Idaho	IDAHO CODE § 72-1349B
Illinois	820 ILL. COMP. STAT. 405/206.1
Iowa	IOWA ADMIN. CODE R. 345-2.3(96)
Kansas	KAN. STAT. ANN. § 44-758
Kentucky	Ky. Dept. for Employment Services, UI-1.2 Letter

Table B3.

States With Special Unemployment Insurance Laws Applicable to Employee Leasing Services (continued)

State	Statute Citation
Louisiana	LA. REV. STAT. ANN. § 1761 TO 1768
Maine	ME. REV. STAT. ANN. TIT 26, § 1221-A
Maryland	MD. REGS. CODE TIT. 9, § 32.01.26
Massachusetts	MASS. REGS. CODE. TIT. 430, § 5.07 THROUGH 5.13
Michigan	MICH. ADMIN. CODE R. 421.190
Minnesota	MINN. STAT. § 268.163
Mississippi	MISS. CODE ANN. § 71-5-11
Missouri	MO. REV. STAT. § 288.032
Montana	MONT. CODE ANN. § 39-8-207
Nebraska	NEB. REV. STAT. § 48-602
New Hampshire	N.H. REV. STAT. ANN. § 277-B:9
New Jersey	N.J. STAT. ANN. § 34: 8-72
New Mexico	N.M. STAT. ANN. § 51-1-52.1
New York	N.Y. LAB. LAW ART. 31, § 923
North Carolina	N.C. GEN. STAT. § 96-8
North Dakota	N.D. CODE § 52-04-24

Table B3.

States With Special Unemployment Insurance Laws Applicable to Employee Leasing Services *(continued)*

State	Statute Citation
Ohio	OHIO ADMIN. CODE § 4141-3-07
Oklahoma	OKLA. STAT. TIT. 40, § 1-209A
Rhode Island	R.I. GEN. LAWS § 44-30-71.4
South Carolina	S.C. CODE ANN. § 40-68-120
Tennessee	TENN. CODE ANN. § 62-43-113
Texas	TEX. LAB. CODE ANN. § 91.044
Utah	UTAH CODE ANN. § 58-59-306
Vermont	VT. STAT. ANN. TIT. 21, § 1033
Washington	WASH. ADMIN. CODE § 50.04.245
Wisconsin	WIS. STAT. § 108.02, 108.065
Wyoming	WYO. STAT. § 27-3-502

State Laws Regarding Exclusive Remedy for Special Employers

Table C1.

States That Apply the Exclusive Remedy Rule to Special Employers

The following states have applied the exclusive remedy provisions of their workers' compensation laws to clients using temporary help or other contract services. A number of states have had multiple court rulings on the issue (e.g., Michigan). This table cites the most recent case by the highest judicial authority in the state that has dealt with the issue.

State	*Case or Statute*
Alabama	ALA. CODE § 25-14-9.
Alaska	Anderson v. Tuboscope Vetco Inc., 9 P.3d 1013 (Alaska 2000)
Arizona	Wiseman v. Dynair Tech of Arizona Inc., 192 Ariz. 413, 966 P.2d 1017 (Ariz. Ct. App. 1998)
Arkansas	National Union Fire Insurance Co. v. Tri-State Iron and Metal Co., 323 Ark. 258, 914 S.W.2d 301 (Ark. 1996); Edgin v. Entergy Operations, 331 Ark. 162, 961 S.W.2d 724 (Ark. 1998).
California	CAL. LABOR CODE § 3602(d)—Workers' Compensation
Colorado	Evans v. Webster, 832 P.2d 951 (Colo. Ct. App. 1991), *cert. denied* 1992 Colo. LEXIS 582 (Colo. July 7, 1992)
Connecticut	Koscak v. Mott Metallurgical Corp., No. CV 94-0536404S, 1996 WL 409232 (Conn. Super. Ct. July 1, 1996)
Delaware	Porter v. Pathfinder Services Inc., 683 A.2d 40 (Del. 1996)

Table C1.

States That Apply the Exclusive
Remedy Rule to Special Employers *(continued)*

State	Case or Statute
District of Columbia	Thomas v. Hycon Inc., 244 F. Supp. 151 (D.D.C. 1965) The court stated that special employers are protected by the exclusive remedy rule even though it was not the issue before the court.
Florida	FLA. STAT. ANN. § 440.11(2)—Workers' Compensation
Georgia	GA. CODE ANN. § 34-9-11(c)—Workers' Compensation
Hawaii	Frank v. Hawaii Planing Mill Foundation, 88 Haw. 140, 963 P.2d 349 (Haw. 1998)
Idaho	IDAHO CODE § 72-103—Workers' Compensation
Illinois	Chaney v. Yetter Manufacturing Co., 315 Ill.App.3d 823, 248 Ill.Dec. 737, 734 N.E.2d 1028 (Ill. App. Ct.), *cert. denied* 192 Ill.2d 685, 252 Ill.Dec. 76, 742 N.E.2d 326 (Ill. 2000)
Indiana	Walters v. Modern Aluminum, 699 N.E.2d 671 (1998)
Iowa	Fletcher v. Apache Hose & Belting Co., 519 N.W.2d 839 (Iowa Ct. App. 1994)
Kansas	Scott v. Altmar, 272 Kan. 1280, 38 P.3d 673 (Kan. 2002)
Kentucky	United States Fidelity & Guaranty Co. v. Technical Minerals Inc., 934 S.W. 2d 266 (Ky. 1996)
Louisiana	Snow v. Lenox International, 662 So. 2d 818 (La. Ct. App. 1995)

Table C1.

States That Apply the Exclusive
Remedy Rule to Special Employers (continued)

State   Case or Statute

State	Case or Statute
Maine	ME. REV. STAT. ANN. tit. 39-A § 104—Workers' Compensation
Maryland	Whitehead v. Safway Steel Products Inc., 304 Md. 67, 497 A.2d 803 (Md. 1985)
Michigan	Kidder v. Miller-Davis Co., 455 Mich. 25, 564 N.W.2d 872 (Mich. 1997)
Minnesota	Danek v. Meldrum Manufacturing & Engineering Co., 312 Minn. 404, 252 N.W.2d 255 (Minn. 1977)
Mississippi	Northern Electric Co. v. Phillips, 660 So.2d 1278 (Miss. 1995)
Missouri	McGuire v. Tenneco Inc., 756 S.W.2d 532 (Mo. 1988)
Montana	MONT. CODE ANN. § 39-8-207(8)(b)—Professional Employer Organizations and Groups Licensing *Note: The Montana PEO licensing statute is the only reference in that state on the application of the exclusive remedy rule to special employers.*
Nebraska	Kaiser v. Millard Lumber Inc., 255 Neb. 943, 587 N.W.2d 875 (Neb. 1999)
Nevada	Antonini v. Hanna Industries, 94 Nev. 12, 573 P.2d 1184 (Nev. 1978)
New Hampshire	Benoit v. Test Systems Inc., 142 N.H. 47, 694 A.2d 992 (N.H. 1997)

Table C1.

States That Apply the Exclusive Remedy Rule to Special Employers *(continued)*

State	Case or Statute
New Jersey	Kelly v. Geriatric and Medical Services Inc., 287 N.J.Super 567, 671 A.2d 631 (N.J. Super. Ct. App Div.), *aff'd without op.* 147 N.J. 42, 685 A.2d 943 (N.J. 1996)
New Mexico	Vigil v. Digital Equipment Corp., 122 N.M. 417, 925 P.2d 883 (N.M. Ct. App.), *cert denied* 122 N.M. 279, 923 P.2d 1164 (N.M. 1996)
New York	CONSOL. LAWS OF N.Y. ANN. § 922.
North Carolina	Poe v. Atlas-Soundelier / American Trading & Production Corp., 132 N.C.App. 472, 512 S.E.2d 760 (N.C. Ct. App.), *cert. denied* 350 N.C. 835, 538 S.E.2d 199 (N.C. 1999)
North Dakota	N.D. CENT. CODE § 65-01-08(2)—Workers' Compensation
Ohio	Campbell v. Central Terminal Warehouse, 56 Ohio St. 2d 173, 383 N.E.2d 135 (Ohio 1978)
Oklahoma	Van Zant v. People Electric Cooperative, 900 P.2d 1008 (Okla. Ct. App.), *cert. denied* (Okla. July 13, 1995)
Oregon	OR. REV. STAT. § 656.018(5)–Workers' Compensation

Table C1.

States That Apply the Exclusive
Remedy Rule to Special Employers (continued)

State   Case or Statute

State	Case or Statute
Pennsylvania	English v. Lehigh County Authority, 286 Pa. Super. 312, 428 A.2d 1343 (Pa. Super. Ct. 1981). But see Swisher v. Caterpillar Inc., 65 Pa. D. & C.4th 32, (Pa.Com.Pl. Dec 23, 2003), in which the lower court relied on the Horner case in Massachusetts and the Edgin case in Arkansas to find that a staffing firm worker who signed a waiver gave up his right to sue any client of the staffing firm, but an appellate court reversed without comment, 888 A.2d 19 (Pa.Super. Sep 06, 2005), and the Pennsylvania Supreme Court refused to hear the matter, 902 A.2d 1242 (Pa. Jun 30, 2006).
Rhode Island	R.I. GEN. LAWS § 28-29-2(6), 28-29-20—Workers' Compensation
South Carolina	Day v. Sanders Brothers Inc. 315 S.C. 95, 431 S.E.2d 629 (S.C. Ct. App. 1993). The court stated that special employers are protected by the exclusive remedy rule even though it was not the issue before the court.
South Dakota	Goodman v. Sioux Steel Co., 475 N.W.2d 563 (S.D. 1991)
Tennessee	Tedder v. Union Planters Corp., No. W1999-01971-COA-R3-CV, 2001 WL 589139 (Tenn. Ct. App. May 29, 2001)
Texas	Garza v. Excel Logistics Inc., 100 S.W.3d 280 (Tex. Ct. App. 2002)
Utah	UTAH CODE ANN. § 34A-2-105—Workers' Compensation

Table C1.

States That Apply the Exclusive
Remedy Rule to Special Employers *(continued)*

State	Case or Statute
Vermont	Candido v. Polymers Inc., 166 Vt. 15, 687 A.2d 476 (Vt. 1996)
Virginia	VA. CODE ANN. § 65.2-803.1(G)—Workers' Compensation
Washington	Novenson v. Spokane Culvert & Fabricating Co., 91 Wash.2d 550, 588 P.2d 1174 (Wash. 1979) The temporary employee must expressly consent to an employment relationship with the client.
West Virginia	Maynard v. Keynard Chemical Co., 626 F.2d 359 (4th Cir. 1980)
Wisconsin	WIS. STAT. ANN. § 102.29(6)—Workers' Compensation

Table C2.

States That Do Not Apply the Exclusive Remedy Rule to Special Employers

State	Case or Statute
Massachusetts	Numberg v. GTE Transport Inc., 34 Mass. App. Ct. 904,607 N.E.2d 1 (Mass. App. Ct. 1993). However, in Horner v. Boston Edison Co., 45 Mass. App. Ct. 139, 695 N.E.2d 1093, *cert. denied* 428 Mass. 1104 (Mass. 1998), the Appeals Court upheld the use of a release with which an employee waived his right to bring claims against any clients of the staffing firm for injuries covered by the state workers' compensation statute.
Wyoming	Wyoming does not have any cases or statutes on whether special employers are protected by the exclusive remedy rule. However, in SOS Staffing Services Inc. v. Fields, 54 P.3d 761 (Wyo. 2002), a "fellow employee" protection case, the Wyoming Supreme Court held that an employment relationship is necessary for the protection to exist and found that the workers' compensation law explicitly states that an assigned staffing firm worker is not an employee of the client. Hence, the court concluded that the worker was not protected from an injury suit by the client's employee.

Internal Revenue Service 20-Factor Test for Determining Who Is an Employee

Rev. Rul. 87-41
1987-1 C.B. 296 (I.R.S.)
Revenue Ruling: Employment Status Under Section 530(D) of the Revenue Act of 1978
Published: 1987
Section 3121. Definitions, 26 CFR 31.3121(d)-1: Who are employees.
(Also Sections 3306, 3401, 31.3306(i)-1, 31.3401(c)-1.)

Employment status under section 530(d) of the Revenue Act of 1978. Guidelines are set forth for determining the employment status of a taxpayer (technical service specialist) affected by section 530(d) of the Revenue Act of 1978, as added by section 1706 of the Tax Reform Act of 1986. The specialists are to be classified as employees under generally applicable common law standards.

Issue

In the situations described below, are the individuals employees under the common law rules for purposes of the Federal Insurance Contributions Act (FICA), the Federal Unemployment Tax Act (FUTA), and the Collection of Income Tax at Source on Wages (chapters 21, 23, and 24 respectively, subtitle C, Internal Revenue Code)? These situations illustrate the application of section 530(d) of the Revenue Act of 1978, 1978-3 (Vol. 1) C.B. xi, 119 (the 1978 Act), which was added by section 1706(a) of the Tax Reform Act of 1986, 1986-3 (Vol. 1) C.B. (the 1986 Act) (generally effective for services performed and remuneration paid after December 31, 1986).

Facts

In each factual situation, an individual worker (Individual), pursuant to an arrangement between one person (Firm) and another person (Client), provides services for the Client as an engineer, designer, drafter, computer programmer, systems analyst, or other similarly skilled worker engaged in a similar line of work.

Situation 1

The Firm is engaged in the business of providing temporary technical services to its clients. The Firm maintains a roster of workers who are available to provide technical services to prospective clients. The Firm does not train the workers but determines the services that the workers are qualified to perform based on information submitted by the workers.

The Firm has entered into a contract with the Client. The contract states that the Firm is to provide the Client with workers to perform computer programming services meeting specified qualifications for a particular project. The Individual, a computer programmer, enters into a contract with the Firm to perform services as a computer programmer for the Client's project, which is expected to last less than one year. The Individual is one of several programmers provided by the Firm to the Client. The Individual has not been an employee of or performed services for the Client (or any predecessor or affiliated corporation of the Client) at any time preceding the time at which the Individual begins performing services for the Client. Also, the Individual has not been an employee of or performed services for or on behalf of the Firm at any time preceding the time at which the Individual begins performing services for the Client. The Individual's contract with the Firm states that the Individual is an independent contractor with respect to services performed on behalf of the Firm for the Client.

The Individual and the other programmers perform the services under the Firm's contract with the Client. During the time the Individual is performing services for the Client, even though the Individual retains the right to perform services for other persons, substantially all of the Individual's working time is devoted to performing services for the Client. A significant portion of the services are performed on the Client's premises. The Individual reports to the Firm by accounting for time worked and describing the progress of the work. The Firm pays the Individual and regularly charges the Client for the services performed by the Individual. The Firm generally does not pay individuals who perform services for the Client unless the Firm provided such individuals to the Client.

The work of the Individual and other programmers is regularly reviewed by the Firm. The review is based primarily on reports by the Client about the performance of these workers. Under the contract between the Individual and the Firm, the Firm may terminate its relationship with the Individual if the review shows that he or she is failing to perform the services contracted for by the Client. Also, the Firm will replace the Individual with another worker if the Individual's services are unacceptable to the Client. In such a case, however, the Individual will nevertheless receive his or her hourly pay for the work completed.

Finally, under the contract between the Individual and the Firm, the Individual is prohibited from performing services directly for the Client and, under the contract between the Firm and the Client, the Client is prohibited from receiving services from the Individual for a period of three months following the termination of services by the Individual for the Client on behalf of the Firm.

Situation 2

The Firm is a technical services firm that supplies clients with technical personnel. The Client requires the services of a systems analyst to complete a project and contacts the Firm to obtain such an analyst. The Firm maintains a roster of analysts and refers such an analyst, the Individual, to the Client. The Individual is not restricted by the Client or the Firm from providing services to the general public while performing services for the Client and in fact does perform substantial services for other persons during the period the Individual is working for the Client. Neither the Firm nor the Client has priority on the services of the Individual. The Individual does not report, directly or indirectly, to the Firm after the beginning of the assignment to the Client concerning (1) hours worked by the Individual, (2) progress on the job, or (3) expenses incurred by the Individual in performing services for the Client. No reports (including reports of time worked or progress on the job) made by the Individual to the Client are provided by the Client to the Firm.

If the Individual ceases providing services for the Client prior to completion of the project or if the Individual's work product is otherwise unsatisfactory, the Client may seek damages from the Individual. However, in such circumstances, the Client may not seek damages from the Firm, and the Firm is not required to replace the Individual. The Firm may not terminate the services of the Individual while he or she is performing services for the Client and may not otherwise affect the relationship between the Client and the Individual. Neither the Individual nor the Client is prohibited for any period after termination of the Individual's services on this job from contracting directly with the other. For referring the Individual to the Client, the Firm receives a flat fee that is fixed prior to the Individual's commencement of services for the Client and is unrelated to the number of hours and quality of work performed by the Individual. The Individual is not paid by the Firm either directly or indirectly. No payment made by the Client to the Individual reduces the amount of the fee that the Client is otherwise required to pay the Firm. The Individual is performing services that can be accomplished without the Individual's receiving direction or control as to hours, place of work, sequence, or details of work.

Situation 3

The Firm, a company engaged in furnishing client firms with technical personnel, is contacted by the Client, who is in need of the services of a drafter for a particular project, which is expected to last less than one year. The Firm recruits the Individual to perform the drafting services for the Client. The Individual performs substantially all of the services for the Client at the office of the Client, using materials and equipment of the Client. The services are performed under the supervision of employees of the Client. The Individual reports to the Client on a regular basis. The Individual is paid by the Firm based on the number of hours the Individual has worked for the Client, as reported to the Firm by the Client or as reported by the Individual and confirmed by the Client. The Firm has no obligation to pay the Individual if the Firm does not receive payment for the Individual's services from the Client. For recruiting the Individual for the Client, the Firm receives a flat fee that is fixed prior to the Individual's commencement of services for the Client and is unrelated to the number of hours and quality of work performed by the Individual. However, the Firm does receive a reasonable fee for performing the payroll function. The Firm may not direct the work of the Individual and has no responsibility for the work performed by the Individual. The Firm may not terminate the services of the Individual. The Client may terminate the services of the Individual without liability to either the Individual or the Firm. The Individual is permitted to work for another firm while performing services for the Client, but does in fact work for the Client on a substantially full-time basis.

Law and Analysis

This ruling provides guidance concerning the factors that are used to determine whether an employment relationship exists between the Individual and the Firm for federal employment tax purposes and applies those factors to the given factual situations to determine whether the Individual is an employee of the Firm for such purposes. The ruling does not reach any conclusions concerning whether an employment relationship for federal employment tax purposes exists between the Individual and the Client in any of the factual situations.

Analysis of the preceding three fact situations requires an examination of the common law rules for determining whether the Individual is an employee with respect to either the Firm or the Client, a determination of whether the Firm or the Client qualifies for employment tax relief under section 530(a) of the 1978 Act, and a determination of whether any such relief is denied the Firm under section 530(d) of the 1978 Act (added by Section 1706 of the 1986 Act).

An individual is an employee for federal employment tax purposes if the individual has the status of an employee under the usual common law rules applicable in determining the employer–employee relationship. Guides for determining that status are found in the following three substantially similar sections of the Employment Tax Regulations: sections 31.3121(d)-1(c); 31.3306(i)-1; and 31.3401(c)-1.

These sections provide that generally the relationship of employer and employee exists when the person or persons for whom the services are performed have the right to control and direct the individual who performs the services, not only as to the result to be accomplished by the work but also as to the details and means by which that result is accomplished. That is, an employee is subject to the will and control of the employer not only as to what shall be done but as to how it shall be done. In this connection, it is not necessary that the employer actually direct or control the manner in which the services are performed; it is sufficient if the employer has the right to do so.

Conversely, these sections provide, in part, that individuals (such as physicians, lawyers, dentists, contractors, and subcontractors) who follow an independent trade, business, or profession, in which they offer their services to the public, generally are not employees.

Finally, if the relationship of employer and employee exists, the designation or description of the relationship by the parties as anything other than that of employer and employee is immaterial. Thus, if such a relationship exists, it is of no consequence that the employee is designated as a partner, coadventurer, agent, independent contractor, or the like.

As an aid to determining whether an individual is an employee under the common law rules, twenty factors or elements have been identified as indicating whether sufficient control is present to establish an employer-employee relationship. The twenty factors have been developed based on an examination of cases and rulings considering whether an individual is an employee. The degree of importance of each factor varies depending on the occupation and the factual context in which the services are performed. The twenty factors are designed only as guides for determining whether an individual is an employee; special scrutiny is required in applying the twenty factors to assure that formalistic aspects of an arrangement designed to achieve a particular status do not obscure the substance of the arrangement (that is, whether the person or persons for whom the services are performed exercise sufficient control over the individual for the individual to be classified as an employee). The twenty factors are described below:

1. **Instructions**. A worker who is required to comply with other persons' instructions about when, where, and how he or she is to work is ordinarily an employee. This control factor is present if the person or persons for whom the services are performed have the RIGHT to require compliance with instructions. See, for example, Rev. Rul. 68-598, 1968-2 C.B. 464, and Rev. Rul. 66-381, 1966-2 C.B. 449.

2. **Training**. Training a worker by requiring an experienced employee to work with the worker, by corresponding with the worker, by requiring the worker to attend meetings, or by using other methods, indicates that the person or persons for whom the services are performed want the services performed in a particular method or manner. See Rev. Rul. 70-630, 1970-2 C.B. 229.

3. **Integration**. Integration of the worker's services into the business operations generally shows that the worker is subject to direction and control. When the success or continuation of a business depends to an appreciable degree upon the performance of certain services, the workers who perform those services must necessarily be subject to a certain amount of control by the owner of the business. See United States v. Silk, 331 U.S. 704 (1947), 1947-2 C.B. 167.

4. **Services rendered personally**. If the Services must be rendered personally, presumably the person or persons for whom the services are performed are interested in the methods used to accomplish the work as well as in the results. See Rev. Rul. 55-695, 1955-2 C.B. 410.

5. **Hiring, supervising, and paying assistants**. If the person or persons for whom the services are performed hire, supervise, and pay assistants, that factor generally shows control over the workers on the job. However, if one worker hires, supervises, and pays the other assistants pursuant to a contract under which the worker agrees to provide materials and labor and under which the worker is responsible only for the attainment of a result,

this factor indicates an independent contractor status. Compare Rev. Rul. 63-115, 1963-1 C.B. 178, with Rev. Rul. 55-593 1955-2 C.B. 610.

6. **Continuing relationship**. A continuing relationship between the worker and the person or persons for whom the services are performed indicates that an employer–employee relationship exists. A continuing relationship may exist where work is performed at frequently recurring although irregular intervals. See United States v. Silk.

7. **Set hours of work**. The establishment of set hours of work by the person or persons for whom the services are performed is a factor indicating control. See Rev. Rul. 73-591, 1973-2 C.B. 337.

8. **Full time required**. If the worker must devote substantially full time to the business of the person or persons for whom the services are performed, such person or persons have control over the amount of time the worker spends working and impliedly restrict the worker from doing other gainful work. An independent contractor on the other hand, is free to work when and for whom he or she chooses. See Rev. Rul. 56-694, 1956-2 C.B. 694.

9. **Doing work on employer's premises**. If the work is performed on the premises of the person or persons for whom the services are performed, that factor suggests control over the worker, especially if the work could be done elsewhere. Rev. Rul. 56-660, 1956-2 C.B. 693. Work done off the premises of the person or persons receiving the services, such as at the office of the worker, indicates some freedom from control. However, this fact by itself does not mean that the worker is not an employee. The importance of this factor depends on the nature of the service involved and the extent to which an employer generally would require that employees perform such services on the employer's premises. Control over the place of work is indicated when the person or persons for whom the services are performed have the right to compel the worker to travel a designated route, to canvass a territory within a certain time, or to work at specific places as required. See Rev. Rul. 56-694.

10. **Order or sequence set**. If a worker must perform services in the order or sequence set by the person or persons for whom the services are performed, that factor shows that the worker is not free to follow the worker's own pattern of work but must follow the established routines and schedules of the person or persons for whom the services are performed. Often, because of the nature of an occupation, the person or persons for whom the services are performed do not set the order of the services or set the order infrequently. It is sufficient to show control, however, if such person or persons retain the right to do so. See Rev. Rul. 56-694.

11. **Oral or written reports**. A requirement that the worker submit regular or written reports to the person or persons for whom the services are performed indicates a degree of control. See Rev. Rul. 70-309, 1970-1 C.B. 199, and Rev. Rul. 68-248, 1968-1 C.B. 431.

12. **Payment by hour, week, month**. Payment by the hour, week, or month generally points to an employer–employee relationship, provided that this method of payment is not just a convenient way of paying a lump sum agreed upon as the cost of a job. Payment made by the job or on straight commission generally indicates that the worker is an independent contractor. See Rev. Rul. 74-389, 1974-2 C.B. 330.

13. **Payment of business and/or traveling expenses**. If the person or persons for whom the services are performed ordinarily pay the worker's business and/or traveling expenses, the worker is ordinarily an employee. An employer, to be able to control expenses, generally retains the right to regulate and direct the worker's business activities. See Rev. Rul. 55-144, 1955-1 C.B. 483.

14. **Furnishing of tools and materials**. The fact that the person or persons for whom the services are performed furnish significant tools, materials, and other equipment tends to show the existence of an employer–employee relationship. See Rev. Rul. 71-524, 1971-2 C.B. 346.

15. **Significant investment**. If the worker invests in facilities that are used by the worker in performing services and are not typically maintained by employees (such as the maintenance of an office rented at fair value from an unrelated party), that factor tends to indicate that the worker is an independent contractor. On the other hand, lack of investment in facilities indicates dependence on the person or persons for whom the services are performed for such facilities and, accordingly, the existence of an employer–employee relationship. See Rev. Rul. 71-524. Special scrutiny is required with respect to certain types of facilities, such as home offices.

16. **Realization of profit or loss**. A worker who can realize a profit or suffer a loss as a result of the worker's services (in addition to the profit or loss ordinarily realized by employees) is generally an independent contractor, but the worker who cannot is an employee. See Rev. Rul. 70-309. For example, if the worker is subject to a real risk of economic loss due to significant investments or a bona fide liability for expenses, such as salary payments to unrelated employees, that factor indicates that the worker is an independent contractor. The risk that a worker will not receive payment for his or her services, however, is common to both independent contrac-

tors and employees and thus does not constitute a sufficient economic risk to support treatment as an independent contractor.

17. **Working for more than one firm at a time**. If a worker performs more than *de minimis* services for a multiple of unrelated persons or firms at the same time, that factor generally indicates that the worker is an independent contractor. See Rev. Rul. 70-572, 1970-2 C.B. 221. However, a worker who performs services for more than one person may be an employee of each of the persons, especially where such persons are part of the same service arrangement.

18. **Making service available to general public**. The fact that a worker makes his or her services available to the general public on a regular and consistent basis indicates an independent contractor relationship. See Rev. Rul. 56-660.

19. **Right to discharge**. The right to discharge a worker is a factor indicating that the worker is an employee and the person possessing the right is an employer. An employer exercises control through the threat of dismissal, which causes the worker to obey the employer's instructions. An independent contractor, on the other hand, cannot be fired so long as the independent contractor produces a result that meets the contract specifications. Rev. Rul. 75-41, 1975-1 C.B. 323.

20. **Right to terminate.** If the worker has the right to end his or her relationship with the person for whom the services are performed at any time he or she wishes without incurring liability, that factor indicates an employer–employee relationship. See Rev. Rul. 70-309.

Rev. Rul. 75-41 considers the employment tax status of individuals performing services for a physician's professional service corporation. The corporation is in the business of providing a variety of services to professional people and firms (subscribers), including the services of secretaries, nurses, dental hygienists, and other similarly trained personnel. The individuals who are to perform the services are recruited by the corporation, paid by the corporation, assigned to jobs, and provided with employee benefits by the corporation. Individuals who enter into contracts with the corporation agree they will not contract directly with any subscriber to which they are assigned for at least three months after cessation of their contracts with the corporation. The corporation assigns the individual to the subscriber to work on the subscriber's premises with the subscriber's equipment. Subscribers have the right to require that an individual furnished by the corporation cease providing services to them, and they have the further right to have such individual replaced by the corporation within a reasonable period of time, but the subscribers have no right to affect the contract between the individual and the corporation. The corporation retains the right to discharge the individuals at any time. Rev. Rul. 75-41 concludes that the individuals are employees of the corporation for federal employment tax purposes.

Rev. Rul. 70-309 considers the employment tax status of certain individuals who perform services as oil well pumpers for a corporation under contracts that characterize such individuals as independent contractors. Even though the pumpers perform their services away from the headquarters of the corporation and are not given day-to-day directions and instructions, the ruling concludes that the pumpers are employees of the corporation because the pumpers perform their services pursuant to an arrangement that gives the corporation the right to exercise whatever control is necessary to assure proper performance of the services; the pumpers' services are both necessary and incident to the business conducted by the corporation; and the pumpers are not engaged in an independent enterprise in which they assume the usual business risks, but rather work in the course of the corporation's trade or business. See also Rev. Rul. 70-630, 1970-2 C.B. 229, which considers the employment tax status of sales clerks furnished by an employee service company to a retail store to perform temporary services for the store.

Section 530(a) of the 1978 Act, as amended by section 269(c) of the Tax Equity and Fiscal Responsibility Act of 1982, 1982-2 C.B. 462, 536, provides, for purposes of the employment taxes under subtitle C of the Code, that if a taxpayer did not treat an individual as an employee for any period, then the individual shall be deemed not to be an employee, unless the taxpayer had no reasonable basis for not treating the individual as an employee. For any period after December 31, 1978, this relief applies only if both of the following consistency rules are satisfied: (1) all federal tax returns (including information returns) required to be filed by the taxpayer with respect to the individual for the period are filed on a basis consistent with the taxpayer's treatment of the individual as not being an employee ("reporting consistency rule"), and (2) the taxpayer (and any predecessor) has not treated any individual holding a substantially similar position as an employee for purposes of the employment taxes for periods beginning after December 31, 1977 ("substantive consistency rule").

The determination of whether any individual who is treated as an employee holds a position substantially similar to the position held by an individual whom the taxpayer would otherwise be permitted to treat as other than an employee for employment tax purposes under section 530(a) of the 1978 Act requires an examination of all the facts and circumstances, including particularly the activities and functions performed by the individuals. Differences in the positions held by the respective individuals that result from the taxpayer's treatment of one individual as an employee and the other individual as other than an employee (for example, that the former individual is a participant in the taxpayer's qualified pension plan or health plan and the latter individual is not a participant in either) are to be disregarded in determining whether the individuals hold substantially similar positions.

Section 1706(a) of the 1986 Act added to section 530 of the 1978 Act a new subsection (d), which provides an exception with respect to the treatment of certain workers. Section 530(d) provides that section 530 shall not apply in the case of an individual who, pursuant to an arrangement between the taxpayer and another person, provides services for such other person as an engineer, designer, drafter, computer programmer, systems analyst, or other similarly skilled worker engaged in a similar line of work. Section 530(d) of the 1978 Act does not affect the determination of whether such workers are employees under the common law rules. Rather, it merely eliminates the employment tax relief under section 530(a) of the 1978 Act that would otherwise be available to a taxpayer with respect to those workers who are determined to be employees of the taxpayer under the usual common law rules. Section 530(d) applies to remuneration paid and services rendered after December 31, 1986.

The Conference Report on the 1986 Act discusses the effect of section 530(d) as follows:

The Senate amendment applies whether the services of [technical service workers] are provided by the firm to only one client during the year or to more than one client, and whether or not such individuals have been designated or treated by the technical services firm as independent contractors, sole proprietors, partners, or employees of a personal service corporation controlled by such individual. The effect of the provision cannot be avoided by claims that such technical service personnel are employees of personal service corporations controlled by such personnel. For example, an engineer retained by a technical services firm to provide services to a manufacturer cannot avoid the effect of this provision by organizing a corporation that he or she controls and then claiming to provide services as an employee of that corporation.

[T]he provision does not apply with respect to individuals who are classified, under the generally applicable common-law standards, as employees of a business that is a client of the technical services firm.

2 H. R. Rep. No. 99-841 (Conf. Rep.), 99th Cong., 2d Sess. II-834 to 835 (1986).

Under the facts of Situation 1 the legal relationship is between the Firm and the Individual, and the Firm retains the right of control to insure that the services are performed in a satisfactory fashion. The fact that the Client may also exercise some degree of control over the Individual does not indicate that the Individual is not an employee. Therefore, in Situation 1, the Individual is an employee of the Firm under the common law rules. The facts in Situation 1 involve an arrangement among the Individual, Firm, and Client, and the services provided by the Individual are technical services. Accordingly, the Firm is denied section 530 relief under section 530(d) of the 1978 Act (as added by section 1706 of the 1986 Act), and no relief is available with respect to any employment tax liability incurred in Situation 1. The analysis would not differ if the acts of Situation 1 were changed to state that the Individual provided the technical services through a personal service corporation owned by the Individual.

In Situation 2, the Firm does not retain any right to control the performance of the services by the Individual and, thus, no employment relationship exists between the Individual and the Firm.

In Situation 3, the Firm does not control the performance of the services of the Individual, and the Firm has no right to affect the relationship between the Client and the Individual. Consequently, no employment relationship exists between the Firm and the Individual.

Holdings

Situation 1. The Individual is an employee of the Firm under the common law rules. Relief under section 530 of the 1978 Act is not available to the Firm because of the provisions of section 530(d).

Situation 2. The Individual is not an employee of the Firm under the common law rules.

Situation 3. The Individual is not an employee of the Firm under the common law rules. Because of the application of section 530(b) of the 1978 Act, no inference should be drawn with respect to whether the Individual in Situations 2 and 3 is an employee of the Client for federal employment tax purposes.

E

Department of Labor Opinion Letter on Joint Employer Obligations for Minimum Wage and Overtime Pay

U.S. Department of Labor
Opinion Letter No. 874, Oct. 1, 1968
Joint Employers—Duty to Keep Records and Pay Overtime

This is in further reference to your letter of August 9, 1968, concerning the application of the Fair Labor Standards Act to certain employees of a company that supplies temporary help to various industries.

With regard to your second question, typically employees of a temporary staffing company working on assignments in various business establishments are joint employers of an employee, each is responsible for compliance with the requirements imposed on an employer under the statute with respect to any work-week when the employee is so employed. However, the employer who actually pays the employee the sums intended as compensation for hours of employment is considered primarily responsible for the keeping of the records required by Regulations, Part 516, and is treated as the one who has the primary duty of compliance as to such hours of employment. Where each employer makes direct payment to the employee, each employer is required to keep the records specified in the record keeping regulations. In any event, a temporary help supplier which acts in the interest of one or more employers in any workweek in relation to any employee whose services it provides should keep the prescribed records with respect to that employee.

You pose a situation in which the ABC Temporary Staffing Company sends Jones to work Monday and Tuesday for a total of 20 hours in the week at the F Company. On Wednesday, Jones is sent to work at G Company for 12 hours; on Thursday and Friday, he works a total of 20 hours at H Company.

The foregoing discussion will answer your questions whether F, G, and H must keep records of the hours Jones has worked or whether it is sufficient that

ABC Company alone keep the records. You also ask if F, G, and H would be liable if the ABC Temporary Staffing Company failed to pay the proper minimum wage. Each individual company is jointly responsible with the temporary staffing company for compliance with the minimum wage requirements of the law during the time the employee worked there. We would consider the ABC Company primarily responsible for the payment of proper overtime compensation in the example you present, since it is through its act that the employee received the assignment which caused overtime to be worked and it has the most direct knowledge of the total number of hours Jones worked in the workweek. Of course, if Jones worked overtime in any week for any of the employers to whom he was assigned by ABC Company, there is no question that such employer would be jointly responsible for the payment of proper overtime compensation for such work, as well as the applicable minimum wage. In addition, we believe we should point out that a number of courts have held in particular joint employment situations that the obligation to pay for overtime work resulting from a totaling of the hours worked for each rests equally on the joint employers. See e.g., Goldberg v. John R. Cowley & Bro. Inc., 292 F.2d 105; McComb v. Midwest Rust Proof Co., 8 Wage Hour Cases 460, 16 Labor Cases 64, 927 (E.D. Mo.); Mitchell v. Sin Jin Products Co., 171 F. Supp. 486 (D. Md.); Wirtz v. Marymax Construction Co., 17 Wage Hour Cases 333 (E.D.N. Mexico).

F

Federal Tax Provisions Regarding Leased Employees—Internal Revenue Code Section 414(n)

Table of Contents

American Staffing Association Answers to the Nine Most Common Questions About Leased Employees Under the Federal Tax Code

1. **Q: What is the technical definition of a "leased employee?"**
   A: Generally, for the purposes of section 414(n), any employee of a service firm who furnishes services to a client under the primary control of the client for 1,500 hours or more in a 12-month period is considered a "leased employee."

2. **Q: Do clients have to provide benefits to leased employees?**
   A: No. Section 414(n) only requires clients to include leased employees in their employee head count for discrimination testing purposes.

3. **Q: Doesn't Erisa require employers to provide benefits to all employees who work 1,000 hours?**
   A: ERISA and section 414(n) have different purposes and requirements. ERISA contains a number of requirements relating to an employer's benefit plans, but they apply only to the employer's own employees. Section 414(n) applies to an employer's use of *outside* employees.

4. **Q: What is the purpose of the IRS "discrimination" tests?**
   A: They are designed to ensure that an employer's benefit plans do not favor higher-paid employees. Generally, they require employers to cover a certain percentage of lower-paid employees and to provide them with benefits similar to those received by higher-paid employees. Plans that meet the tests are eligible for favorable tax treatment. Coverage tests apply to retirement plans and to certain fringe benefits such as group life insurance, cafeteria plans, and self-insured health plans.

5. **Q: Does section 414(n) apply to all benefit plans that are subject to coverage testing?**
   A: No. Section 414(n) applies to retirement plans and to certain fringe benefits such as group life insurance and cafeteria plans. It does not apply to the coverage testing of group health plans (but it does apply in determining whether such plans are subject to COBRA or to certain Medicare "coordination-of-benefits" rules).

6. **Q: Why are clients concerned about leased employees?**
   A: Clients with tax-qualified benefit plans are concerned that including leased employees in their employee count will cause their plans to fail the coverage tests and lose their tax-favored status. If a plan fails the coverage tests, an employer could lose its tax deduction for the cost of benefits, and its employees could be immediately taxed on the value of the benefits earned.

7. **Q: Are there exceptions to the rule requiring clients to count leased employees?**
   A: Yes. Congress intended that a client not have to count leased employees for coverage testing purposes if its total use of such persons is less than 5% of its lower-paid workforce, and provided the client's plans are not "top-heavy." Of course, in such a case, the client's plans should also expressly exclude leased employees from coverage.

8. **Q: What if the number of leased employees furnishing services to a client is 5% or more?**
   A: The client will have to count all leased employees when applying the coverage tests applicable to any benefit plans to which section 414(n) applies.

9. **Q: Who is responsible for keeping track of the number of leased employees?**
   A: Legally, it is the client's responsibility to keep records to determine whether outside employees work long enough to be considered leased employees. Temporary staffing firms can, of course, assist in the record-keeping regarding the employees they assign.

United States Code Annotated

Title 26. Internal Revenue Code

Subtitle A. Income Taxes

Chapter 1. Normal Taxes and Surtaxes

Subchapter D. Deferred Compensation, etc.

Part I. Pension, Profit-Sharing, Stock Bonus Plans, etc.

Subpart B. Special Rules

Current through P.L. 106-180, approved Mar. 17, 2000

Section 414. Definitions and Special Rules

(n) Employee Leasing

(1) In general. For purposes of the requirements listed in paragraph (3), with respect to any person (hereinafter in this subsection referred to as the "recipient") for whom a leased employee performs services

    (A) the leased employee shall be treated as an employee of the recipient, but

    (B) contributions or benefits provided by the leasing organization which are attributable to services performed for the recipient shall be treated as provided by the recipient.

(2) Leased employee. For purposes of paragraph (1), the term "leased employee" means any person who is not an employee of the recipient and who provides services to the recipient if

    (A) such services are provided pursuant to an agreement between the recipient and any other person (in this subsection referred to as the "leasing organization"),

    (B) such person has performed such services for the recipient (or for the recipient and related persons) on a substantially full-time basis for a period of at least 1 year, and

    (C) such services are performed under primary direction or control by the recipient.

(3) Requirements. For purposes of this subsection, the requirements listed in this paragraph are

    (A) paragraphs (3), (4), (7), (16), (17), and (26) of section 401(a),

    (B) sections 408(k), 408(p), 410, 411, 415, and 416, and

    (C) sections 79, 106, 117(d), 120, 125, 127, 129, 132, 137, 274(j), 505, and 4980B.

(4) Time when first considered as employee.

    (A) In general. In the case of any leased employee, paragraph (1) shall apply only for purposes of determining whether the requirements listed in paragraph (3) are met for periods after the close of the period referred to in paragraph (2)(B).

    (B) Years of service. In the case of a person who is an employee of the recipient (whether by reason of this subsection or otherwise), for purposes of the requirements listed in paragraph (3), years of service for the recipient shall be determined by taking into account any period for which such employee would have been a leased employee but for the requirements of paragraph (2)(B).

(5) Safe harbor.

    (A) In general. In the case of requirements described in subparagraphs (A) and (B) of paragraph (3), this subsection shall not apply to any leased employee with respect to services performed for a recipient if

        (i) such employee is covered by a plan which is maintained by the leasing organization and meets the requirements of subparagraph (B), and

        (ii) leased employees (determined without regard to this paragraph) do not constitute more than 20 percent of the recipient's non-highly compensated work force.

    (B) Plan requirements. A plan meets the requirements of this subparagraph if

        (i) such plan is a money purchase pension plan with a nonintegrated employer contribution rate for each participant of at least 10 percent of compensation,

        (ii) such plan provides for full and immediate vesting, and

        (iii) each employee of the leasing organization (other than employees who perform substantially all of their services for the leasing organization) immediately participates in such plan. Clause (iii) shall not apply to any individual whose compensation from the leasing organization in each plan year during the 4-year period ending with the plan year is less than $1,000.

    (C) Definitions. For purposes of this paragraph

        (i) Highly compensated employee. The term "highly compensated employee" has the meaning given such term by section 414(q).

        (ii) Nonhighly compensated work force. The term "nonhighly compensated work force" means the aggregate number of individuals (other than highly compensated employees).

(I) who are employees of the recipient (without regard to this subsection) and have performed services for the recipient (or for the recipient and related persons) on a substantially full-time basis for a period of at least 1 year, or

(II) who are leased employees with respect to the recipient (determined without regard to this paragraph).

(iii) Compensation. The term "compensation" has the same meaning as when used in section 415; except that such term shall include

(I) any employer contribution under a qualified cash or deferred arrangement to the extent not included in gross income under section 402(e)(3) or 402(h) (1)(B),

(II) any amount which the employee would have received in cash but for an election under a cafeteria plan (within the meaning of section 125), and

(III) any amount contributed to an annuity contract described in section 403(b) pursuant to a salary reduction agreement (within the meaning of section 3121(a)(5)(D)).

(6) Other rules. For purposes of this subsection

(A) Related persons. The term "related persons" has the same meaning as when used in section 144(a)(3).

(B) Employees of entities under common control. The rules of subsections (b), (c), (m), and (o) shall apply.

(o) Regulations

The Secretary shall prescribe such regulations (which may provide rules in addition to the rules contained in subsections (m) and (n) as may be necessary to prevent the avoidance of any employee benefit requirement listed in subsection (m)(4) or (n)(3) or any requirement under section 457 through the use of

(1) separate organizations,

(2) employee leasing, or

(3) other arrangements.

The regulations prescribed under subsection (n) shall include provisions to minimize the recordkeeping requirements of subsection (n) in the case of an employer which has no top-heavy plans (within the meaning of section 416(g)) and which uses the services of persons (other than employees) for an insignificant percentage of the employer's total workload.

Internal Revenue Bulletin 1984-2 CB 469— Notice 84-11 (July 16, 1984)

Section 414(n) Employee Leasing Provision of the Tax Equity and Fiscal Responsibility Act of 1982

This Notice provides questions and answers relating to the employee leasing provisions of section 414(n) of the Internal Revenue Code as added by the Tax Equity and Fiscal Responsibility Act of 1982 (Pub. L. 97-248, 1982-2 C.B. 462) (TEFRA).

Until applicable regulations are published, the guidance provided by these questions and answers may be relied upon to comply with the provisions of section 414(n). The Service will apply these rules in issuing determination letters, opinion letters, and other rulings with respect to qualified retirement plans. If future regulations are more restrictive than the guidance in this Notice, the regulations will be applied without retroactive effect. However, no inference should be drawn regarding issues not raised which may be suggested by a particular question or answer or as to why certain questions and not others are included.

The determination of whether an organization is a "leasing organization" for purposes of section 414(n) will be based upon the facts and circumstances of each case. Taxpayers that utilize the services of leased employees may request a determination as to whether their plan qualifies by following the determination letter procedure issued in Notice 83-12, 1983-2 C.B. 412 (relating to procedures for obtaining determination letters on the qualification of pension, profit-sharing, and stock bonus plans that have been amended to comply with the changes made by the Tax Equity and Fiscal Responsibility Act of 1982). With regard to item 5 of Notice 83-12 (relating to the requirement that the employer provide information regarding what retirement benefits are provided for leased employees), the employer must supply information regarding the leasing organization's retirement benefits only if the recipient is relying on such benefits for purposes of qualification of the recipient's plan.

Q-1. How did TEFRA change the law with regard to employee leasing?

A-1. TEFRA amended the Internal Revenue Code to provide that for purposes of certain employee benefit provisions, a "leased employee" generally shall be treated as an employee of the person for whom such leased employee performs services (the "recipient" of the services) even though such individual is a common law employee of the leasing organization.

Q-2. For purposes of which employee benefit provisions will a "leased employee" be treated as an employee of the recipient?

A-2. A leased employee will be treated as an employee of the recipient for purposes of the following employee benefit requirements:

(1) Section 401(a) (relating to the exclusive benefit rule);

(2) Sections 401(a)(3) and 410 (relating to minimum participation requirements);

(3) Section 401(a)(4) (relating to the requirement that contributions or benefits do not discriminate in favor of employees who are officers, shareholders, or highly compensated);

(4) Section 401(a)(7) and 411 (relating to minimum vesting standards);

(5) Sections 401(a)(16) and 415 (relating to limitations on contributions and benefits);

(6) Section 404 (relating to deductions for contributions);

(7) Section 408(k) (relating to simplified employee pensions); and

(8) Section 416 (relating to top-heavy plans).

Q-3. How do the provisions of section 414(n) relate to the "common law employee" rules?

A-3. The provisions of section 414(n) operate independently of the "common law employee" rules. Thus, if an individual is considered an employee of the recipient under the common law rules, such individual is an employee of the recipient for all purposes and without regard to the provisions of section 414(n). For example, an individual who is a common law employee of an organization (a "recipient") will continue to be an employee of the recipient even though the recipient formally "leases" the individual from a separate entity that maintains a safe harbor plan described in section 414(n)(5). In such cases, the fact that the "leasing" organization maintains a safe harbor plan does not affect the treatment of the individual as a common law employee of the recipient.

Q-4. When is section 414(n) effective?

A-4. Section 414(n) applies to taxable years of the recipient beginning after December 31, 1983.

Q-5. What is a leased employee for purposes of section 414(n)?

A-5. A leased employee is any person who performs services for a recipient if:

(1) such services are provided pursuant to an agreement between the recipient and any other person (the "leasing organization"),

(2) such person has performed such services on a substantially full-time basis for a period of at least one year, and

(3) such services are of a type historically performed in the business field of the recipient by employees.

Q-6. **Must the agreement referred to in paragraph (1) of A-5 between the recipient and the leasing organization be in writing?**

A-6. No, an oral contract between the recipient and the leasing organization will satisfy the "agreement" requirement.

Q-7. **What standards are used to determine if a person has performed services on a substantially full-time basis for a period of at least one year?**

A-7. A person is considered to have performed services on a substantially full-time basis for a period of at least one year if: (1) during any consecutive 12-month period such person has performed at least 1500 hours of service for the recipient, or (2) during any consecutive 12-month period such person performs services for the recipient for a number of hours of service at least equal to 75 percent of the average number of hours that are customarily performed by an employee of that recipient in the particular position. The performance of services for a recipient includes the performance of services for an organization related to the recipient in accordance with section 103(b)(6)(C). For example, assume that Corporation X leases Individual A from Leasing Company Y to perform bookkeeping duties. Leasing Company Y does not maintain a retirement plan. It is customary for bookkeepers who are employed by Corporation X to perform services 35 hours per week or 1820 hours per year. During the next consecutive 12-month period, A performs 1450 hours of service for X. A does not meet the first test of "substantially full-time" because A did not perform 1500 hours of service. However, A does meet the second test for "substantially full-time" because A performed services for a number of hours at least equal to 75 percent of the number of hours that are customarily performed by an employee in that particular position (.75 ? 1820 hours = 1365 hours customarily performed). Therefore, A is a "leased employee" of Corporation X.

Q-8. **For purposes of determining if an employee has performed services for the recipient on a substantially full-time basis for at least one year, does the one-year period include service of the employee prior to the effective date of section 414(n)?**

A-8. Yes. For example, in the case of a recipient that is a calendar year taxpayer if, as of January 1, 1984, an individual has been performing services for the recipient on a substantially full-time basis for one year or more and the other requirements of section 414(n)(2) are met, such individual is a "leased employee" as of January 1, 1984. In addition, any period of service performed by the employee as a common law employee of the recipient is taken into account for purposes of determining whether the employee has performed services on a substantially full-time basis for a period of at least one year. For example, assume that Individual B has been a common law employee of Corporation X for a period of 3 years. On April 1, 1984, B terminates his employment with X. On May 1, 1984, B is hired by and becomes a common law employee of Leasing Company Z. Leasing Company Z is not related to Corporation X. Z enters into a contract with Corporation X to provide leased employees. On May 2, 1984, Individual B is leased to Corporation X. Corporation X does not maintain direct control over Individual B's day to day activities sufficient for B to be considered a common law employee of X. Individual B is considered to be a leased employee of X for purposes of section 414(n) as of May 2, 1984, because prior service performed by Individual B for the recipient as a common law employee is taken into account for purposes of determining whether an individual has performed services on a substantially full-time basis for a period of at least one year.

Q-9. **Will a recipient's retirement plan be denied qualification if the plan covers an individual who would otherwise be a leased employee but for the fact that such individual does not meet the "substantially full-time" standard?**

A-9. No. In the case where a recipient's retirement plan covers an individual who would be a leased employee for purposes of section 414(n), but such individual does not meet either of the tests in answer 7 for determining "substantially full-time," the plan will not lose its qualified status or otherwise be denied qualification.

Q-10. **What is the meaning of the requirement that services be of a type historically performed in the business field of the recipient by employees?**

A-10. Services will be considered of a type historically performed by employees in the business field of the recipient if it is not unusual for the services to be performed by employees of organizations in the recipient's business field in the United States.

Q-11. **Are there any exceptions to the application of the provisions of section 414(n)?**

A-11. Generally, no. Except as provided in section 414(n)(5) (relating to safe harbor plans of leasing organizations), as long as the three requirements of section 414(n)(2) and questions and answers 5 through 10 are met, the provisions of section 414(n) apply. However, the Service will consider suggestions made by the public regarding employee leasing arrangements that might be excepted from the provisions of section 414(n) in regulations.

Q-12. **If, as of January 1, 1984, an individual is considered to be a leased employee, how are that individual's years of service determined for purposes of participation and vesting under the recipient's retirement plan?**

A-12. For purposes of both participation and vesting, the entire period for which the leased employee has performed services for the recipient must be taken into account in accordance with section 414(n)(4), including periods before the effective date of section 414(n). Therefore, if the recipient is a calendar year taxpayer and the recipient's retirement plan requires one year of service before an employee may participate, and a leased employee began performing services for the recipient on January 1, 1981, the leased employee's service for participation purposes will be considered to have commenced on January 1, 1981. However, because the individual does not become a leased employee until January 1, 1984, such leased employee need not begin to participate in the plan until January 1, 1984. Therefore, section 414(n) does not require the recipient to provide retroactive benefits for the leased employee for years of service prior to January 1, 1984.

Q-13. **How does the plan maintained by the leasing organization treat the leased employee for purposes of the applicable pension requirements?**

A-13. The leased employee continues to be the common law employee of the leasing organization. Therefore, for purposes of coverage, vesting, contributions and benefits, a plan maintained by the leasing organization must take into consideration all of the leased employee's service for the leasing organization (including periods during which the employee was leased by the leasing organization to a recipient) and compensation for services for or on behalf of the leasing organization.

Q-14. **Must a leased employee participate in the plan maintained by the recipient?**

A-14. No. Section 414(n)(1)(A) requires only that a leased employee be treated as an employee; it does not require that a leased employee be a participant in the recipient's qualified plan.

For example, assume that for 1984 Company X (a calendar year taxpayer) has 500 common law employees who have completed one or more years of service. In addition, X maintains a qualified profit-sharing plan in which 400 of these employees participate. The plan requires an employee to complete one year of service before participation, but does not impose a minimum age requirement. Also, section 414(n) requires that Company X treat 25 leased employees as its own employees for 1984.

Considering only the common law employees, X's plan satisfies the coverage requirements of section 410(b)(1) because it benefits 80 percent (400/500) of X's employees who have completed one or more years of service. But X's plan also must consider the 25 leased employees in applying the coverage requirements of section 410(b)(1) for 1984. If none of the 25 leased employees is permitted to participate under X's plan for 1984, the plan will benefit 76.2 percent (400/525) of its employees and thus will satisfy section 410(b)(1)(A). Thus, X's plan is not required to benefit any of the 25 leased employees for 1984. (But see question and answer 16, relating to plan amendments.)

Q-15. **May leased employees who must be treated as employees of the recipient under section 414(n) be excluded as a class from participation in the recipient's plan?**

A-15. Yes. A plan maintained by a recipient may exclude from participation all leased employees who must be treated as employees under section 414(n) so long as the plan otherwise satisfies either the percentage or the fair cross-section test of section 410(b)(1) by taking such leased employees into account.

Q-16. **Must a plan maintained by a recipient be amended to provide explicitly for the treatment of leased employees who must be treated as employees under section 414(n)?**

A-16. Yes. How leased employees will be treated under a recipient's plan depends on the terms of the plan. Therefore, if an organization utilizes the services of leased employees, the plan must specifically provide how leased employees will be treated under the recipient's plan.

Q-17. **How does the plan maintained by the recipient determine the contributions or benefits to be provided on behalf of the leased employee?**

A-17. For purposes of providing a leased employee with contributions or benefits that are based on compensation, a plan maintained by the recipient must determine the portion of the leased employee's total compensation received from or on behalf of the leasing organization that is attributable to the performance of services for the recipient. For purposes of providing a leased employee with contributions or benefits based on years of service, the principles of question and answer 12 are applicable.

Q-18. Section 414(n)(5) provides that section 414(n) shall not apply to any leased employee if such employee is covered by a "safe harbor" plan maintained by the leasing organization. Must the leasing organization cover all of its employees under a safe harbor plan?

A-18. Generally, no. A leasing organization need not cover every employee it leases under its safe harbor plan but may cover some employees and not others. However, the safe harbor plan is still required to qualify under the rules of section 401(a) and thus must satisfy the coverage rules of section 410(b) and the antidiscrimination rules of section 401(a)(4). In addition, any leased employee not covered by the safe harbor plan is subject to the general rule of section 414(n).

Q-19. If a plan maintained by a leasing organization provides a fully and immediately vested 7 1/2 percent nonintegrated contribution for each year during which a common law employee of the leasing organization is considered a leased employee of a recipient, does such plan meet the immediate participation requirement of a safe-harbor plan?

A-19. No. In order to be treated as a safe harbor plan with respect to a leased employee, a plan maintained by a leasing organization must provide for immediate participation for such leased employee at the start of the 12-month period used to determine if the employee is a leased employee under section 414(n). For example, assume that a common law employee of the leasing organization begins performing services for a recipient on July 1, 1984. Between July 1, 1984, and July 1, 1985, the employee performs more than 1500 hours of service for the recipient. Therefore, as of July 1, 1985, the recipient must treat the employee as its own employee for purposes of the pension requirements listed in section 414(n)(3). If, as of July 1, 1984, the employee was a participant in the leasing organization's qualified plan, the leasing organization's plan will be considered to satisfy the immediate participation requirement for a safe harbor plan with respect to that employee. This is true even if the employee was hired by the leasing organization on January 1, 1984, and did not become a participant in the plan until July 1, 1984, the date on which the employee began providing services for the recipient.

However, in no case does the immediate participation rule require that an individual be a participant in a safe harbor plan before the effective date of section 414(n). Therefore, in the case of a recipient that is a calendar year taxpayer, if an individual is a leased employee as of January 1, 1984, (in accordance with the rules of answer 8), such individual need not become a participant in the safe harbor plan before January 1, 1984.

Small Business Job Protection Act of 1996
104th Congress, 2nd Session
House of Representatives
Report 104-737
August 1, 1996—Ordered to be printed
Mr. Archer, from the committee of conference, submitted the following.

Conference Report
[To accompany H.R. 3448]
The committee of conference on the disagreeing votes of the two Houses on the amendments of the Senate to the bill (H.R. 3448), to provide tax relief for small businesses, to protect jobs, to create opportunities, to increase the take home pay of workers, to amend the Portal-to-Portal Act of 1947 relating to the payment of wages to employees who use employer owned vehicles, and to amend the Fair Labor Standards Act of 1938 to increase the minimum wage rate and to prevent job loss by providing flexibility to employers in complying with minimum wage and overtime requirements under that Act, having met, after full and free conference, have agreed to recommend and do recommend to their respective Houses as follows:

17. Treatment of Leased Employees
(Sec. 1454 of the House bill and the Senate amendment.)

Present Law
An individual (a leased employee) who performs services for another person (the recipient) may be required to be treated as the recipient's employee for various employee benefit provisions, if the services are performed pursuant to an agreement between the recipient and any other person (the leasing organization) who is otherwise treated as the individual's employer (sec. 414(n)). The individual is to be treated as the recipient's employee only if the individual has performed services for the recipient on a substantially full-time basis for a year, and the services are of a type historically performed by employees in the recipient's business field.

An individual who otherwise would be treated as a recipient's leased employee will not be treated as such an employee if the individual participates in a safe harbor plan maintained by the leasing organization meeting certain requirements. Each leased employee is to be treated as an employee of the recipient, regardless of the existence of a safe harbor plan, if more than 20 percent of an employer's nonhighly compensated workforce are leased.

House Bill

Under the House bill, the present-law "historically performed" test is replaced with a new test under which an individual is not considered a leased employee unless the individual's services are performed under primary direction or control by the service recipient. As under present law, the determination of whether someone is a leased employee is made after determining whether the individual is a common-law employee of the recipient. Thus, an individual who is not a common-law employee of the service recipient could nevertheless be a leased employee of the service recipient. Similarly, the fact that a person is or is not found to perform services under primary direction or control of the recipient for purposes of the employee leasing rules is not determinative of whether the person is or is not a common-law employee of the recipient.

Whether services are performed by an individual under primary direction or control by the service recipient depends on the facts and circumstances. In general, primary direction and control means that the service recipient exercises the majority of direction and control over the individual. Factors that are relevant in determining whether primary direction or control exists include whether the individual is required to comply with instructions of the service recipient about when, where, and how he or she is to perform the services, whether the services must be performed by a particular person, whether the individual is subject to the supervision of the service recipient, and whether the individual must perform services in the order or sequence set by the service recipient. Factors that generally are not relevant in determining whether such direction or control exists include whether the service recipient has the right to hire or fire the individual and whether the individual works for others.

For example, an individual who works under the direct supervision of the service recipient would be considered to be subject to primary direction or control of the service recipient even if another company hired and trained the individual, had the ultimate (but unexercised) legal right to control the individual, paid his wages, withheld his employment and income taxes, and had the exclusive right to fire him. Thus, for example, temporary secretaries, receptionists, word processing personnel and similar office personnel who are subject to the day-to-day control of the employer in essentially the same manner as a common-law employee are treated as leased employees if the period of service threshold is reached.

On the other hand, an individual who is a common-law employee of Company A who performs services for Company B on the business premises of Company B under the supervision of Company A would generally not be considered to be under primary direction or control of Company B. The supervision by Company A must be more than nominal, however, and not merely a mechanism to avoid the literal language of the direction or control test.

An example of the situation in the preceding paragraph might be a work crew that comes into a factory to install, repair, maintain, or modify equipment or machinery at the factory. The work crew includes a supervisor who is an employee of the equipment (or equipment repair) company and who has the authority to direct and control the crew, and who actually does exercise such direction and control. In this situation, the supervisor and his or her crew are required to comply with the safety and environmental precautions of the manufacturer, and the supervisor is in frequent communication with the employees of the manufacturer. As another example, certain professionals (e.g., attorneys, accountants, actuaries, doctors, computer programmers, systems analysts, and engineers) who regularly make use of their own judgment and discretion on matters of importance in the performance of their services and are guided by professional, legal, or industry standards, are not leased employees even though the common law employer does not closely supervise the professional on a continuing basis, and the service recipient requires the services to be performed on site and according to certain stages, techniques, and timetables. In addition to the example above, outside professionals who maintain their own businesses (e.g., attorneys, accountants, actuaries, doctors, computer programmers, systems analysts, and engineers) generally would not be considered to be subject to such primary direction or control.

Under the direction or control test, clerical and similar support staff (e.g., secretaries and nurses in a doctor's office) generally would be considered to be subject to primary direction or control of the service recipient and would be leased employees provided the other requirements of section 414(n) are met.

In many cases, the "historically performed" test is overly broad, and results in the unintended treatment of individuals as leased employees. One of the principal purposes for changing the leased employee rules is to relieve the unnecessary hardship and uncertainty created for employers in these circumstances. However, it is not intended that the direction or control test enable employers to engage in abusive practices. Thus, it is intended that the Secretary interpret and apply the leased employee rules in a manner so as to prevent abuses. This ability to prevent abuses under the leasing rules is in addition to the present-law authority of the Secretary under section 414(o). For example, one potentially abusive situation exists where the benefit arrangements of the service recipient overwhelmingly favor its highly compensated employees, the employer has no or very few nonhighly compensated common-law employees, yet the employer makes substantial use of the services of nonhighly compensated individuals who are not its common-law employees.

Effective date.—The provision is effective for years beginning after Dec. 31, 1996, except that the House bill would not apply to relationships that have been previously determined by an IRS ruling not to involve leased employees. In applying the leased employee rules to years beginning before the effective date, it is intended that the Secretary use a reasonable interpretation of the statute to apply the leasing rules to prevent abuse.

Senate Amendment

The Senate amendment is the same as the House bill.

Conference Agreement

The conference agreement follows the House bill and the Senate amendment.

IRS Technical Advice Memorandum: Retirement Plans May Exclude Leased Employees

IRS TAM on Section 410: Minimum Participation Standards
Document Date: Jul. 28, 1999
Manager, EP Determinations, Cincinnati, OH

I. Issues

Whether Plan 1 and Plan 2 may exclude from plan participation employees who are either (1) not reported on the payroll records of affiliated companies as common law employees (even if a court or administrative agency determines that such individuals are common law employees and not independent contractors) or (2) are identified by either a specified job code or work status code on the employer's payroll records, and still satisfy the requirements of section 410(a) of the Internal Revenue Code and section 1.410(a)-3(d) of the Income Tax Regulations.

Whether plan eligibility requirements cause Plan 1 and Plan 2 to fail to satisfy the requirement that a plan must be a definite written program.

Whether section 11.04 of Plan 1 and sections 11.02, 13.06(e), and 14.02(a) of Plan 2, which provide for an involuntary cashout of a participant's benefit if the present value of the vested portion of such participant's account is $3,500 or less at the time of the distribution, satisfy the requirement of section 411(a)(11) and section 417(e) of the Code and the regulations thereunder.

II. Facts

In September of 1997, the Internal Revenue Service received an Application for Determination for Employee Benefit Plan, Form 5300, for Plans 1 and 2. The Plans were initially effective March 1, 1996, and have calendar plan years. The taxpayer submitted proposed amendments to the plans on March 2, 1998.

Section 2.14 of Plan 1 and section 2.21 of Plan 2, as amended March 2, 1998, state that "an individual shall only be treated as an employee if he or she is reported on the payroll records of an affiliated company as a common law employee. This term does not include any other common law employee or any leased employee. In particular, it is expressly intended that individuals not treated as common law employees by the Affiliated Companies on their payroll records are to be excluded from Plan participation even if a court or administrative agency determines that such individuals are common law employees and not independent contractors." Neither "common law employees" nor "independent contractors" are defined in the Plan document.

Section 3.02 of Plan 2 excludes "special assignment employees" from plan participation. The special assignment classification includes two types of workers: those with job code "Y" (Sections 2.14 and 3.03(a)) and those with work status code "X" (section 3.03(b)). The "X" and "Y" work code dictate how these workers are compensated and other terms of their employment. Specifically, "Y" code workers are hired to perform work on specific contracts with specific deadlines for specific compensation and benefits. These benefits include participation in other employer retirement plans. "X" code workers are members of the salaried employee union who have been laid off and are on the inactive seniority list. Pursuant to an agreement between the union and the employer, these former employees are hired for a predetermined period of time to complete a specific task or project. The agreement further provides that they be paid the prevailing contract salary rate and that they are not entitled to participate in the employer's retirement plans.

Section 11.04(a) of Plan 1 as amended March 2, 1998, provides in general that upon a participant's retirement or termination of employment, if the present value of the vested portion of the participant's account is $3,500 or less at the time of the distribution, the vested portion will be distributed to him as soon as practicable following the next valuation date after retirement or termination occurs.

Section 11.02 of Plan 2 as amended March 2, 1998, provides that in the event a participant becomes a terminated participant, if the total value of his or her vested account is $3,500 or less at the time of the annuity starting date, he or she will receive a total distribution of his or her account as soon as practicable.

Section 13.06(e) of Plan 2 as amended March 2, 1998, provides that with respect to a participant who has an outstanding loan balance at the time he or she terminates employment with the affiliated companies or dies and whose vested account and outstanding loan balance does not exceed $3,500 on the annuity starting date, the outstanding loan balance will be treated as a distribution.

Section 14.02(a) of Plan 2 as amended March 2, 1998, provides that if the total value of the deceased participant's account is $3,500 or less on the annuity starting date, a total distribution shall be made automatically to the designated beneficiary.

III. Law and Rationale

Issue 1. Section 410(a) Requirements

Section 410(a) of the Code provides, in general, that a trust will not qualify under section 401(a) if the plan of which it is a part requires, as a condition of participation, that an employee complete a period of service with the employer or employers maintaining the plan extending beyond the later of the date on which the employee attains the age of 21; or the date on which he completes 1 year of service (or two years of service in the case of a plan that meets 410(a)(1)(B)(1))).

Section 1.410(a)-3(d) of the Income Tax Regulations states that "Section 410(a) and section 1.410(a)-4 relate solely to age and service conditions and do not preclude a plan from establishing conditions, other than conditions relating to age or service, which must be satisfied by plan participants. For example, such provisions would not preclude a qualified plan from requiring, as a condition of participation, that an employee be employed within a specific job classification."

Section 1.410(a)-3(a)(1) of the regulations, however, provides that "plan provisions may be treated as imposing age and service requirements even though the provisions do not specifically refer to age or service. Plan provisions which have the effect of imposing an age and service requirement with the employer or employers maintaining the plan will be treated as if they imposed an age or service requirement."

Section 1.401-1(a)(2) of the regulations provides, in relevant part, that a qualified pension, profit sharing, or stock bonus plan is a definite written program and arrangement which is communicated to the employees and which is established and maintained by the employer.

Revenue Ruling 74-466, 1974-2 C.B. 131, holds that a plan which excludes nonsalaried employees unless such employees satisfy alternative eligibility requirements "approved by the trustees" that are not defined or described in the plan fails to satisfy the qualification requirement that a plan have a definite written program and arrangement as described in section 1.401-1(a)(2) of the regulations.

It is important to address these plan provisions in the context in which they arise. Many plans simply state that employees are eligible to participate, or that common law employees are eligible to participate. These provisions mean the same thing.[1] *In National Mutual Ins. Co. v. Darden*, 503 U.S. 318 (1992), the Supreme Court held that, for purposes of the Employee Retirement Income Security Act of 1974 (ERISA), common law agency principles are applied in determining whether an individual is an employee. The Court did not address how the term "employee" is defined under the Internal Revenue Code. However, the same common law standard is applied for Code purposes. Section 3121(d) of the Code and section 31.3121(d)-f(c)(2) of the Employment Tax Regulations provide that an employee includes any individual who, under the usual common law rules applicable in determining the employer–employee relationship, has the status of an employee. The analysis of a common law employment relationship typically arises in the context of determining whether an individual is a common law employee or an Independent contractor for purposes of employment taxes. This analysis is equally applicable in determining whether an individual is a common law employee of the employer for purposes of section 401(a) of the code. See *Professional & Executive Leasing, Inc. v. Commissioner*, 89 T.C. 225, 231 (1987); *Edward L. Burnette, O.D., PA. v. Commissioner*, 68 T.C. 387, 397 (1977); *Packard v. Commissioner*, 63 T.C. 621, 629 (1975).

Determining whether a particular worker is an independent contractor or an employee can be difficult, for it's based on facts and circumstances.[2] The entity that engages a worker typically makes the initial determination of whether a worker is an independent contractor or a common law employee. However, that initial determination of a worker's status can subsequently be determined (by the entity, the Internal Revenue Service, or the courts) to have been erroneous, so that workers who were initially treated as independent contractors are retroactively reclassified as common law employees. This reclassification could have a direct effect upon whether the reclassified workers are eligible to participate in any employee benefit plans of the employer. However, plan participation does not flow automatically from reclassification. Instead, plan terms must be examined to determine whether or not the recharacterized workers participate in the plan.

Vizcaino v. Microsoft Corp., 97 F.3d 1187 (9th Cir. 1996), illustrates how retroactive reclassifications can affect participation in qualified retirement plans.[3] The *Vizcaino* decision involves workers who were initially classified as independent contractors but were later determined to be common law employees for employment tax purposes. The workers claimed benefits under Microsoft's benefit plans, including its plan containing a cash or deferred arrangement described in section 401(k) of the Code (401(k) plan). The 401(k) plan limited participation to employees on Microsoft's U.S. payroll. The court concluded that the workers at issue were common law employees and thus were eligible, under the plan's terms, to participate in the 401(k) plan.[4]

Many employers have amended their retirement plans in the wake of this decision in an attempt to protect their plans against the uncertainty that may be created by retroactive determinations that workers are employees rather than independent contractors. Typically, such amendments provide that workers engaged as independent contractors, or workers not paid through the payroll system will not be eligible to participate in the plan, even if the classification as an independent contractor is later determined to be erroneous.

Section 410(a) of the Code precludes an employer from limiting participation on the basis of age or service, except as specifically permitted in that section. Section 410(a) does not otherwise limit an employer's ability to design its retirement plan to exclude (or to cover) whichever classifications of employees that it chooses to exclude (or to cover). Similarly, section 1.410(a)-3(d) of the regulations does not preclude an employer from excluding workers based on conditions other than conditions that are age or service related. Indeed, this provision permits an employer to condition participation on "those employees being employed within a specification [sic] job classification." The section 410(a) inquiry ends with a determination that the plan's exclusion is not age or service related.[5]

As indicated previously, employers have legitimate reasons to exclude from plans workers who were not engaged as common law employees. If the worker is, in fact, an independent contractor, the employer would be precluded from covering the individual under its plan, absent some specific statutory rule, such as the individual's status as a based employee under section 414(n) of the Code. Even if the worker is not, in fact, an independent contractor, the employer has a legitimate business interest in knowing the cost of the worker's compensation package at the time the worker is engaged.

A tax-qualified retirement plan that conditions participation on status as a common law employee need not define that term, for the standard articulated in *Darden* will be applicable absent some special definition in the plan. With respect to the case at issue, section 410(a) of the Code does not preclude a qualified plan from excluding retroactively reclassified employees from participating in the plan. A worker's status is based on facts and circumstances. Making a determination as to whether a common law employment relationship exists is not always straightforward. An employer, making the initial classification of a worker's status, has legitimate concerns in protecting its plan from the consequences of retroactive reclassifications if a mistake is made. Nothing in section 410(a) prevents an employer from addressing these concerns through preventative measures similar to the plan language provided by the taxpayer.

The District contends that the plan language excluding workers identified by work codes in the taxpayer's payer records does not satisfy the requirements of section 410(a) of the Code for the same reasons that plan language excluding independent contractors fails to satisfy section 410(a). We disagree with this argument that plan language excluding independent contractors fails to satisfy section 410(a). As stated earlier, independent contractors are generally precluded from participating in the plan of an employer based on the exclusive benefit rule described in section 401(a). Section 410(a) provides, in part, that a trust shall not constitute a qualified trust if the plan requires as a condition of participation in the plan that an employee complete a period of service with the employer extending beyond the later of the date that the employee attains age 21 or the date the employee completes one year of service. Independent contractors are not employees (except of themselves) and, thus, the section 410(a) minimum age and service conditions are irrelevant for purposes of determining whether independent contractors can be excluded from a qualified plan of an entity that engages them.

Here the plan excludes workers based on a payroll code. Such an exclusion could potentially be an indirect age or service exclusion, and hence impermissible. This question cannot be answered merely by examining the plan document. Instead, an examination of facts external to the plan document would be necessary to conclude that the plan improperly excluded employees based on age or service. As we previously indicated, there are no facts present to indicate that this plan provision, excluding workers by codes, violates section 410(a) of the Code. Consequently, this exclusion does not violate section 410(a).

Issue 2. Definite Written Program Requirement

The District contends that the definite written program requirement is not satisfied because there is no specific, objective criteria. In the plan identifying common law employees and further, that allowing the employer to define an individual as an employee only if the employee is reported on the payroll records of an affiliated company gives the employer discretion in determining who can participate in the plan by specifying how they are paid, i.e., on the payroll or by some other method such as accounts payable. Basically, the District presents the same contention as under section 410 of the Code with respect to the plan's exclusion of independent contractors, namely, that it is not possible to determine from the plan document which employees will participate in the plan.

We believe that, for the same reasons that we discussed with reference to section 410(a) of the Code, the definite written program requirement is not violated by the exclusion of workers who were engaged as independent contractors but later determined to be employees. Although it can be difficult to determine accurately whether a worker is an independent contractor or an employee, the terms have independent legal significance. Further, the reference to the payroll system is in no sense ambiguous. Given the plan language, workers, whether engaged as employees on the payroll or in some other status, can determine whether they are covered by the plan. So, too, can the employer, trustees, and plan administrator.

As we have indicated, we believe that a plan must be definite as to which workers are covered and which workers are not and that the employer must communicate this essential fact to the employees. We agree with the District that the plan terms cannot leave the determination of which employees are covered to the employer's discretion and that section 1.401-1(a)(2) of the regulations would be violated by plan provisions that permitted such discretion. Clearly, an employee should be able to enforce his or her rights based on the written plan document, and a plan that is not definite enough to enable an employee to determine coverage status so as to enforce rights is fatally flawed.

Section 402(a)(l) of ERISA has a comparable requirement that retirement plans "be established and maintained pursuant to a written agreement." The ERISA conference report in explaining this requirement stated that a written plan is to be required in order that every employee may, on examining the plan document, determine exactly what his rights and obligations are under the plan. A written plan is required so the employees may know who is responsible for operating the plan. Conference Report 93-1260(1974) (reprinted in 1974-3 C.B. 415). We believe that this ERISA requirement is a corollary to the Code requirement of a definite written program that has long been required of a tax-qualified retirement plan. This requirement first appeared in Reg. 103, Sec. 19. 1655(a)(1)-1(a), which was added by T.D. 5278, for taxable years beginning after December 31, 1941.

A plan does not fail this requirement simply because facts extrinsic to the plan document need to be examined to determine which workers are covered by the plan. For example, if a plan covers certain classifications of employees, facts and circumstances must be examined to determine whether a particular worker fits into the covered classifications.

The Code contains pension plan rules that are premised on the fact that plans may cover particular classifications of employees. There are rules that recognize that a plan may cover collectively bargained employees or non-collectively bargained employees in section 410(b)(3) and section 413(b). Also, section 410(b)(2)(A) recognizes that a plan may benefit "such employees as qualify under a classification set up by the employer."

Further, section 1.410(a)-3(d) of the regulations recognizes that a plan may limit its coverage to specified job classifications.

The Service has published revenue rulings describing situations in which qualified plans covered only certain classifications of employees. This limited coverage was not raised as an issue involving impermissible discretion. In Rev. Rul. 70-384, 1970-2 C.B. 87, the plan covered only supervisors. In Rev. Rul.

74-256, 1974-1 C.B. 94, the plan covered salaried employees in contrast to hourly employees. In Rev. Rul. 70-283, 1970-2 CR. 26, the plan covered nonunion employees.

Just because a plan can cover a particular category of employees and because it is permissible for an employer, in the exercise of its business judgment, to assign a worker to a particular category, does not mean that every category set forth in a plan is acceptable. We disagree with the taxpayer's suggestion that no further inquiry is appropriate. A category like the impermissible category discussed in Rev. Rul. 74-466, 1974-2 C.B. 131 (employees approved by the trustees) is not acceptable. There may be other categories that leave the employer arbitrary and unbridled discretion and that are based on no independent business reason such that the category does not satisfy the definite written program requirement. For example, if the plan said that it covered employees who were on a list and there was no business reason for the list and a particular worker could be added to or removed from the list by the employer at any time, then an argument could be made that such a plan provision fails the definite written program requirement. We do not now suggest that such an argument be raised. We believe such a plan provision would be unusual and that a plan that meets the test below will be acceptable.

We believe the appropriate inquiry as to whether or not a particular category is acceptable is whether, given the particular facts of the employer and the plan provision, is it clear whether or not a particular employee is or is not in the plan. That is, is it clearly understood by the employees, the plan administrator, and the plan fiduciaries when they examine all the facts, which employees are covered by the plan and which employees are excluded? If this question can be answered in the affirmative, then the plan passes the definite written program requirement. Whether the question is being asked as to the present situation or is being asked on a retrospect [sic] basis, the test is the same. Thus, what is definite today should be definite tomorrow and the same answer should obtain with respect to a particular worker. On the other hand, if given knowledge of the same facts a reasonable person would not be able to tell who was covered or who was excluded, then the plan fails the test. Similarly, if the answer can change with respect to a particular employee when the question is asked on a retrospective basis, the classification is suspect.

We now turn to the facts in this case to see if the use of work and job codes in the context of the employer's business satisfies the definite written program requirement. The "X" code workers that are excluded are basically rehired union employees who are on an inactive seniority list. The "Y" code workers that are excluded are hired to work on specific contracts and have a different compensation package, including coverage in another retirement plan. Here, the excluded workers know who they are. Further, it is undisputed that if any person looked at the facts with respect to a particular worker that person would know if the worker fit within the enumerated categories. Nor is there any question that at a subsequent time, an employee could be retroactively determined to have been a member of these excluded classes. Further, the employer has demonstrated that there is a business purpose for these categories. For these reasons, we believe that the plans satisfy the definite written program requirement.

Issue 3. Cash-Out Requirements

Prior to the enactment of the Taxpayer Relief Act of 1997 (TRA'97), section 411(a)(11)(A) of the Code provided that if the present value of any nonforfeitable accrued benefit exceeded $3,500, a plan met the requirements of section 411(a)(11) only if such plan provided that such benefit could not be immediately distributed without the consent of the participant. TRA'97 changed this cash-out limit to $5,000, effective for plan years beginning after August 5, 1997.

Interpreting the law prior to the enactment of TRA'97, section 1.411(a)-11(c)(3) of the regulations provides that the written consent of a participant is required before the commencement of the distribution of any portion of the participant's accrued benefit if the present value of the nonforfeitable total accrued benefit is greater than $3,500. If the present value does not exceed $3,500, the consent requirements are deemed satisfied, and the plan may distribute such portion to the participant as a single sum. The regulation further provides that, if the present value determined at the time of a distribution to the participant exceeds $3,500, then the present value at any subsequent time is deemed to exceed $3,500; this is commonly referred to as the "lookback rule."

Section 1.417(e)1(b)(2) of the regulations provides that written consent of the participant and, if the participant is married at the annuity starting date and the benefit is to be paid in a form other than a qualified joint and survivor annuity (QJSA), the participant's spouse (or if either the participant or the spouse has died, the survivor) is required before the commencement of the distribution of any part of an accrued benefit if the present value of the nonforfeitable benefit is greater than $3,500. No consent is required before the annuity starting date if the present value of the nonforfeitable benefit is not more than

$3,500. If the present value of the accrued benefit at the time at any distribution exceeds $3,500, the present value of the accrued benefit at any subsequent time will be deemed to exceed $3,500.

Effective December 31, 1998, final and temporary regulations were published under Code sections 411(a)(7), 411(a)(11), and 417(e)(1). These regulations provide guidance relating to the increase from $3,500 to $5,000 of the limit on distributions from qualified retirement plans that can be made without participant consent. This increase is contained in TRA'97.

In addition, these regulations eliminate, for most distributions, the "lookback rule" pursuant to which the qualified plan benefits of certain participants are deemed to exceed this limit on mandatory distributions.

In determining whether a participant's nonforfeitable accrued benefit may be distributed without consent during plan years beginning on or after August 6, 1997, the now cash-out limit of $5,000 is permitted to be applied as though it were in effect for any plan years, including those beginning before August 6, 1997. In addition, these temporary regulations eliminate for many distributions the "lookback rule" under section 1.411(a)-11(c)(3) of the regulations. Under these regulations, a plan may provide that the present value of a participant's nonforfeitable accrued benefit may be distributed without consent if that present value does not exceed the cash-out limit as determined at the time of the current distribution without regard to the present value of the participant's benefit at the time of an earlier distribution. However, section 1.411(a)-11T(c)(3)(1) of the temporary regulations, which in effect eliminates the "lookback rule," applies only to distributions made on or after March 22, 1999.

In this case, the plan amendment fails to satisfy section 1.411(a) 11(c)(3) of the regulations which applies to distributions made on or before March 22, 1999. Thus, the plan provisions in section 11.04 relating to mandatory distributions that do not require employee consent fail to satisfy section 411(a)(11)(A) of the Code for the period from the effective date of the amendment of March 2, 1998, through March 21, 1999.

IV. Conclusions

We conclude that Plans 1 and 2 may exclude from plan participation employees who are either (1) not reported on the payroll records of affiliated companies as common law employees (even if a court or administrative agency determines that such individuals are common law employees and not independent contractors) or (2) are identified by either a specified job code or work status code on the employer's payroll records, and still satisfy the requirements of section 410(a) of the Internal Revenue Code and section 1.410(a)-3(d) of the Income Tax Regulations.

We further conclude that the eligibility provisions of Plan 1 and Plan 2 do not prevent each Plan from satisfying the requirement that a plan must be a definite written program.

Section 11.04 of Plan 1, and sections 11.02, 13.06, and 14.02 of Plan 2 as provided in the proposed amendments of March 2, 1998, fail to satisfy the requirements of section 411(a)(11) of the Code and sections 1.411(a)-11(c)(3) of the Income Tax Regulations for the period from March 2, 1998 through March 21, 1999.

Notes

1. The term "employee," as used in a qualified plan, may include certain individuals who are not common law employees. For example, an independent contractor may be treated as an employee with respect to a plan established by the independent contractor by reason of section 401(c) of the Code. Similarly, a full-time life insurance salesman is treated as an employee for qualified plan purposes. These statutory expansions of the term are not relevant for purposes of this technical advice memorandum.

2. Revenue Ruling 87-41, 1987-1 C.B. 296, contains a list of twenty factors courts had applied in determining whether a common law employment relationship exists. However, in order to better reflect the factors courts now appear to consider relevant, the Internal Revenue Service now makes this determination by exploring three primary categories of evidence: behavioral control, financial control, and relationship of the parties.

3. The discussion of this case is, of course, based solely on published court opinions.

4. The court remanded the case for a "determination of any questions of individual eligibility for benefits that may remain following issuance of this opinion and for calculation of the damages or benefits due the various class members." Vizcaino v. Microsoft Corp. 97 F.3d 1187, 1200 (9th Cir. 1996), aff'd, 120 F.3d 1006 (9th Cir. 1997). See also Vizcaino v. Microsoft Corp. 173 F.3d 713 (9th Cir. 1999).

5. Exclusions permitted under section 410(a) may cause a plan to fail to meet the coverage standards of section 410(b). The latter is a separate inquiry, which is not at issue in this case.

H

Equal Employment Opportunity Commission Guidelines on Application Of EEO Laws to Contingent Workers

DATE: 12/03/97

1. SUBJECT: Enforcement Guidance: Application of EEO Laws to Contingent Workers Placed by Temporary Employment Agencies and Other Staffing Firms.

2. PURPOSE: This document provides guidance regarding the application of the anti-discrimination statutes to temporary, contract, and other contingent employees.

3. EFFECTIVE DATE: Upon receipt.

4. EXPIRATION DATE: As an exception to EEOC Order 205.001, Appendix B, Attachment 4, Section a(5), this Notice will remain in effect until rescinded or superseded.

5. ORIGINATOR: Title VII/EPA/ADEA Division, Office of Legal Counsel.

6. INSTRUCTIONS: File after Section 605 of Volume II of the Compliance Manual.

Executive Summary

This Guidance addresses the application of the federal employment discrimination statutes to individuals placed in job assignments by temporary employment agencies, contract firms, and other firms that hire workers and place them in job assignments with the firms' clients. The term "staffing firm" is used in this document to refer to these types of firms.

Staffing firm workers are generally covered under the anti-discrimination statutes. This is because they typically qualify as "employees" of the staffing firm, the client to whom they are assigned, or both. Thus, staffing firms and the clients to whom they assign workers may not discriminate against the workers on the basis of race, color, religion, sex, national origin, age, or disability.

The guidance makes clear that a staffing firm must hire and make job assignments in a non-discriminatory manner. It also makes clear that the client must treat the staffing firm worker assigned to it in a non-discriminatory manner, and that the staffing firm must take immediate and appropriate corrective action if it learns that the client has discriminated against one of the staffing firm workers. The document also explains that staffing firms and their clients are responsible for ensuring that the staffing firm workers are paid wages on a non-discriminatory basis. Finally, the guidance describes how remedies are allocated between a staffing firm and its client when the EEOC finds that both have engaged in unlawful discrimination.

\s\

Gilbert F. Casellas, Chairman

Table of Contents

Introduction

This Guidance addresses the application of Title VII of the Civil Rights Act of 1964 (Title VII), the Age Discrimination in Employment Act (ADEA), the Americans with Disabilities Act (ADA), and the Equal Pay Act (EPA) to individuals placed in job assignments by temporary employment agencies and other staffing firms, i.e., "contingent workers." The term "contingent workers" generally refers to workers who are outside an employer's "core" work force, such as those whose jobs are structured to last only a limited period of time, are sporadic, or differ in any way from the norm of full-time, long-term employment.

This guidance focuses on a large subgroup of the contingent work force—those who are hired and paid by a "staffing firm," such as a temporary employment agency or contract firm, but whose working conditions are controlled in whole or in part by the clients to whom they are assigned.

Recent statistics compiled by the National Association of Temporary and Staffing Services (NATSS) show that the temporary help industry currently employs more than 2.3 million individuals.[1] That number represents a 100% increase since 1991, when 1.15 million individuals were employed in temporary help jobs. NATSS statistics also show that the professional segment of the temporary help industry (including occupations in accounting, law, sales, and management) has risen significantly.

A 1995 survey by the Bureau of Labor Statistics (BLS) showed that workers paid by temporary employment agencies were more likely to be female and African American than workers in traditional job arrangements,[2] while workers provided by contract firms were disproportionately male.[3] BLS found that workers paid by temporary help agencies were heavily concentrated in administrative support and laborer occupations and earned 60% of the traditional worker wage.[4] The largest proportion of contract workers was employed in the services industry, and female contract workers earned slightly less than traditional workers while male contract workers earned more. BLS also found that contract and temporary workers had lower rates of health insurance and pension coverage than traditional workers, and that the majority of temporary workers would have preferred traditional work arrangements.

Staffing firms may assume that they are not responsible for any discrimination or harassment that their workers confront at the clients' work sites. Similarly, some clients of staffing firms may assume that they are not the employers of temporary or contract workers assigned to them, and that they therefore have no EEO obligations toward these workers. However, as this guidance explains, both staffing firms and their clients share EEO responsibilities toward these workers.

The Commission has addressed in previous guidance several of the coverage issues discussed in this document.[5] However, because use of contingent workers is increasing, it is important to set out an updated and unified policy that more specifically explains how the anti-discrimination laws apply to this segment of the work force.

This document provides guidance concerning the following issues:

■ coverage under the EEO laws, including coverage of workers assigned to federal agencies;

■ liability of staffing firms and/or clients for discriminatory hiring, assignment, or wage practices;

■ liability of staffing firms and/or clients for unlawful discrimination or harassment at the assigned work site; and

■ allocation of damages where both the staffing firm and its client violate EEO laws.

Staffing Service Work Arrangements

The activities of the following types of staffing firms are addressed in this guidance:[6]

Temporary Employment Agencies

Unlike a standard employment agency, a temporary employment agency employs the individuals that it places in temporary jobs at its clients' work sites. The agency recruits, screens, hires, and sometimes trains its employees. It sets and pays the wages when the worker is placed in a job assignment, withholds taxes and social security, and provides workers' compensation coverage. The agency bills the client for the services performed.

While the worker is on a temporary job assignment, the client typically controls the individual's working conditions, supervises the individual, and determines the length of the assignment.

Contract Firms

Under a variety of arrangements, a firm may contract with a client to perform a certain service on a long-term basis and place its own employees, including supervisors, at the client's work site to carry out the service. Examples of contract firm services include security, landscaping, janitorial, data processing, and cafeteria services.

Like a temporary employment agency, a contract firm typically recruits, screens, hires, and sometimes trains its workers. It sets and pays the wages when the worker is placed in a job assignment, withholds taxes and social security, and provides workers' compensation coverage.

The primary difference between a temporary agency and a contract firm is that a contract firm takes on full operational responsibility for performing an ongoing service and supervises its workers at the client's work site.

Other Types of Staffing Firms

There are many variants on the staffing firm/client model. For example, "facilities staffing" is an arrangement in which a staffing firm provides one or more workers to staff a particular client operation on an ongoing basis, but does not manage the operation.

Under another model, a client of a staffing firm puts its workers on the firm's payroll, and the firm leases the workers back to the client. The purpose of this arrangement is to transfer responsibility for administering payroll and benefits from the client to the staffing firm. A staffing firm that offers this service does not recruit, screen, or train the workers.

The term "staffing firm" is used in this document to describe generically these types of firms, although more specific terms are used where necessary for purposes of clarity.

Coverage Issues

This section sets forth criteria for determining whether a staffing firm worker qualifies as an "employee" within the meaning of the anti-discrimination statutes or an independent contractor; whether the staffing firm and/or its client qualifies as the worker's employer(s); and whether the staffing firm or its client can be liable for discriminating against the worker even if it does not qualify as the worker's employer. This section also discusses coverage of staffing firm workers assigned to jobs in the Federal Government and coverage of workers assigned to jobs in connection with welfare programs. Finally, this section explains the method for counting workers of a staffing firm or its client to determine whether either entity has the minimum number of employees to be covered under the applicable anti-discrimination statute.

1. Are staffing firm workers "employees" within the meaning of the federal employment discrimination laws?

Yes, in the great majority of circumstances.[7] The threshold question is whether a staffing firm worker is an "employee" or an "independent contractor." The worker is a covered employee under the anti-discrimination statutes if the right to control the means and manner of her work performance rests with the firm and/or its client rather than with the worker herself. The label used to describe the worker in the employment contract is not determinative. One must consider all aspects of the worker's relationship with the firm and the firm's client.[8] As the Supreme Court has emphasized, there is "no shorthand formula or magic phrase that can be applied to find the answer… all incidents of the relationship must be assessed with *no one factor being decisive.*"[9] Factors that indicate that the worker is a covered employee include:[10]

a) the firm or the client has the right to control when, where, and how the worker performs the job;

b) the work does not require a high level of skill or expertise;

c) the firm or the client rather than the worker furnishes the tools, materials, and equipment;

d) the work is performed on the premises of the firm or the client;

e) there is a continuing relationship between the worker and the firm or the client;

f) the firm or the client has the right to assign additional projects to the worker;

g) the firm or the client sets the hours of work and the duration of the job;

h) the worker is paid by the hour, week, or month rather than for the agreed cost of performing a particular job;

i) the worker has no role in hiring and paying assistants;

j) the work performed by the worker is part of the regular business of the firm or the client;

k) the firm or the client is itself in business;

l) the worker is not engaged in his or her own distinct occupation or business;

m) the firm or the client provides the worker with benefits such as insurance, leave, or workers' compensation;

n) the worker is considered an employee of the firm or the client for tax purposes (i.e., the entity withholds federal, state, and social security taxes);

o) the firm or the client can discharge the worker; and

p) the worker and the firm or client believe that they are creating an employer–employee relationship.

This list is not exhaustive. Other aspects of the relationship between the parties may affect the determination of whether an employer–employee relationship exists. Furthermore, not all or even a majority of the listed criteria need be met. Rather, the fact-finder must make an assessment based on all of the circumstances in the relationship between the parties.

EXAMPLE 1:

A temporary employment agency hires a worker and assigns him to serve as a computer programmer for one of the agency's clients. The agency pays the worker a salary based on the number of hours worked as reported by the client. The agency also withholds social security and taxes and provides workers' compensation coverage. The client establishes the hours of work and oversees the individual's work. The individual uses the client's equipment and supplies and works on the client's premises. The agency reviews the individual's work based on reports by the client. The agency can terminate the worker if his or her services are unacceptable to the client. Moreover, the worker can terminate the relationship without incurring a penalty. In these circumstances, the worker is an "employee."

2. Is a staffing firm worker who is assigned to a client an employee of the firm, its client, or both?

Once it is determined that a staffing firm worker is an "employee," the second question is who is the worker's employer. The staffing firm and/or its client will qualify as the worker's employer(s) if, under the factors described in Question 1, one or both businesses have the right to exercise control over the worker's employment. As noted above, no one factor is decisive, and it is not necessary even to satisfy a majority of factors. The determination of who qualifies as an employer of the worker cannot be based on simply counting the number of factors. Many factors may be wholly irrelevant to particular facts. Rather, all of the circumstances in the worker's relationship with each of the businesses should be considered to determine if either or both should be deemed his or her employer. If either entity qualifies as the worker's employer, and if that entity has the statutory minimum number of employees (see Question 6), then it can be held liable for unlawful discriminatory conduct against the worker. If both the staffing firm and its client have the right to control the worker, and each has the statutory minimum number of employees, they are covered as "joint employers."[11]

a. Staffing Firm

The relationship between a staffing firm and each of its workers generally qualifies as an employer–employee relationship because the firm typically hires the worker, determines when and where the worker should report to work, pays the wages, is itself in business, withholds taxes and social security, provides workers' compensation coverage, and has the right to discharge the worker. The worker generally receives wages by the hour or week rather than by the job and often has a continuing relationship with the staffing firm. Furthermore, the intent of the parties typically is to establish an employer–employee relationship.[12] In limited circumstances, a staffing firm might not qualify as an employer of the workers that it assigns to a client. For example, in some circumstances, a client puts its employees on the staffing firm's payroll solely in order to transfer the responsibility of administering wages and insurance benefits. This is often referred to as employee leasing. If the firm does not have the right to exercise any control over these workers, it would not be considered their "employer."[13]

b. Client

A client of a temporary employment agency typically qualifies as an employer of the temporary worker during the job assignment, along with the agency. This is because the client usually exercises significant supervisory control over the worker.[14]

EXAMPLE 2:
Under the facts of Example 1, above, the temporary employment agency and its client qualify as joint employers of the worker because both have the right to exercise control over the worker's employment.

EXAMPLE 3:
A staffing firm hires charging party (CP) and sends her to perform a long term accounting project for a client. Her contract with the staffing firm states that she is an independent contractor. CP retains the right to work for others, but spends substantially all of her work time performing

services for the client, on the client's premises. The client supervises CP, sets her work schedule, provides the necessary equipment and supplies, and specifies how the work is to be accomplished. CP reports the number of hours she has worked to the staffing firm. The firm pays her and bills the client for the time worked. It reviews her work based on reports by the client and has the right to terminate her if she is failing to perform the requested services. The staffing firm will replace her with another worker if her work is unacceptable to the client.

In these circumstances, despite the statement in the contract that she is an independent contractor, both the staffing firm and the client are joint employers of CP.[15]

Clients of contract firms and other types of staffing firms also qualify as employers of the workers assigned to them if the clients have sufficient control over the workers, under the standards set forth in Question 1, above.[16] For example, the client is an employer of the worker if it supplies the work space, equipment, and supplies, and if it has the right to control the details of the work to be performed, to make or change assignments, and to terminate the relationship. On the other hand, the client would not qualify as an employer if the staffing firm furnishes the job equipment and has the exclusive right, through on-site managers, to control the details of the work, to make or change assignments, and to terminate the workers.

EXAMPLE 4:

A staffing firm provides janitorial services for its clients. It hires the workers and places them on each client's premises under the supervision of the contract firm's own managerial employees. The firm's manager sets the work schedules, assigns tasks to the janitors, provides the equipment they need to do the job, and supervises their work performance. The client has no role in controlling the details of the work, making assignments, or setting the hours or duration of the work. Nor does the client have authority to discharge the worker. In these circumstances, the staffing firm is the worker's exclusive employer; its client is not a joint employer.

EXAMPLE 5:

A staffing firm provides landscaping services for clients on an ongoing basis. The staffing firm selects and pays the workers, provides health insurance, and withholds taxes. The firm provides the equipment and supplies necessary to do the work. It also supervises the workers on the clients' premises. Client A reserves the right to direct the staffing firm workers to perform particular tasks at particular times or in a specified manner, although it does not generally exercise that authority. Client A evaluates the quality of the workers' performance and regularly reports its findings to the firm. It can require the firm to remove the worker from the job assignment if it is dissatisfied. The firm and the Client A are joint employers.

3. **Can a staffing firm or its client be liable for unlawfully discriminating against a staffing firm worker even if it does not qualify as the worker's employer?**
    An entity that has enough employees to qualify as an employer under the applicable EEO statute can be held liable for discriminating against an individual who is not its employee. The anti-discrimination statutes not only prohibit an employer from discriminating against its own employees, but also prohibit an employer from interfering with an individual's employment opportunities with another employer.[17] Thus, a staffing firm that discriminates against its client's employee or a client that discriminates against a staffing firm's employee is liable for unlawfully interfering in the individual's employment opportunities.[18]

EXAMPLE 6:
A staffing firm assigned one of its employees to maintain and repair a client's computers. The firm supplied all the tools and direction for the repairs. The technician was on the client's premises only sporadically over a three to four week period and worked independently while there. The client did not report to the firm about the number of hours worked or about the quality of the work. The client had no authority to make assignments or require work to be done at particular times. After a few visits, the client asked the contract firm to assign someone else, stating that it was not satisfied with the worker's computer repair skills. However, the worker believes that the true reason for the client's action was racial bias.

The client does not qualify as a joint employer of the worker because it had no ongoing relationship with the worker, did not pay the worker or firm based on the hours worked, and had no authority over hours, assignments, or other aspects of the means or manner by which the work was achieved. However, if the client's request to replace the worker was due to racial bias, and if the client had fifteen or more employees, it would be liable for interfering in the worker's employment opportunities with the staffing firm.

EXAMPLE 7:

A company puts its employees on the payroll of a staffing firm solely in order to transfer the responsibility of administering wages and insurance benefits for the company's workers. The staffing firm administers a health insurance policy for its client's workers that does not cover AIDS-related illness. Two workers file ADA charges against the staffing firm and the client. The staffing firm claims that it is not an employer of the workers and therefore falls outside ADA coverage.

The staffing firm does not qualify as a joint employer of the workers because it does not have the requisite degree of control—it did not hire the workers, establish their wage rates or hours, control the conditions of work, manage personnel disputes, or have the right to fire the workers. Nevertheless, the firm shares liability with its client for the discriminatory health insurance plan if it has fifteen or more employees of its own to fall under the coverage of the ADA.[19] This is because the firm's administration of the insurance plan interferes in the workers' access to employment opportunities or benefits.[20]

4. **Do the same coverage principles apply when a staffing firm assigns a worker to a federal agency?**

The principles regarding joint employer coverage are the same. Thus, a federal agency qualifies as a joint employer of an individual assigned to it if it has the requisite control over that worker, as discussed in Questions 1 and 2. If so, and if the agency discriminates against the individual, it is liable whether or not the individual is on the federal payroll.[21]

In contrast to private employers, a federal agency that does not qualify as a joint employer of the worker assigned to it cannot be found liable for discrimination under a "third party interference" theory. This is because Title VII, the ADEA, and Section 501 of the Rehabilitation Act only permit claims against the federal government by "employees or applicants for employment."[22]

5. **Are workers participating in work-related activities in connection with welfare programs protected by the federal employment discrimination laws? If so, who is the employer of such a worker? What types of claims might arise?**

a. Employee Status

Welfare recipients participating in work-related activities[23] are protected by the federal anti-discrimination statutes if they are "employees" within the meaning of the federal employment discrimination laws.[24] See Question 1. The simple fact of participation in one of these activities is not dispositive of the question of whether the federal employment discrimination laws apply. Rather, the same analysis applies which is used to determine whether any other worker is covered by the federal employment discrimination laws. Under the criteria that have been set out, welfare recipients would likely be considered employees in most of the work activities described in the new welfare law, including unsubsidized and subsidized public and private sector employment, work experience, and on-the-job training programs.[25] On the other hand, individuals engaged in activities such as vocational education, job search assistance, and secondary school attendance would probably not be covered.[26]

b. Employer Status

While some workers participating in these programs will have a single employer, others may have joint employers. For example, a state or local welfare agency may function as a staffing firm and the "direct" employer may function as the client. In some cases, a state or local welfare agency may contract with a temporary employment agency to place the welfare recipients in job assignments. The determination of whether any or all of these entities are employers of the worker is based on the same criteria set forth in answer to Questions 1 and 2 that apply to any other employment situation. The fact that an entity does not pay the worker a salary does not, by itself, defeat a finding of an employment relationship. Moreover, even if an entity is not the worker's employer, it can be found liable under the employment discrimination laws based on the interference theory explained in the answer to Question 3.

c. Types of Claims

Types of claims which may arise include, for example, harassment, discriminatory assignments, discriminatory termination, failure to provide reasonable accommodation to persons covered under the Americans with Disabilities Act, and retaliation.

6. Which workers are counted when determining whether a staffing firm or its client is covered under Title VII, the ADEA, or the ADA?

The staffing firm and the client each must count every worker with whom it has an employment relationship.[27] Although a worker assigned by a staffing firm to a client may not appear on the client's payroll, (s)he must be counted as an employee of both entities if they qualify as joint employers.[28] Questions 1 and 2, above, set forth the legal standards for determining whether a worker has an employment relationship with either the staffing firm or its client, or both.

The Supreme Court has made clear that a respondent must count each employee from the day that the employment relationship begins until the day that it ends, regardless of whether the employee is present at work or on leave on each working day during that period.[29] Thus, a client of a staffing firm must count each worker assigned to it from the first day of the job assignment until the last day. The staffing firm also must count the worker as its employee during every period in which the worker is sent on a job assignment.

Staffing firms are typically covered under the anti-discrimination statutes, because their permanent staff plus the workers that they send to clients generally exceeds the minimum statutory threshold. Clients may or may not be covered, depending on their size. In cases where questions are raised regarding coverage, the investigator should ask the respondent to name and provide records regarding every individual who performed work for it, including all individuals assigned by staffing firms and any temporary, seasonal, or other contingent workers hired directly by the respondent. If the investigator has questions about the documents produced and cannot otherwise obtain the necessary information, he or she may consider deposing the respondent. The investigator should then determine which of the named individuals qualified as employees of the respondent rather than independent contractors, according to the standards set forth in Questions 1 and 2, above.

Discriminatory Assignment Practices

A staffing firm is obligated, as an employer, to make job assignments in a nondiscriminatory manner.[30] It also is obligated as an employment agency to make job referrals in a nondiscriminatory manner. The staffing firm's client is liable if it sets discriminatory criteria for the assignment of workers. The following question and answer explore these issues in detail.

7. **If a worker is denied a job assignment by a staffing firm because its client refuses to accept the worker for discriminatory reasons, is the staffing firm liable? Is the client?**

a. Staffing Firm

The staffing firm is liable for its discriminatory assignment decisions. Liability can be found on any of the following bases: 1) as an employer of the workers assigned to clients (for discriminatory job assignments); 2) as a third party interferer (for discriminatory interference in the workers' employment opportunities with the firm's client); and/or 3) as an employment agency for (discriminatory job referrals).[31]

The fact that a staffing firm's discriminatory assignment practice is based on its client's requirement is no defense. Thus, a staffing firm is liable if it honors a client's discriminatory assignment request or if it knows that its client has rejected workers in a protected class for discriminatory reasons and for that reason refuses to assign individuals in that protected class to that client. Furthermore, the staffing firm is liable if it administers on behalf of its client a test or other selection requirement that has an adverse impact on a protected class and is not job-related for the position in question and consistent with business necessity. 42 U.S.C. § 2000e-2(k).

b. Client

A client that rejects workers for discriminatory reasons is liable either as a joint employer or third party interferer if it has the requisite number of employees to be covered under the applicable anti-discrimination statute.

EXAMPLE 8:

A staffing firm that provides job placements for nurses receives a job order from an individual client for a white nurse to provide her with home-based nursing care. The firm agrees to refer only white nurses for the job. The firm is violating Title VII, both as an employment agency for its discriminatory referral practice and as an employer for the discriminatory job assignment. The client is not covered by Title VII because she does not have fifteen or more employees.

EXAMPLE 9:

A temporary employment agency receives a job order for a temporary receptionist. The client requires that the individual assigned to it speak English fluently because a large part of the job entails communication with English-speaking persons who call the client or who come to the client's work place. The agency assigns an Asian American individual who speaks English fluently, but with an accent. The client insists that the agency replace her with someone who can speak unaccented English. The agency complies with that request and sends an individual who speaks English fluently with no accent.

The Asian American individual files a charge with the EEOC. The investigator determines that English fluency was necessary for the job. However, he further determines that CP's accent does not interfere with her ability to communicate and that she has effectively performed similar jobs. The investigator properly concludes that both the client and the staffing firm are liable for terminating CP on the basis of her national origin.

EXAMPLE 10:
A staffing firm provides machine operators to its clients. One of its clients requires that all workers assigned to it pass a certain paper and pencil test. The firm administers the test to its available workers and refers only those who pass the test. An African American individual who is denied an assignment with the client files charges against both the staffing firm and its client, alleging that administration of the test results in the disproportionate exclusion of African Americans. An investigation shows that the test does have an adverse impact on African Americans and does not accurately measure the skills that are necessary for job performance. Therefore, both the staffing firm and its client are in violation of Title VII.

Discrimination at Work Site

A client of a staffing firm is obligated to treat the workers assigned to it in a nondiscriminatory manner. Where the client fails to fulfill this obligation, and the staffing firm knows or should know of the client's discrimination, the firm must take corrective action within its control.[32] The following questions and answers explore these issues in detail.

8. **If a client discriminates against a worker assigned by a staffing firm, who is liable?**

Client: If the client qualifies as an employer of the worker (see Questions 1 and 2), it is liable for discriminating against the worker on the same basis that it would be liable for discriminating against any of its other employees.

Even if the client does not qualify as an employer of the worker, it is liable for discriminating against that individual if the client's misconduct interferes with the worker's employment opportunities with the staffing firm, and if the client has the minimum number of employees to be covered under the applicable discrimination statute. See Question 3.

Staffing Firm: The firm is liable if it participates in the client's discrimination. For example, if the firm honors its client's request to remove a worker from a job assignment for a discriminatory reason and replace him or her with an individual outside the worker's protected class, the firm is liable for the discriminatory discharge. The firm also is liable if it knew or should have known about the client's discrimination and failed to undertake prompt corrective measures within its control.[33]

The adequacy of corrective measures taken by a staffing firm depends on the particular facts. Corrective measures may include, but are not limited to: 1) ensuring that the client is aware of the alleged misconduct; 2) asserting the firm's commitment to protect its workers from unlawful harassment and other forms of prohibited discrimination; 3) insisting that prompt investigative and corrective measures be undertaken; and 4) affording the worker an opportunity, if (s)he so desires, to take a different job assignment at the same rate of pay. The staffing firm should not assign other workers to that work site unless the client has undertaken the necessary corrective and preventive measures to ensure that the discrimination will not recur. Otherwise, the staffing firm will be liable along with the client if a worker later assigned to that client is subjected to similar misconduct.[34]

EXAMPLE 11:

A temporary receptionist placed by a temporary employment agency is subjected to severe and pervasive unwelcome sexual comments and advances by her supervisor at the assigned work site. She complains to the agency, and the agency informs its client of the allegation. The client refuses to investigate the matter, and instead asks the agency to replace the worker with one who is not a "troublemaker." The agency tells the worker that it cannot force the client to take corrective action, finds the worker a different job assignment, and sends another worker to complete the original job assignment.

The client is liable as an employer of the worker for harassment and for retaliatory discharge.

The temporary employment agency also is liable for the harassment and retaliatory discharge because it knew of the misconduct and failed to undertake adequate corrective action. Informing the client of the harassment complaint was not sufficient—the agency should have insisted that the client investigate the allegation of harassment and take immediate and appropriate corrective action. The agency should also have asserted the right of its workers to be free from unlawful discrimination and harassment, and declined to assign any other workers until the client undertook the necessary corrective and preventive measures. The agency unlawfully participated in its client's discriminatory misconduct when it acceded to the client's request to replace the worker with one who was not a "troublemaker." If the replacement worker is subjected to similar harassment, the agency and the client will be subject to additional liability.

> EXAMPLE 12:
> A staffing firm provides computer services for a company that has more than 15 employees. The staffing firm assigns an individual to work on-site for that client. When the client discovers that the worker has AIDS, it tells the staffing firm to replace him because the client's employees fear infection. The staffing firm alerts the client that they are both prohibited from discriminating against the worker, and that such a discharge would violate the ADA. The client nevertheless continues to insist that the firm remove the worker from the work assignment and replace him with someone else. The staffing firm has no choice but to remove the worker. However, it declines to replace him with another worker to complete the assignment because to do so would constitute acquiescence in the discrimination. Furthermore, the firm offers the worker a different job assignment at the same rate of pay. The client is liable for the discriminatory discharge, either as an employer or third party interferer. The staffing firm is not liable because it took immediate and appropriate corrective action within its control.

9. **If a staffing firm sends its employee on a job assignment with a federal agency and the individual is subjected to discrimination while on the assignment, is the federal agency liable? Is the staffing firm? What procedures should the individual follow in filing a complaint?**
    The federal agency is liable for discriminating against the worker if it qualifies as an employer of the worker. If the federal agency does not qualify as an employer of the staffing firm worker under the criteria in Questions 1 and 2, it will not be liable for discriminating against that worker under the statutes enforced by the EEOC. A federal agency is liable for employment discrimination under these statutes only where it has sufficient control to be deemed an employer of the worker. See Question 4.

The staffing firm is liable if it participated in the federal agency's discrimination or if it knew or should have known of the discrimination and failed to intervene, under the principles discussed in Question 8, above.

If the staffing firm worker seeks to pursue a complaint against the federal agency as his or her employer, (s)he should contact an EEO Counselor at the federal agency within 45 days of the date of the alleged discrimination. If the individual also seeks to pursue a claim against the staffing firm, (s)he should file a separate charge with an EEOC field office. In such circumstances, the EEOC investigator should alert the individual as to the different time frames and procedures in the federal and private sectors.[35] The investigator should also contact the EEO office of the federal agency once the individual files the federal sector complaint in order to coordinate the federal and private sector investigations.[36]

Discriminatory Wage Practices

A staffing firm may not discriminate in the payment of wages on the basis of race, sex, religion, national origin, age, or disability. Its clients share that obligation.

10. **If a staffing firm assigns a male and female to a client to perform substantially equal work, and the female is paid a lower wage than the male, would the firm and/or the client be subject to Equal Pay Act or Title VII liability?**

Under the EPA, men and women must receive equal pay for equal work.[37] The jobs need not be identical, but they must be substantially equal. It is job content, not job titles, that determines whether jobs are substantially equal. Specifically, a sex-based wage disparity violates the EPA if the jobs are in the same establishment, require substantially equal skill, effort, and responsibility, are performed under similar working conditions, and if no statutory defense applies. Wage differences that are not based on sex, but on bona fide distinctions between temporary and permanent workers, can be justified under the EPA as based on a "factor other than sex."[38] Both the staffing firm and its client are liable for a violation of the Equal Pay Act if they both qualify as "employers" of the worker bringing the complaint.[39]

A violation of the EPA also constitutes a violation of Title VII as long as there is Title VII coverage.[40] Furthermore, a sex-based wage disparity violates Title VII even if the jobs are not substantially equal under EPA standards if there is other evidence of wage discrimination.[41] Moreover, an entity with fifteen or more employees is liable under Title VII for wage discrimination even if it does not qualify as an employer of the worker assigned to it, if the wage discrimination interferes in the worker's employment opportunities.

EXAMPLE 13:

A temporary employment agency assigned CP (female) to a temporary job as a hospital aide. CP discovered that the agency had also assigned a male to a temporary job as an "orderly" at the same hospital at a higher wage. CP files charges against the agency and the hospital, alleging that her job and that of the male orderly were substantially equal, and that the wage disparity violated the Equal Pay Act and Title VII. CP's charge against the hospital also challenges a disparity between her wages and those of permanent male aides and orderlies at the hospital.

The investigator determines that the temporary employment agency and the hospital were joint employers of CP and that both entities had control over the rates of pay for the hospital aide and orderly jobs. The investigator also determines that the temporary aide and orderly jobs were substantially equal under EPA standards, and that no defense applies. Therefore, he finds that the agency and the hospital are both liable under the EPA and Title VII on the claim that the temporary aide and orderly should have received the same wage. The investigator further determines that the wage differential between the temporary and permanent aide and orderly jobs was based on a factor other than sex, since the hospital paid all its temporary workers less than permanent workers filling the same jobs, regardless of sex. Therefore, "no cause" is found on this latter claim.

Allocation of Remedies

11. If the Commission finds reasonable cause to believe that both a staffing firm and its client have engaged in unlawful discrimination, how are back wages and damages allocated between the respondents?

Where the combined discriminatory actions of a staffing firm and its client result in harm to the worker, the two respondents are jointly and severally liable for back pay, front pay, and compensatory damages. This means that the complainant can obtain the full amount of back pay, front pay, and compensatory damages from either one of the respondents alone or from both respondents combined.[42] Punitive damages under Title VII and the ADA[43] and liquidated damages under the ADEA[44] are individually assessed against and borne by each respondent in accordance with its respective degree of malicious or reckless misconduct.[45] This is because punitive damages are designed not to compensate the victim for his or her harm, but to punish the respondent.[46] Of course, no respondent can be required to pay a sum of future pecuniary damages, damages for emotional distress, and punitive damages, in excess of its applicable statutory cap. The investigator should contact the legal unit in his or her office for advice in determining how to allocate damages between the parties.

Computation of Monetary Relief

The first step is to compute lost wages (including back and front pay), compensatory damages for both pecuniary loss and emotional distress, and punitive damages.[47] This computation should be made without regard to the statutory caps on damages[48] and, except for punitive damages, without regard to either respondent's ability to pay.[49] This initial computation will establish the charging party's total wage and other compensable losses, as well as the full calculation of punitive damages.

Back Pay, Front Pay, and Past Pecuniary Damages

The next step is to determine the allocation between the respondents of back and front pay and past pecuniary damages. The charging party can obtain the full amount of these remedies because they are not subject to the statutory caps. The Commission can pursue the entire amount from either the staffing firm or the client, or from both combined.[50] However, the total amount actually paid cannot exceed the sum of back and front wages and past pecuniary damages owed to the worker.

Application of the Statutory Cap on Damages

The final step is to determine each respondent's liability for compensatory and punitive damages subject to the statutory caps. The total amount paid by a respondent for compensatory damages for emotional distress and future pecuniary harm, and for punitive damages, cannot exceed its statutory cap. Thus, while the initial determination of the appropriate amount of compensatory and/or punitive damages is made without regard to the caps, the caps may affect the allocation of damages between two respondents as well as the total damages paid to the charging party. In applying the caps to the actual allocation of damages, the following principles apply:

For compensatory damages subject to the caps, each respondent is responsible for any portion of the total damages up to its cap.

For punitive damages, each respondent is only responsible for the damages which have been assessed against it and only up to its applicable statutory cap.

After the fact-finder has determined the amount of compensatory damages for emotional distress and future pecuniary harm, and the amount of punitive damages for which either or both respondents are liable, these amounts should be allocated between the two respondents in order to yield the maximum payable relief for the charging party.

If the total compensatory damages are within the sum of the two respondents' caps, the damages should be allocated to assure that the full amount is paid.

If one or both respondents are liable for punitive damages as well as compensatory damages, and the total sum of damages is within the applicable caps, the damages should be allocated, both between the respondents and between compensatory and punitive damages for each respondent, to assure full payment. Thus, each respondent should pay the full amount of punitive damages for which it is liable, and any portion of the compensatory damages up to its statutory cap.

If the sum of damages exceeds the sum of the applicable caps, the damages should be allocated, both between the respondents and between compensatory and punitive damages for each respondent, to maximize the payment to the charging party.

EXAMPLE 14:

CP was assigned by Staff Serve to work as a security guard at a store called Value, U.S.A. ("Value"). CP was subjected to persistent and egregious racial epithets by two supervisory employees of the store. CP complained several times to both a higher level manager at Value and to a supervisor at Staff Serve, but neither took any action to address the problem. After being subjected to egregious racial epithets that involved his family, CP informed the manager at Value and the supervisor at Staff Serve that the situation was intolerable. These individuals told CP to stop complaining and to live with these epithets as the price of holding the job. CP stopped reporting to work and asked Staff Serve to assign him elsewhere, but the firm failed to do so. CP was unable to find work for eight months.

CP files a charge against Staff Serve and Value. The investigator determines that both are liable for the racial harassment and constructive discharge. The investigator further determines that CP is due $40,000 in back pay and $60,000 in damages for emotional distress and that Staff Serve and Value are jointly and severally liable for these amounts.

Although Value's conduct was at least as egregious as Staff Serve's, the investigator determines that Value's financial position is relatively weak, and that a punitive damage award of $30,000 against Value is appropriate, as compared to $50,000 for Staff Serve.

Staff Serve employs 137 employees (counting its regular staff people and the workers it has sent on assignment) and is subject to the $100,000 damages cap. Value employs 45 workers and is subject to the $50,000 cap on damages.

In conciliation, the investigator determines that Staff Serve and Value should work out a division of the $40,000 in back pay, for which they are jointly and severally liable. The investigator further determines that the damages should be allocated as follows: Staff Serve should pay $40,000 and Value $20,000 in compensatory damages, and Staff Serve should pay $50,000 and Value $30,000 in punitive damages. CP can thus obtain the full amount of damages due him, with neither respondent's liability exceeding its cap.

EXAMPLE 15:
Same facts as in Example 14, but CP only names Staff Serve as a respondent because Value has gone bankrupt. The sum of compensatory and punitive damages assessed by the Commission is $110,000 ($60,000 for emotional distress and $50,000 in punitive damages assessed against Staff Serve). The Commission pursues $100,000 in combined damages due to Staff Serve's statutory cap. The Commission and Staff Serve may agree to deduct the $10,000 in excess of the caps from either the emotional distress or the punitive damages. The Commission also pursues the full $40,000 in back pay from Staff Serve, which is not subject to the cap.

EXAMPLE 16:
Same facts as Example 14, except that both Staff Serve and Value are subject to the $50,000 cap. CP could obtain only a total of $100,000 in damages, even though the sum of compensatory and punitive damages was $140,000. The investigator works with CP and the respondents to determine how to allocate the damages between compensatory and punitive damages. The full amount of back pay remains payable since it is not subject to the caps.

Charge Processing Instructions

When a charge is filed by a worker who was hired by a temporary agency, contract firm, or other staffing firm and who alleges discrimination by the staffing firm or the firm's client, consider the following questions (refer to the questions and answers in the guidance for detailed information):

I. Coverage

1. **Is the charging party (CP) an employee or an independent contractor? (Q&A 1)**

Determine whether the right to control the means and manner of CP's work performance rested with the staffing firm and/or the client or with the worker herself. Consider the factors listed in Question and Answer 1 of this guidance and all other aspects of CP's relationship to the firm and its client.

If CP is an independent contractor, dismiss the charge for lack of jurisdiction. If CP is an employee, determine who qualifies as his or her employer. It is possible that both the staffing firm and its client qualify as joint employers. In that regard consider the following:

2. **Is CP an employee of the staffing firm? (Q&A 2(a))**

Consider the factors listed in Question 1 as they apply to the relationship between CP and the staffing firm.

3. **Is CP an employee of the firm's client? (Q&A 2(b))**

Consider the factors listed in Question 1 as they apply to the relationship between CP and the client.

Even if the client does not qualify as CP's employer, it is still covered under the applicable anti-discrimination statute if it interfered on a discriminatory basis with CP's employment opportunities with the staffing firm and has the requisite number of employees. (Q&A 3) The same is true if the staffing firm does not qualify as CP's employer. However, a federal agency can only be held liable as an employer, not as a third-party interferer. (Q&A 4)

If CP is a welfare recipient alleging discrimination in a work-related activity connected with a welfare program, the above considerations apply to determine coverage. (Q&A 5) In such circumstances, the state or local welfare agency may function as a staffing firm and the employer for whom CP performed work as the client.

4. **If there is a question about coverage, does the staffing firm and/or the client have the minimum number of employees to be covered under the applicable anti-discrimination statute? (Q&A 6)**

Ask the respondent to name and provide records regarding each individual who performed work for it during the applicable time period, including individuals assigned by staffing firms and any temporary, seasonal, or other contingent workers hired directly by the respondent. Determine which of these individuals qualified as employees rather than independent contractors.

II. Assignment Practices (Q&A 7)

If CP alleges that a staffing firm declined to assign him or her to its client for discriminatory reasons, consider the following questions:

1. **Does the evidence show that the staffing firm denied CP a job assignment for discriminatory reasons?**

If so, the staffing firm is liable as an employer of CP for its discriminatory assignment practice, as a third party interferer, and/or as an employment agency for its discriminatory referral practice.

2. **Does the evidence show that the client set discriminatory criteria for assignments by the staffing firm?**

If so, the client is liable either as a joint employer of CP or a third party interferer.

III. Discrimination at Work Site (Q&A 8, 9)

If CP alleges that (s)he was subjected to discrimination while performing a job assignment for the staffing firm's client, consider the following questions:

1. **Client: Does the evidence show that the client discriminated against CP?**

If so, the client is liable as CP's employer or as a third party interferer. However, if the client is a federal agency it can only be held liable as an employer.

2. **Staffing firm:**

a. **Does the evidence show that the staffing firm participated in its client's discrimination, e.g., by honoring the client's discriminatory request to replace CP with someone outside his or her protected class?**

b. **Does the evidence show that the staffing firm knew or should have known of its client's discrimination and failed to take immediate and appropriate corrective measures within its control?**

If the answer to (a) or (b) is "yes," the staffing firm is liable for its discrimination.

IV. Discriminatory Wage Practices (Q&A 10)

If CP alleges that the staffing firm paid discriminatory wages for his or her work for the firm's client, consider the following:

1. **Is there an Equal Pay Act violation? Did the staffing firm assign a person of the opposite sex to the same client to perform substantially equal work and pay that individual a higher wage?**

   If so, the staffing firm is liable for the EPA violation. The client also can be found liable if it qualified as CP's joint employer.

2. **Is there a violation of Title VII, the ADEA, or the ADA?**

   A violation of the EPA also constitutes a violation of Title VII as long as there is Title VII coverage.

   A sex-based wage disparity violates Title VII even if the jobs are not substantially equal under EPA standards, if there is other evidence of wage discrimination. Title VII also prohibits wage discrimination based on race, national origin, and religion.

   If the respondent committed wage discrimination in violation of Title VII, the ADEA, or the ADA, it is liable as CP's employer or as a third party interferer.

V. Allocation of Remedies (Q&A 11)

If both the staffing firm and its client have unlawfully discriminated against CP, remedies can be allocated as follows:

1. CP can obtain the full amount of back pay, front pay, and compensatory damages from either respondent or from both combined.

2. Punitive damages under Title VII and the ADA, and liquidated damages under the ADEA, are individually assessed against each respondent according to its degree of malicious or reckless misconduct.

3. The total amount paid by a respondent for future pecuniary damages, damages for emotional distress, and punitive damages cannot exceed its statutory cap.

Damages should be allocated between the respondents in a way that maximizes the payable relief to CP. Contact the legal unit for advice in determining the allocation.

Notes

1. June 18, 1997, News Release of the National Association of Temporary and Staffing Services.

2. Seasonal and temporary foreign employees performing work for companies in this country form another category of the contingent workforce. The Commission intends to address at a future date particular issues regarding coverage of these workers.

3. Bureau of Labor Statistics, U.S. Dept. of Labor, Report 900, Contingent and Alternative Employment Arrangements (August 1995).

4. For a discussion of wage data for contingent workers, see Steven Hipple and Jay Stewart, Earnings and benefits of workers in alternative work arrangements, Monthly Labor Review 46 (October 1996).

5. See Policy Statement on control by third parties over the employment relationship between an individual and his/her direct employer, Compliance Manual Section 605, Appendix F (BNA) 605:0087 (5/20/87); Policy Statement on the concepts of integrated enterprise and joint employer, Compliance Manual Section 605, Appendix G (BNA) 605:0095 (5/6/87); Policy Statement on Title VII Coverage of Independent Contractors, Compliance Manual Section 605, Appendix H (BNA) 605:0105 (9/4/87); and Policy Statement: What constitutes an employment agency under Title VII, how should charges against employment agencies be investigated, and what remedies can be obtained for employment agency violations of the Act? Compliance Manual (BNA) N:3935 (9/20/91).

    The above-referenced policy documents set forth some general principles regarding coverage under the anti-discrimination statutes, and they remain in effect. The current guidance explains more specifically how the coverage principles apply to workers who are hired by staffing firms and placed in job assignments with the firms' clients.

6. For a detailed explanation of the various types of staffing service work arrangements, see Edward A. Lenz, Co-Employment—A Review of Customer Liability Issues in the Staffing Services Industry, 10 The Labor Lawyer 195, 196-99 (1994).

7. See, infra, cases cited in notes 12, 14, and 15.

8. The coverage principles set forth here apply not only to workers who are hired by staffing firms and assigned to the firms' clients, but also to temporary, seasonal, part-time, and other contingent workers who are hired directly by employers.

9. Nationwide Mutual Insurance Co. v. Darden, 503 U.S. 318, 324 (1992) (quoting National Labor Relations Board v. United Ins. Co. of America, 390 U.S. 254, 258 (1968)) (emphasis added).

10. The listed factors are drawn from Darden, 503 U.S. at 323–324 (quoting Community for Creative Non-Violence v. Reid, 490 U.S. 730, 751–752 (1989)); Rev. Ruling 87-41, 1987-1 Cum. Bull. 296 (cited in Darden, 503 U.S. at 325); and Restatement (Second) of Agency § 220(2) (1958) (cited in Darden, 503 U.S. at 325). The Court in Darden held that the "common law" test governs who qualifies as an "employee" under the Employee Retirement Income Security Act of 1974 (ERISA). That test, as described by the Court, is indistinguishable from the "hybrid test" for determining an employment relationship adopted by the EEOC in the Policy Statement on Title VII Coverage of Independent Contractors, Compliance Manual Section 605, Appendix G (BNA) 605:0105 (9/4/87). Although the Supreme Court has not had occasion to address the standards that govern who is an "employee" under Title VII, the ADEA, and the ADA, the rationale in Darden should apply. This is because the ERISA definition of "employee" that the Court interpreted in Darden is identical to the definition of "employee" in Title VII, the ADEA, and the ADA.

    Courts have stated that the definition of "employee" is broader under the Fair Labor Standards Act (FLSA), of which the Equal Pay Act is a part, than under the other EEO statutes. However, there is no significant functional difference between the tests. Under the FLSA, employees are those who, as a matter of economic reality, are dependent upon the business to which they render service. See 29 C.F.R. § 1620.8 (1996); Hodgson v. Griffin & Brand of McAllen Inc., 471 F.2d 235 (5th Cir.) (under FLSA's "economic realities" test, fruit and vegetable company qualified as joint employer of harvest workers supplied by crew leaders), reh'g denied, 472 F.2d 1405 (5th Cir.), cert. denied, 414 U.S. 819 (1973). All three tests (common law, hybrid, and economic realities) consider similar factors and often result in the same conclusions as to "employee" status.

11. For additional guidance on criteria for determining whether two or more entities are joint employers of a charging party, see EEOC's Policy Statement on the concepts of integrated enterprise and joint employer, Compliance Manual Section 605, Appendix G (BNA) 605:0095 (5/6/87).

12. For cases holding that a staffing firm is an "employer" of the workers it sends on job assignments, see Magnuson v. Peak Technical Services Inc., 808 F. Supp. 500, 508 (E.D. Va. 1992) (personnel firm that provided employees to clients pursuant to service contracts and the worker that it assigned to one of its clients "clearly had the type of direct employer–employee relationship that is typically the subject of Title VII lawsuits"), aff'd mem., 40 F.3d 1244 (4th Cir. 1994); Amarnare v. Merrill, Lynch, Pierce, Fenner & Smith, 611 F. Supp. 344, 349 (D.C.N.Y. 1984) (worker paid by "Mature Temps" employment agency and assigned to Merrill Lynch for temporary job assignment was employee of both Mature Temps and Merrill Lynch during period of assignment), aff'd mem., 770 F.2d 157 (2d Cir. 1985); Cf. NLRB v. Western Temporary Services Inc., 821 F.2d 1258, 1266–67 (7th Cir. 1987) (NLRB correctly determined that temporary employment service and its client were joint employers of temporary worker); Maynard v. Kenova Chemical Company, 626 F.2d 359, 362 (4th Cir. 1980) (temporary employee injured while working on defen-

dant's premises could not sue defendant in tort because he was employee of both defendant and temp agency, and workers' compensation provided sole remedy).

The Commission disagrees with the rulings of the District Court of Delaware in Williams v. Caruso, 966 F. Supp. 287 (D. Del. 1997), and Kellam v. Snelling Personnel Services, 866 F. Supp. 812 (D. Del. 1994), aff'd mem., 65 F.3d 162 (3d Cir. 1996). In Williams, the court ruled that a temporary employment agency was not a Title VII employer of a temporary worker whom it hired and placed in a job assignment. The court followed its earlier reasoning in Kellam, in which it declined to count the workers assigned by a temporary employment agency as its employees on the ground that the agency did not supervise the workers on a day-to-day basis. In the Commission's view, the court in both cases placed undue emphasis on daily supervision of job tasks and underestimated the significance of other factors indicating an employment relationship.

13. See, e.g., Astrowsky v. First Portland Mortgage Corp., 887 F. Supp. 332 (D. Me. 1995) (holding that employee leasing firm was not a joint employer of workers that it leased back to original employer; firm only processed paychecks and made tax withholdings but did not exercise any control over employees; original employer remained exclusive employer of the workers for purposes of EEO coverage).

14. See Reynolds v. CSX Transportation Inc., 115 F.3d 860 (11th Cir. 1997) (finding that temporary employment agency's client qualified as employer of worker assigned to it and upholding jury award for retaliation by client); King v. Booz-Allen & Hamilton Inc., No. 83 Civ. 7420 (MJL), 1987 WL 11546, n.3 (S.D.N.Y. May 21, 1987) (finding that plaintiff who was paid by temporary employment agency and assigned to work at Booz-Allen was an employee of Booz-Allen); Amarnare, 611 F. Supp. at 349 (finding that temporary employment agency's client qualified as joint employer of worker assigned to it).

15. See Rev. Rul. 87-41, 1987-1 Cum. Bull. 296, 298–99, cited in Nationwide Mutual Insurance Company v. Darden, 503 U.S. 318, 324 (1992) (concluding on above facts that the staffing firm was the individual's employer, but not addressing the status of the client vis-à-vis the worker).

16. For examples of cases finding that a client of a staffing firm can qualify as a joint employer of the worker assigned to it, see Poff v. Prudential Insurance Co. of America, 882 F. Supp. 1534 (E.D. Pa. 1995) (where plaintiff was hired by computer services contractor and assigned to work on-site at insurance company, issue of fact existed as to whether insurance company exercised sufficient control over the manner and means by which plaintiff's work was accomplished to qualify as employer); Magnuson, 808 F. Supp. at 508-10 (where car company contracted with staffing firm for plaintiff's services and assigned her to work at its car dealership, genuine issue of fact was raised as to whether car company, dealership, and staffing firm all qualified as her joint employers); Guerra v. Tishman East Realty, 52 Fair Empl. Prac. Cas. (BNA) 286 (S.D.N.Y. 1989) (security guard employed by management firm who worked in building owned by insurance company could seek to prove that insurance company exercised sufficient control over him to qualify as his "employer"); EEOC v. Sage Realty, 507 F. Supp. 599 (S.D.N.Y. 1981) (building management company that contracted with cleaning company for services of building lobby attendant qualified as joint employer of lobby attendant; contractor carried lobby attendant on its payroll but management company supervised her day-to-day work).

For examples of cases finding that the client did not qualify as a joint employer of the contract worker because the client did not have sufficient control over the worker, see Rivas v. Federacion de Asociaciones Pecuarias, 929 F.2d 814 (1st Cir. 1991) (client of shipping services contractor was not a joint employer of workers who unloaded ships; although client set time for ship unloading, had some disciplinary authority over foremen, and directed order of unloading, contractor selected, scheduled, and supervised the workers and handled disciplinary matters); King v. Dalton, 895 F. Supp. 831 (E.D. Va. 1995) (Navy was not joint employer of worker assigned by contract firm to work on project due to insufficient direct supervisory control over the daily details of the plaintiff's work).

17. See 42 U.S.C. § 2000e-2(a) (Title VII), 29 U.S.C. § 623(a) (ADEA), and 42 U.S.C. § 12112(a) (ADA), which do not limit their protections to a covered employer's own employees, but rather protect an "individual" from discrimination. Section 503 of the ADA, 42 U.S.C. § 12203(b), additionally makes it unlawful to "interfere with any individual in the exercise or enjoyment of...any right granted or protected by this chapter." The EPA, 29 U.S.C. § 206, limits its protections to an employer's own employees, and therefore third-party interference theory does not apply.

For cases allowing staffing firm workers to bring claims against the firms' clients as third-party interferers, see King v. Chrysler Corp., 812 F. Supp. 151 (E.D. Mo. 1993) (cashier employed by company that operated cafeteria on automobile company's premises could sue automobile company for failing to take sufficient corrective action to remedy sexually hostile work environment; Title VII does not specify that employer committing an unlawful employment practice must employ the injured individual); Fairman v. Saks Fifth Avenue, 1988 U.S. Dist. LEXIS 13087 (W.D. Mo. 1988) (plaintiff who was employed by cleaning contractor to perform cleaning duties at store and who was allegedly discharged due to her race could proceed with Title VII action against store; store claimed that it was not plaintiff's employer because it did not pay her wages, supervise her or terminate her; however, even if the store was not plaintiff's employer, it could be sued for improperly interfering with her employment opportunities with the cleaning contractor); Amarnare, 611 F. Supp. at 349 (temporary employee assigned by "Mature Temps" to work for Merrill Lynch could challenge discrimination by Merrill Lynch either on basis that Merrill Lynch was her joint employer or that Merrill Lynch interfered with her employment opportunities with Mature Temps).

18. See Policy Statement on control by third parties over the employment relationship between an individual and his/her direct employer, Compliance Manual Section 605, Appendix F (BNA) 605:0087 (5/20/87).

19. While Title I of the ADA only applies to entities with fifteen or more employees, the Commission has not yet addressed the scope of the interference provision in Section 503, which applies to all titles of the ADA and does not contain a specific coverage limitation. See note 17.

20. See Carparts Distribution Ctr. v. Automotive Wholesalers, 37 F.3d 12, 17–18 (1st Cir. 1994) (trade association and its administering trust for health benefit plan provided by plaintiff's employer were sued under Title I for limiting coverage of AIDS; court held that defendants were covered under Title I if they functioned as plaintiff's employer with respect to his health care coverage or if they affected plaintiff's access to employment opportunities); Spirt v. Teachers Insurance and Annuity Ass'n, 691 F.2d 1054, 1063 (2d Cir. 1982) (association that managed retirement plans for college and university employees could be found liable for using sex-based mortality tables to calculate benefits; although association was not plaintiff's "employer" in any commonly understood sense, the term "employer" under Title VII encompasses any party who significantly affects worker's access to employment opportunities), vacated and remanded sub nom Long Island University v. Spirt, 463 U.S. 1223 (1983), reinstated on remand, 735 F.2d 23 (2d Cir.), cert. denied, 469 U.S. 883 (1984).

21. See Mares v. Marsh, 777 F.2d 1066 (5th Cir. 1985) (in determining whether individual is a federal employee for purposes of Title VII coverage, key issue is extent to which government exercises control over that individual). For guidance on procedures in handling joint federal sector/private sector complaints, see Question 9.

22. 42 U.S.C. § 20003-16(a) (Title VII); 29 U.S.C. § 633(a) (ADEA); 29 U.S.C. § 794a (Rehabilitation Act, incorporating remedies, procedures, and rights set forth in 42 U.S.C. § 2000e-16). See King v. Dalton, 895 F. Supp. at 836 n.7 (plain terms of § 2000e-16 require a plaintiff to be an employee of the defendant agency); Spirides v. Reinhardt, 613 F.2d 826, 829 (D.C. Cir. 1979) (§ 2000e-16 "cover[s] only those individuals in a direct employment relationship with a government employer").

23. A variety of work and work-related activities may be required as a condition of receipt of welfare, food stamps, or other benefits. Under the Personal Responsibility and Work Opportunity Reconciliation Act of 1996, P.L. 104-193, 110 Stat. 2105 (1996), for example, welfare recipients may be required to perform work activities, which are defined to include unsubsidized employment, subsidized private or public sector employment, work experience, on-the-job training, job search and job readiness assistance, community service programs, vocational educational or job skills training, educational activities, or child care services. Section 103 of the Welfare Reform Act, 110 Stat. 2133, amending Part A of Title IV of the Social Security Act, 42 U.S.C. § 601, et seq. See also Section 824 of the Welfare Reform Act, 110 Stat. 2323, amending Section 6 of the Food Stamp Act of 1977, 7 U.S.C. § 2015.

24. The Balanced Budget Act of 1997, P.L. 105-33, 111 Stat. 251 (1997), requires each state that receives a grant from the Secretary of Labor as a "welfare-to-work state" to establish a procedure for handling complaints by participants in work activities who allege certain violations, including gender discrimination. The Act does not preempt application of Title VII, the ADEA, the ADA, or the EPA. See Morton v. Mancari, 417 U.S. 535, 550 (1973). Therefore, welfare recipients who perform work activities and qualify as "employees" are covered under the anti-discrimination statutes enforced by the EEOC.

25. Title VII specifically makes it unlawful to discriminate in admission to or employment in any program established to provide apprenticeship or other training. 42 U.S.C. § 2000e-2(d). The ADA and the ADEA also prohibit discrimination in job training and apprenticeship programs. 42 U.S.C. § 12112(a); 29 C.F.R. § 1625.21.

26. The Commission notes that other federal statutes prohibit discrimination in federally assisted education and training programs. See, e.g., Title VI of the Civil Rights Act of 1964, 42 U.S.C.§ 2000d, et seq.; Title IX of the Education Amendments of 1972, 42 U.S.C. § 1681, et seq., and Section 504 of the Rehabilitation Act of 1973, 29 U.S.C. § 794. Complaints about discrimination in education or other non-employment programs should be referred to the Offices for Civil Rights in the federal agencies that fund such programs.

27. Title VII and the ADA apply to any employer who has fifteen or more employees for each working day in each of twenty or more calendar weeks in the current or preceding calendar year. 42 U.S.C. § 2000e(b). The ADEA applies to any employer who has twenty or more employees for each working day in each of twenty or more calendar weeks in the current or preceding calendar year. 29 U.S.C. § 630(b). Counting issues do not arise in EPA claims because that Act applies to any employer who has more than one employee engaged in commerce or in the production of goods for commerce, unless an exception applies. 29 C.F.R. § 1620.1–1620.7.

28. Cf. 29 C.F.R. § 825.106(d) (1996) (under the Family and Medical Leave Act, employees jointly employed by two employers must be counted by both employers, whether or not they are maintained on both employers' payrolls, in determining employer coverage and employee eligibility).

29. EEOC & Walters v. Metropolitan Educ. Enterprises, 117 S. Ct. 660 (1997). For guidance on how to count employees when determining whether a respondent satisfies the jurisdictional prerequisite for coverage, see Enforcement Guidance on Equal Employment Opportunity Commission & Walters v. Metropolitan Educational Enterprises, 117 S. Ct. 660 (1997), Compliance Manual (BNA) N:2351 (5/2/97).

30. Staffing firms and their clients are subject to the same record preservation requirements as other employers that are covered by the anti-discrimination statutes. They therefore must preserve all personnel records that they have made relating to job assignments or any other aspect of a staffing firm worker's employment for a period of one year from the date of the making of the record or the personnel action involved, whichever occurs later. Personnel records relevant to a discrimination charge or an action brought by the EEOC or the U.S. Attorney General must be preserved until final disposition of the charge or action. 29 C.F.R. § 1602.14, 1627.3(b). The Commission can pursue an enforcement action where the respondent fails to keep records pertaining to all its contingent and non-contingent employees and applicants for employment.

31 Section 701(c) of Title VII defines the term "employment agency" as "any person regularly undertaking with or without compensation to procure employees for an employer or to procure for employees opportunities to work for an employer and includes an agent of such a person." For further guidance, see Policy Guidance: What constitutes an employment agency under Title VII, how should charges against employment agencies be investigated, and what remedies can be obtained for employment agency violations of the Act? Compliance Manual (BNA) N:3935 (9/29/91).

32. The questions and answers in this section assume that the staffing firm is an "employer" of the worker.

33. See EEOC Guidelines on Sexual Harassment, 29 C.F.R. § 1604.11(3) (1996) (an employer is liable for harassment of its employee by a nonemployee if it knew or should have known of the misconduct and failed to take immediate and appropriate corrective action within its control). See also Caldwell v. ServiceMaster Corp. and Norrell Temporary Services, 966 F. Supp. 33 (D.D.C. 1997) (joint employer temporary agency is liable for discrimination against temporary worker by agency's client if agency knew or should have known of the discrimination and failed to take corrective measures within its control); Magnuson v. Peak Technical Servs., 808 F. Supp. 500, 511-14 (E.D. Va. 1992) (where plaintiff was subjected to sexual harassment by her supervisor during a job assignment, three entities could be found liable: staffing firm that paid her salary and benefits, automobile company that contracted for her services, and retail car dealership to which she was assigned; staffing firm and automobile company were held to standard for harassment by nonemployees, under which an entity is liable if it had actual or constructive knowledge of the harassment and failed to take immediate and appropriate corrective action within its control); EEOC v. Sage Realty, 507 F. Supp. 599, 612–613 (S.D.N.Y. 1981) (cleaning contractor and joint employer building management company found jointly liable for sex discrimination against lobby attendant on contractor's payroll where management company required attendant to wear revealing costume that subjected her to harassment by passersby, and where plaintiff was discharged for refusing to continue wearing outfit; court rejected contractor's argument that management company was exclusively liable because it had set the costume requirement; contractor knew of plaintiff's complaints of harassment, and there was no evidence that it was powerless to remedy the situation); cf. Capitol EMI Music Inc., 311 N.L.R.B. No. 103, 143 L.R.R.M. (BNA) 1331 (May 28, 1993) (in joint employer relationships in which one employer supplies employees to the other, National Labor Relations Board holds both joint employers liable for unlawful employee termination or other discriminatory discipline if the non-acting joint employer knew or should have known that the other employer acted against the employee for unlawful reasons and the former has acquiesced in the unlawful action by failing to protest it or to exercise any contractual right it might possess to resist it).

34. Cf. Paroline v. Unisys Corp., 879 F.2d 100, 107 (4th Cir. 1989) (employer is liable where it anticipated or reasonably should have anticipated that plaintiff would be subjected to sexual harassment yet failed to take action reasonably calculated to prevent it; "[a]n employer's knowledge that a male worker has previously harassed female employees other than the plaintiff will often prove highly relevant in deciding whether the employer should have anticipated that the plaintiff too would become a victim of the male employee's harassing conduct"), vacated in part on other grounds, 900 F.2d 27 (4th Cir. 1990).

35. If the federal agency refuses to accept the complaint based on a belief that the staffing firm worker is not its employee, the worker can file an appeal with the Commission's Office of Federal Operations.

36. If the federal agency does not wish to coordinate the investigations, then the EEOC office should proceed independently. If the federal agency refuses to provide documents or testimony requested by the EEOC investigator, the Commission can issue a subpoena to compel production of the evidence.

37. The EPA applies to any employer that has more than one employee engaged in commerce or in the production of goods for commerce, unless a statutory exception applies. 29 U.S.C. § 203(s).

38. See Compliance Manual Section 708.5(3) (BNA) 708:0023. As that subsection explains, in determining whether a wage differential between temporary and permanent employees is based on a factor other than sex, the following issues should be considered: 1) whether the wage differential is applied uniformly to males and females; 2) whether the differential conforms with the nature and duration of the job; and 3) whether the differential conforms with a nondiscriminatory customary practice within the industry and establishment.

39. See 29 C.F.R. § 1620.8 (1996) (two or more employers may be jointly or severally responsible for compliance with EPA requirements applicable to employment of a particular employee). For guidance on elements of an EPA claim, see Compliance Manual Sections 704 and 708 (BNA) 704:001 and 708:001, et seq. Cf., 29 C.F.R. § 791.2 (1996) (regulations issued by Wage and Hour Division, Department of Labor, on Joint Employment Relationship under FLSA) (joint employers are individually and jointly responsible for compliance with FLSA, including overtime requirements).

    The EPA, unlike Title VII, the ADA, and the ADEA, only permits claims by employees against their employers, not against third-party interferers.

40. If the EEOC determines that the client had no involvement or control over the wages paid to the worker, it may decline to pursue relief against the client.

41. For guidance on wage discrimination claims under Title VII, see Compliance Manual Section 633 (BNA) 633:001, et seq. Title VII prohibits wage discrimination on the basis of race, national origin, and religion, as well as sex.

42. However, even where there is joint liability, neither a charging party nor the Commission is obliged to pursue a claim against both entities; nor does one party have a right to bring the other into the proceeding or a right of contribution from the other. See Northwest Airlines Inc. v. Transport Workers Union of America, 451 U.S. 77, 91–95 (1981); EEOC v. Gard Corp. v. Tall Services Inc., 795 F. Supp. 1070, 1071–72 (D. Kan. 1992).

43. Punitive damages are not available against federal, state, and local government agencies.

44. Liquidated damages under the ADEA are punitive in nature. Trans World Airlines v. Thurston, 469 U.S. 111, 125 (1985). Therefore, each respondent individually bears a liquidated damages award under the ADEA.

45. See Hafner v. Brown, 983 F.2d 570, 573 (4th Cir. 1992) (holding under 42 U.S.C. § 1983 that compensatory damages are joint and several but punitive damages are borne by each defendant individually); Erwin v. County of Manitowoc, 872 F.2d 1292, 1296 (7th Cir. 1989) (same); Bosco v. Serhant, 836 F.2d 271, 280–81 (7th Cir. 1987) (tort

principles require joint and several liability for compensatory damages but not punitive damages), cert. denied, 108 S. Ct. 2824 (1988); Hurley v. Atlantic City Police Dept., 933 F. Supp. 396, 420–23 (D.N.J. 1996) (reaching same conclusion in a Title VII case).

46. The respondents are also jointly and severally liable for liquidated damages in EPA claims because such damages are compensatory in nature. Laffey v. Northwest Airlines, 740 F.2d 1071, 1096 (D.C. Cir. 1984), cert. denied, 469 U.S. 1181 (1985); Marshall v. Bruner, 668 F.2d 748, 753 (3d Cir. 1982).

47. Compensatory and punitive damages are available in Title VII and ADA cases, and in retaliation cases under the ADEA and the EPA. The ADEA and EPA damages, which are not subject to statutory caps, are available pursuant to a 1977 amendment to the Fair Labor Standards Act that authorizes both legal and equitable relief for retaliation claims. 29 U.S.C. § 216(b). See Moskowitz v. Trustees of Purdue University, 5 F.3d 279, 283–84 (7th Cir. 1993) (FLSA amendment allows common law damages where plaintiff is retaliated against for exercising his rights under ADEA); Soto v. Adams Elevator Equip. Co., 941 F.2d 543, 551 (7th Cir. 1991) (FLSA amendment authorizes compensatory and punitive damages for retaliation claims under EPA, in addition to lost wages and liquidated damages).

48. 42 U.S.C. § 1981a(c)(2).

49. The financial position of the respondent is a relevant factor in assessing punitive damages. City of Newport v. Fact Concerts Inc., 453 U.S. 47, 270 (1981).

For guidance on the various factors to consider in calculating compensatory and punitive damages, see Enforcement Guidance: Compensatory and Punitive Damages Available under § 102 of the Civil Rights Act of 1991, Compliance Manual (BNA) N:6071 (7/14/92).

50. See EEOC v. Sage Realty, 507 F. Supp. 599, 612–13 (finding two joint employers responsible for harassment of worker and holding them jointly and severally liable for back pay).

EEOC Guidelines on Application of the Americans With Disabilities Act to Contingent Workers

DATE: 12/22/00

1. SUBJECT: EEOC Enforcement Guidance on the Application of the ADA to Contingent Workers Placed by Temporary Agencies and Other Staffing Firms

2. PURPOSE: This enforcement guidance explains how some provisions of Title I of the Americans with Disabilities Act of 1990 apply to staffing firms and their clients.

3. EFFECTIVE DATE: Upon receipt.

4. EXPIRATION DATE: As an exception to EEOC Order 205.001, Appendix B, Attachment 4, § a(5), this Notice will remain in effect until rescinded or superseded.

5. ORIGINATOR: ADA Division, Office of Legal Counsel.

6. INSTRUCTIONS: File after Section 902 of Volume II of the Compliance Manual.

\s\

Ida L. Castro, Chairwoman

Table of Contents

Introduction

Staffing firms provide "opportunities to build a work history, experience different types of jobs, and increase…employment marketability and earning potential through enhancement of work skills."[1] A recent study suggests that employment through the staffing firm industry can provide "[a] critical means for people with disabilities to move from unemployment to competitive permanent employment."[2] Because less than one-third of Americans with severe disabilities are employed,[3] the opportunity to enter the workforce and to move to stable, permanent employment through staffing firms should be fully encouraged and facilitated. There is still uncertainty, however, about how some provisions of Title I of the Americans with Disabilities Act of 1990 (ADA)[4] apply to staffing firms and their clients.[5] For this reason, the U.S. Equal Employment Opportunity Commission (EEOC or the Commission) has determined that further guidance is necessary to promote full access by people with disabilities to this important source of employment.

This guidance addresses unique ADA issues not addressed in the EEOC's 1997 enforcement guidance on the application of the EEO laws to contingent work arrangements (Contingent Workers Guidance).[6] For example, the ADA has requirements regarding disability-related inquiries and medical examinations, reasonable accommodation, and qualification standards that screen out individuals on the basis of disability.[7] The ADA also prohibits an employer from participating in a contractual or other arrangement or relationship that has the effect of subjecting its own qualified applicant or employee with a disability to prohibited discrimination.[8] This guidance should be used in conjunction with the Contingent Workers Guidance, as well as with other EEOC enforcement guidance on specific ADA topics such as reasonable accommodation and disability-related questions and medical examinations.

Basic staffing firm work arrangements involving temporary employment agencies, contract firms, facilities staffing firms, lease-back firms, and welfare-to-work programs are described in the Contingent Workers Guidance.[9] The term "staffing firm" is used in this document to describe generically all of these types of work arrangements, although more specific terms are used where necessary for clarity.

The Contingent Workers Guidance discusses several bases on which a staffing firm, its client, or both may be liable for violations of the federal employment discrimination laws.[10] These bases of liability may be summarized as follows:

A staffing firm or its client that qualifies as an employer of a staffing firm worker[11] may be liable for:

■ its own discrimination against the worker; or
■ discrimination by the other entity if it either:
■ participates in the discrimination; or
■ knew or should have known of the discrimination and failed to take corrective action within its control.[12]

A staffing firm that does not qualify as a worker's employer may still be liable for discrimination if it:

■ interferes with the worker's ADA rights;[13] or
■ qualifies as an employment agency, in that it refers potential employees to employers or provides employers with the names of potential employees.[14]

Finally, a client that does not qualify as a staffing firm worker's employer still may be liable if it interferes with the worker's ADA rights, except if that client is a federal agency.[15]

Disability-Related Inquiries and Medical Examinations

A. In General

Under the ADA, a covered entity, including a staffing firm, may not make disability-related inquiries or require medical examinations before making an offer of employment. A covered entity may do several things before an offer of employment, however, to evaluate whether an applicant is qualified for the job, including asking about an applicant's ability to perform specific job functions; asking about an applicant's non-medical qualifications and skills, such as education, work history, and required certifications and licenses; and asking applicants to describe or demonstrate how they would perform job tasks.

In general, a covered entity may not ask questions on an application or in an interview about whether an applicant will need reasonable accommodation to perform the functions of the job. This is because these questions are likely to elicit information about whether an applicant has a disability. Under certain circumstances, however, a covered entity may ask an applicant whether she or he needs a reasonable accommodation to perform the functions of the job, and if so, what type.[16] These questions are permitted where:

▪ the covered entity reasonably believes that the applicant will need a reasonable accommodation because of an obvious disability;

▪ the covered entity reasonably believes that the applicant will need a reasonable accommodation because of a hidden disability that the applicant has voluntarily disclosed; or

▪ an applicant has voluntarily disclosed that s/he needs a reasonable accommodation to perform the job.[17]

A covered entity may ask disability-related questions or require medical examinations after it has made an offer of employment and before the applicant begins work duties, if it does so for all entering employees in the same job category, regardless of disability.[18]

Disability-related inquiries and medical examinations of employees are permitted only if they are job-related and consistent with business necessity or in other limited circumstances.[19]

B. Offer of Employment

Since an employer has considerable latitude in asking disability-related questions or requiring medical examinations after an offer is made, it is critical to determine what constitutes a job offer in the context of staffing firm arrangements.

1. Does a staffing firm's offer to place an individual on its roster for possible consideration in the future for temporary work assignments with its clients constitute an "offer of employment" under the ADA?

No. None of the factors indicating a relationship of employment[20] between an individual and a staffing firm or staffing firm's client exist when the individual is placed on the roster. Typically, a staffing firm and an individual applying for a temporary work assignment with the staffing firm do not intend to create an employer–employee relationship at this stage. The parties merely agree that: (1) the staffing firm will consider the individual for specific work assignments in the future; and (2) the individual will consider accepting assignments in the future depending on his or her availability and the desirability of the assignment.

Additionally, no job functions or duties are performed until after the staffing firm worker accepts an offer of an assignment with a client. Performance of job functions is implicitly included among the factors that show that a relationship is one of employment. For example, the most critical factor—the staffing firm's and/or client's control over when, where, and how the worker performs work duties—is necessarily absent when no job functions are being performed.

EXAMPLE 1:

CP applies for work with Jobmart, a temporary employment agency. A Jobmart associate interviews CP to find out about his skills, education, experience, and the types of work assignments he would be willing to accept. The associate informs CP that the agency will contact him when an appropriate assignment becomes available. Jobmart has not made CP an offer of employment, and therefore may not make disability-related inquiries or require medical examinations.

2.   What constitutes an offer of employment to a staffing firm worker?

Generally, the offer occurs when a staffing firm worker is given an assignment with a particular client. After a staffing firm offers an individual an actual work assignment with one of its clients and the individual accepts the offer, the factors indicating an employment relationship are present. Once an individual has been given an assignment with a client, the staffing firm typically pays wages, withholds taxes and social security, and provides benefits and workers' compensation coverage to the individual, while the client typically controls when, where, and how the individual performs work duties.[21] Therefore, a staffing firm or client violates the ADA if it asks disability-related questions or requires a medical examination of an individual before an assignment to a particular client is made.[22]

Some staffing firms have contracts with numerous clients to provide similar services on a long-term basis, such as janitorial, security, landscaping, etc. Typically, such firms place their own employees, including supervisors, at the clients' work sites and assume full operational responsibility for providing ongoing services. Under such circumstances, an offer of employment may occur prior to the designation of a particular location where work is to be performed, as long as the workers are guaranteed positions somewhere and specific assignments are made soon after the offer.

EXAMPLE 2:

Clean Sweep is a contract firm that hires workers to perform housekeeping duties at its clients' offices. Clean Sweep assumes full operational responsibility for providing housekeeping services. Because of the high turnover in housekeeping jobs, Clean Sweep knows that each week several positions will become available at its clients' offices, but it often does not know which clients will need workers until a day or two before the assignment is supposed to begin. Clean Sweep tells CP to report to its office on Monday morning at 8 a.m. to be given an assignment. Clean Sweep has made CP an offer of employment.

3. **To what extent may a staffing firm or its client make disability-related inquiries or require medical examinations after an offer of employment has been made?**

    After a staffing firm offers an applicant an actual work assignment with a client and before his or her duties begin, the staffing firm or client may ask any disability-related questions or require any medical examinations it chooses, as long as it does so for all individuals entering the same job category.[23] Of course, the offer of a work assignment may be conditioned on the results of post-offer disability-related questions and medical examinations.

EXAMPLE 3:

After CP is interviewed for laboratory technician positions, Tempsmart offers him an assignment with a federal agency's research laboratory. The federal agency requires that all of its laboratory technicians be tested for Hepatitis B and C before starting work. Since an offer of employment has been made to CP, Tempsmart may, consistent with the ADA, require the tests for Hepatitis B and C. The federal agency also may require the tests, consistent with the Rehabilitation Act.

If, however, a qualified individual is screened out because of a disability, the staffing firm or client must show that the exclusionary criterion is "job-related and consistent with business necessity," and that there was no reasonable accommodation that would have enabled the individual to meet the criterion.[24] In addition, if an offer is withdrawn for reasons related to safety, the employer must show that the individual poses a "direct threat."[25] (For more information about a staffing firm's or client's use of qualification standards, including the results of medical examinations that screen out individuals on the basis of disability, see Question 11).

4. **If a staffing firm or client requires a medical examination, may it revoke an offer of employment if the results of the examination are not received before the assignment begins?**

Yes. Because the ADA allows an employer to obtain medical information only after an offer of employment (as long as it does so for all entering employees in the same job category), where an applicant is unable to provide requested medical information before an assignment begins, the staffing firm or client may revoke the offer.

EXAMPLE 4:

Same facts as example 3. The laboratory technician position that CP is offered is scheduled to begin in three days. If CP is unable to provide the results of tests for Hepatitis B and C before then, the offer may be revoked.

Where possible, staffing firms should notify applicants ahead of time of medical information or examinations needed for certain types of work assignments. This enables applicants to obtain in advance the information needed for specific assignments that may need to be filled on short notice.[26]

EXAMPLE 5:

Same facts as example 3, except that Tempsmart notifies CP at the interview that he will have to be tested for Hepatitis B and C before he begins most laboratory technician assignments. A week later, at 3:00 P.M., when the federal agency requests a laboratory technician who can begin work the next morning, Tempsmart offers the assignment to CP and reminds him that the agency requires him to be tested for Hepatitis B and C. Because of Tempsmart's advance notice, CP has already been tested by his own physician. The physician faxes the results to Tempsmart in time for CP to start the next day.

C. Disability-Related Inquiries and Medical Examinations of Employees

5. **May a staffing firm or client ask disability-related questions or require a medical examination of a staffing firm worker once s/he is employed (i.e., during the work assignment)?**

Yes, if the questions or examinations are job-related and consistent with business necessity.[27] Generally, a disability-related inquiry or medical examination of an employee may be "job-related and consistent with business necessity" when an employer "has a reasonable belief, based on objective evidence, that: (1) an employee's ability to perform essential job functions will be impaired by a medical condition; or (2) an employee will pose a direct threat[28] due to a medical condition."[29] Disability-related inquiries and medical examinations that follow up on a request for reasonable accommodation when the disability or need for accommodation is not known or obvious, as well as certain types of periodic medical examinations and monitoring, also may be job-related and consistent with business necessity. Additionally, such questions or examinations of staffing firm workers while they are on a work assignment are permitted if they are required by another federal law or regulation.[30]

The questions or examinations must not exceed the scope of the specific medical condition and its effect on the staffing firm worker's ability, with or without reasonable accommodation, to perform essential job functions or to work without posing a direct threat.[31] Thus, for example, if a staffing firm worker asks for a reasonable accommodation, and the disability and/or the need for accommodation is not obvious, the staffing firm or its client may ask the worker for reasonable documentation of his/her disability and functional limitations.[32] Like any medical information that an employer has about an applicant or employee, information obtained as the result of lawful disability-related inquiries or medical examinations of an employee must be kept confidential.[33]

Reasonable Accommodation and Undue Hardship

The ADA requires employers to provide reasonable accommodation to the known physical or mental limitations of otherwise qualified individuals with disabilities who are employees or applicants for employment, unless it would impose undue hardship.[34] Undue hardship means significant difficulty or expense and focuses on the resources and circumstances of the particular employer in relation to the cost or difficulty of providing a specific accommodation.[35] The ADA also prohibits employers from denying employment opportunities to qualified applicants or employees with disabilities because of the need to provide a reasonable accommodation.[36]

6. **Which entity—the staffing firm or its client—is obligated to provide a reasonable accommodation for the application process?**

Typically, only the staffing firm is an applicant's prospective employer[37] during the application process because it has not yet identified the client for which the applicant will work. In such cases, only the staffing firm is obligated to provide a reasonable accommodation for the application process.

EXAMPLE 6:

Workfast, a staffing firm, requires all applicants to fill out a job application form. CP, who is substantially limited in her ability to perform manual tasks because of muscular dystrophy, tells a Workfast associate that she will need assistance in filling out the application form. Workfast alone is obligated to provide the accommodation, absent undue hardship.

Where a client sends an applicant to apply for work with it through a staffing firm, the client will usually qualify as a prospective employer and, as such, will be obligated along with the staffing firm to provide reasonable accommodation for the application process.

EXAMPLE 7:

EconoShop sends all applicants for temporary positions to apply through Workfast, a staffing firm. EconoShop and Workfast are both obligated to provide reasonable accommodations for the application process for individuals with disabilities who are applicants for temporary positions with EconoShop.

While a client is generally not required to provide reasonable accommodations for the application process, a client that qualifies as a joint employer of staffing firm workers may still violate the ADA if it continues to obtain workers through a staffing firm although it knows or has reason to know that the firm does not provide reasonable accommodation for the application process. This is because a client that qualifies as a joint employer of staffing firm workers may be liable for a staffing firm's discrimination if the client knows or has reason to know of the discrimination and fails to take corrective action within its control.[38]

EXAMPLE 8:

A federal agency hires graphic artists through Sleek Design, a contract firm. Individuals with disabilities have complained to the federal agency that Sleek Design has denied them reasonable accommodations needed for the application process. Assuming that the federal agency qualifies as the joint employer of staffing firm workers, it will violate the Rehabilitation Act if it continues to obtain workers through Sleek Design.

7. **Where a staffing firm and its client are joint employers of a staffing firm worker with a disability, are both obligated to provide a reasonable accommodation that the worker needs on the job?**

Yes. Because each qualifies as an employer of the staffing firm worker, each is obligated to provide a reasonable accommodation needed on the job, absent undue hardship,[39] if it has notice of the need for the accommodation.

EXAMPLE 9:

Just-jobs, a temporary employment agency, sends CP, who is deaf, to perform maintenance work for XYZ Corp. Both qualify as CP's employer because Just-jobs hires CP and pays his wages, and XYZ supervises and directs CP's work. CP informs Just-jobs that he will need a sign language interpreter for a one-hour safety orientation program that XYZ Corp. requires all employees to attend. Just-jobs lets XYZ know about CP's need for an interpreter. Just-jobs and XYZ are both obligated to provide a reasonable accommodation.

If it is not clear what accommodation should be provided, both entities should engage in an informal interactive process with the worker to clarify what s/he needs and to identify the appropriate reasonable accommodation.[40]

It may be mutually beneficial for the staffing firm and its clients to specify in their contracts with one another which entity will provide reasonable accommodations that are required on the job or how the costs of accommodations will be shared. In this way, the question of which entity will provide an accommodation can be anticipated and resolved before a request is actually received, thereby eliminating unnecessary delay in providing the accommodation. A staffing firm and its clients may, through a contract, allocate responsibility for providing reasonable accommodations in any way they choose. Any contractual arrangement between a staffing firm and a client, however, does not alter their obligations under the ADA.[41]

8. **Can a staffing firm or its client claim undue hardship if a reasonable accommodation cannot be provided quickly enough to enable a staffing firm worker to begin, or to complete, a temporary work assignment in a timely manner?**

Yes. Some temporary jobs become available on short notice and last for only a brief period of time, during which certain tasks must be completed. In such cases, a staffing firm or client can establish undue hardship by showing that the work assignment had to be filled on short notice and that the accommodation could not be provided quickly enough to enable the staffing firm worker to timely begin or complete a temporary work assignment.

EXAMPLE 10:

CP applies with All-temps for craft work. CP wears a prosthesis in place of her missing left hand and is substantially limited in her ability to perform manual tasks. In mid-October, All-temps offers CP a temporary assignment, to begin the next day, as a wood cutter with Masters, a manufacturer of small wooden toys. The assignment is to last for two weeks, during which time Masters needs to complete production of a specified number of toys in anticipation of holiday sales that will begin in November. CP tells All-temps that she can perform the job with a reasonable accommodation—an inexpensive adaptive device that she has used to perform similar work for other employers. Because neither All-temps nor Masters has the device, it must be ordered, and it will take about a week to receive. The accommodation results in an undue hardship for both All-temps and Masters.

EXAMPLE 11:

Same facts as example 10, except that the temporary work assignment does not begin for three weeks. Because there is adequate time for All-temps and Masters to provide the requested reasonable accommodation, neither can show undue hardship.

The fact that a staffing firm and its client have a very short period of time within which to provide an accommodation will not alone constitute undue hardship. For example, it is often possible to quickly provide qualified sign language interpreters for people who are deaf. Resources are also available to provide readers for people who are blind on short notice. Staffing firms and their clients should anticipate these types of requests for reasonable accommodations and plan for how to provide them expeditiously when a request is made. (See Question 7 above.)

9. **Where a staffing firm and its client are both obligated to provide a reasonable accommodation for a staffing firm worker with a disability, how should cost-related undue hardship be assessed?**

Where a staffing firm and its client are both obligated to provide a reasonable accommodation, the following principles apply:

■ Where a reasonable accommodation would involve significant expense[42] for both the staffing firm and the client, even if their resources were combined, both can show undue hardship.

EXAMPLE 12:

CP applies for temporary work with All-temps and is offered an assignment with XYZ Corp. Because of her disability, CP needs adaptive equipment to use XYZ's machines. Neither All-temps nor XYZ Corp. has sufficient resources of its own to purchase the equipment. Moreover, even when All-temps' and XYZ Corp.'s assets are combined, acquisition of the equipment would still result in significant expense. All-temps and XYZ Corp. can show undue hardship.

Where the resources of the staffing firm and the client together are sufficient to provide an accommodation without undue hardship, either entity may still show undue hardship if it can demonstrate that:
▪ its resources alone are insufficient to provide the reasonable accommodation without undue hardship; and
▪ it made good faith, but unsuccessful, efforts to obtain contribution from the other entity.[43]

EXAMPLE 13:

Same facts as example 12, except that the adaptive equipment would not result in significant expense when the resources of the two are combined. All-temps makes good faith efforts to get XYZ to contribute to the cost of the equipment, but XYZ refuses. All-temps can show undue hardship. XYZ Corp. cannot show undue hardship, even if its own resources would have been insufficient to provide the accommodation, because it refused to contribute to the accommodation's cost.

Where a reasonable accommodation would have resulted in significant expense for a staffing firm, and it has made good faith, but unsuccessful, efforts to obtain a contribution to the cost from the client, it has an undue hardship defense. However, it should offer the worker the next available assignment for which s/he is qualified.[44] To avoid future liability for participating in the discriminatory conduct of the client, the staffing firm should inform the client of its obligation to provide reasonable accommodation and it should not assign other workers to that work site until the client agrees to abide by its ADA obligation to provide reasonable accommodation.[45]

Where a reasonable accommodation would have resulted in significant expense for a client and it has made good faith, but unsuccessful, efforts to obtain a contribution to the cost from the staffing firm, the client has an undue hardship defense. To avoid future liability for participating in the discriminatory conduct of the staffing firm, the client should inform the staffing firm of its obligation to provide reasonable accommodation and it should not obtain other workers through the staffing firm until the firm agrees to abide by its ADA obligation to provide reasonable accommodation.[46]

EXAMPLE 14:

X-Perts, a staffing firm, receives a request from its client, Clutter Corp., a manufacturer of household appliances, to fill a position editing its operating manuals. CP, a staffing firm worker who is blind, needs adaptive equipment to perform the editing work on Clutter's computers. The equipment would result in significant expense for either X- Perts or Clutter Corp. alone, but together they can provide the full cost without either one incurring undue hardship. Both X-Perts and Clutter Corp. must contribute to the cost of the adaptive equipment.

If X-Perts refuses to contribute to the cost of the accommodation, it has violated the ADA. Clutter Corp. can show undue hardship, but should inform X-Perts of its commitment to provide reasonable accommodation and should not obtain other workers through X-Perts until X-Perts agrees to abide by its ADA obligation to provide reasonable accommodation.

If Clutter Corp. refuses to contribute, it has violated the ADA. X-Perts can show undue hardship, but should offer the worker the next available assignment for which the worker is qualified. X-Perts also should inform Clutter Corp. of its commitment to provide reasonable accommodation and should not assign other workers to that work site until Clutter Corp. agrees to abide by its ADA obligation to provide reasonable accommodation.

Where an entity's own resources are sufficient to provide an accommodation without undue hardship, it must do so, even if the other entity refuses to contribute to the cost of the accommodation.

EXAMPLE 15:

Same facts as example 14, except that Clutter Corp. can provide the accommodation alone without undue hardship. Clutter Corp. asks X-Perts, the staffing firm, to pay part of the cost of the accommodation, but X-Perts refuses. Clutter Corp. must still provide the accommodation and does not have an undue hardship defense.[47]

A staffing firm or client that refuses to contribute to the cost of a reasonable accommodation may be liable for a failure to provide a reasonable accommodation, even if the other entity provides it.[48]

10. Where a staffing firm and its client are joint employers of a staffing firm worker with a disability, may one entity claim undue hardship where providing the accommodation is solely within the other's control?

Yes, if it can demonstrate that it has made good faith, but unsuccessful, efforts to obtain the other's cooperation in providing the reasonable accommodation.[49]

A staffing firm that asserts undue hardship under these circumstances should offer the worker the next available work assignment for which s/he is qualified, should inform the client of its commitment to provide reasonable accommodation, and should not assign other workers to that work site until the client agrees to abide by its ADA obligation to provide reasonable accommodation.

A client that asserts undue hardship under these circumstances should inform the staffing firm of its commitment to provide reasonable accommodation, and it should not obtain other workers through the staffing firm until the staffing firm agrees to abide by its ADA obligation to provide reasonable accommodation.[50]

EXAMPLE 16:
CP, who has Down Syndrome, has been sent by Goodstaff, a staffing firm, to various clients to work as a kitchen helper performing simple food preparation tasks. CP has no difficulty performing any of the tasks but, because of his disability, he sometimes gets confused about the order in which the tasks are to be done. As a reasonable accommodation, Goodstaff has provided CP with posters picturing the tasks in the proper sequence that have enabled him to perform his job functions correctly. Goodstaff provides CP with posters for a kitchen helper position with Bon Banquet and offers to adjust them to Bon Banquet's business practices, if necessary. Bon Banquet refuses to let CP use the posters, however, and discharges him when he is unable to complete the tasks in the right order. Goodstaff can show undue hardship, but should offer CP the next available position for which CP is qualified. Goodstaff should also inform Bon Banquet of its commitment to provide reasonable accommodation and should not assign other workers to that work site until Bon Banquet agrees to abide by its ADA obligation to provide reasonable accommodation.

Qualification Standards, Employment Tests, and Other Selection Criteria

The ADA prohibits an employer from using a qualification standard, employment test, or other selection criterion that screens out or tends to screen out an individual with a disability or class of individuals with disabilities, unless the standard, test, or criterion, as used by the covered entity, is job-related for the position to which it is being applied and consistent with business necessity.[51] If the standard, test, or criterion is shown to be job-related and consistent with business necessity, an employer still must consider whether there is a reasonable accommodation that will enable an otherwise qualified individual with a disability to satisfy it.[52] With regard to health and safety standards that screen out qualified individuals because of disability, an employer must demonstrate that the requirement, as applied to an individual, satisfies the "direct threat" standard.[53]

11. Is a staffing firm that uses a qualification standard to disqualify a worker because of his/her disability liable for violating the ADA? Is the client also liable?

Where the staffing firm and client are joint employers of staffing firm workers, the following principles apply to the use of qualification standards (including the use of the results of medical examinations):

A staffing firm will be liable for violating the ADA where:

▪ it applies a qualification standard, either directly or at its client's direction, that screens out an individual on the basis of disability and is not job-related and consistent with business necessity; or

▪ it knows or has reason to know that a client is applying a qualification standard that is not job-related and consistent with business necessity to screen out a staffing firm worker on the basis of disability and fails to take corrective action within its control.

A client will be liable for violating the ADA where:

▪ it applies a qualification standard, either directly or through a staffing firm, that screens out an individual on the basis of disability and is not job-related and consistent with business necessity; or

▪ it knows or has reason to know that a staffing firm is applying a qualification standard that is not job-related and consistent with business necessity to screen out a staffing firm worker on the basis of disability and fails to take corrective action within its control.

If the qualification standard is job-related and consistent with business necessity, the staffing firm and client must consider whether there is a reasonable accommodation that will enable a staffing firm worker with a disability to meet the standard.

EXAMPLE 17:
XYZ Corp. hires temporary secretaries through Quality Workers. XYZ tells Quality Workers that it requires all secretaries to have a driver's license. CP applies for secretarial positions with Quality Workers and is offered a position with XYZ. Quality Workers withdraws its offer when it discovers that CP does not have a driver's license because of his disability. XYZ Corp. requires its secretaries to have a driver's license so that they can run errands for XYZ's executives, although it is not an essential function of the job. Having a driver's license, therefore, is not job-related and consistent with business necessity. XYZ and Quality Workers have violated the ADA.

EXAMPLE 18:
Same facts as example 17, except that XYZ does not tell Quality Workers about the driver's license requirement. CP, however, informs Quality Workers that, when he showed up at XYZ's offices, XYZ refused to allow him to perform the secretarial job because he did not have a driver's license. CP further explains that he does not have a driver's license because of his epilepsy. In this situation, Quality Workers must take corrective action within its control in order to avoid liability under the ADA. Quality Workers should offer CP the next available position for which he is qualified, inform XYZ of its ADA obligations, and should not assign other workers to XYZ until it agrees to abide by these obligations.

12. How does the ADA apply to the administration and use of pre-employment tests in contingent work arrangements?

Many staffing firms administer their own pre-employment tests to screen applicants or administer tests at the direction of a client. Under the ADA, a covered entity must provide reasonable accommodations to an individual with a disability to ensure that a test accurately measures what it purports to measure, and not the particular skills (e.g., sensory, manual, or speaking skills) that are affected by the disability, unless these are the skills the test is actually intended to measure.[54] Moreover, where a test does measure the skills affected by an applicant's disability, a covered entity may not use the test results to exclude the individual, unless it can show that the skill is necessary to perform an essential function and that there is either no reasonable accommodation available to enable the individual to perform the function, or any necessary accommodation would result in undue hardship.[55] In other words, use of the test results must be job-related and consistent with business necessity.

In the context of contingent work arrangements, therefore, the following principles apply where the staffing firm and client qualify as joint employers of staffing firm workers with disabilities:

A staffing firm will be liable under the ADA if it:

▪ fails to provide a necessary reasonable accommodation, absent undue hardship, in connection with a pre-employment test that it administers to an individual with a disability either directly or on a client's behalf;

▪ uses the results of a test that it administers directly or on a client's behalf to exclude an individual with a disability, where the use of such results is not job-related and consistent with business necessity; or

▪ knows or has reason to know that a client is administering or using pre-employment tests in a manner that discriminates against staffing firm workers with disabilities on the basis of disability and fails to take corrective action within its control.

A client will be liable under the ADA if it:

▪ fails to provide a necessary reasonable accommodation, absent undue hardship, for an individual with a disability in connection with any test administered by the client directly or by the staffing firm on the client's behalf;

▪ uses the results of any pre-employment test administered by it directly, or by the staffing firm on its behalf, to exclude an individual on the basis of disability, where the use of such results is not job-related and consistent with business necessity; or

▪ knows or has reason to know that a staffing firm is administering or using pre-employment tests in a manner that discriminates against staffing firm workers with disabilities on the basis of disability and fails to take corrective action within its control.

EXAMPLE 19:
Pro-staff, a staffing firm, gives a pre-employment test to all applicants for temporary positions designed to measure their aptitude for performing certain types of jobs. The test is made up of one hundred multiple choice

questions, and an applicant records his or her answers by punching a small hole on the answer sheet next to his or her chosen response. A machine then grades the test. CP, who has quadriplegia that substantially limits his ability to perform manual tasks, requests, as a reasonable accommodation, that he be allowed to give his answers orally to someone who can record them to ensure that each hole is completely punched. Assuming that the accommodation would not result in undue hardship, Pro-staff will violate the ADA by refusing to provide it.

EXAMPLE 20:

Same facts as example 19. CP and other individuals with disabilities inform Items Inc., which qualifies as a joint employer of staffing firm workers, that Pro-staff is refusing to provide reasonable accommodations for the pre-employment test. Because Items Inc. knows or has reason to know that Pro-staff is violating the ADA by failing to provide reasonable accommodations for qualified applicants with disabilities, Items Inc. must inform Pro-staff of its obligation to provide reasonable accommodation and should not obtain other workers through Pro-staff until Pro-staff agrees to abide by this ADA obligation.[56]

EXAMPLE 21:

Stock-up, a grocery store, hires cashiers, stockers, inventory clerks, and maintenance workers through Super-temps, a staffing firm. Stock-up asks Super-temps to administer a math test to applicants for all of Stock-up's positions and instructs Super-temps not to refer anyone for any of the positions who has not passed the test. CP, who has mental retardation that substantially limits his cognitive abilities, is unable to pass the test, even with a reasonable accommodation. The test is not job-related and consistent with business necessity for the stocker or maintenance worker positions. Super-temps and Stock-up, therefore, will violate the ADA if they exclude CP from these positions based on his test results, assuming he can perform the essential functions of the jobs with or without a reasonable accommodation.

Notes

1. Peter David Blanck, The Emerging Role of the Staffing Industry in the Employment of Persons with Disabilities: A Case Report on Manpower Inc. (Iowa City, Iowa), 1998, at 6 [hereinafter Manpower Report].

2. Id.

3. Bureau of the Census, U.S. Department of Commerce, Disabilities Affect One-Fifth of All Americans: Proportion Could Increase in Coming Decades (Census Brief No. 97-5, 1997).

4. 42 U.S.C. § 12101–12117, 12201–12213 (1994) (codified as amended). Pursuant to the Rehabilitation Act Amendments of 1992, the ADA's employment standards apply to all nonaffirmative action employment discrimination claims of individuals with disabilities who are federal employees or applicants for federal employment. Pub. L. No. 102-569 § 503(b), 106 Stat. 4344, 4424 (1992) (codified as amended at 29 U.S.C. § 791(g) (1994)). Accordingly, the analysis in the guidance applies to federal sector complaints of nonaffirmative action employment discrimination arising under section 501 of the Rehabilitation Act of 1973. It also applies to employment discrimination under section 504 of the Rehabilitation Act. 29 U.S.C. § 793(d), 794(d) (1994).

5. See, e.g., People with Disabilities—Temporary Employment Options, President's Committee on Employment of People With Disabilities, at http:// www.pcepd.gov (last visited December 4, 2000). www.pcepd.gov.

6. Enforcement Guidance: Application of EEO Laws to Contingent Workers Placed by Temporary Employment Agencies and Other Staffing Firms, 8 FEP Manual (BNA) 405:7551 (1997) [hereinafter Contingent Workers Guidance]. This enforcement guidance can be found on EEOC's Web site, eeoc.gov.

7. See EEOC Enforcement Guidance on Reasonable Accommodation and Undue Hardship Under the Americans with Disabilities Act, 8 FEP Manual (BNA) 405:7601 (1999) [hereinafter Reasonable Accommodation Guidance]; Enforcement Guidance: Disability-Related Inquiries and Medical Examinations of Employees Under the Americans with Disabilities Act (ADA) of 1990, 8 FEP Manual (BNA) 405:7701 (2000) [hereinafter Disability-Related Inquiries and Medical Examinations of Employees]; Enforcement Guidance: Preemployment Disability-Related Questions and Medical Examinations, 8 FEP Manual (BNA) 405:7191 (1995) [hereinafter Preemployment Questions and Examinations]. These enforcement guidance documents can be found on EEOC's Web site, eeoc.gov.

8. 42 U.S.C. § 12112(b)(2) (1994); 29 C.F.R. § 1630.6 (2000).

9. Contingent Workers Guidance, supra note 6, at 3–4, 8 FEP at 405:7551, 7553.

10. Id. at 7–13 (Q&As 2–3), 8 FEP at 405:7555–59.

11. To determine whether a staffing firm or its client qualifies as the employer of a staffing firm worker, see id. at 7–11 (Q&A 2), 8 FEP at 405:7555–58. A staffing firm worker must qualify as an "applicant" or "employee" within the meaning of federal anti-discrimination statutes of at least one of the entities in order for there to be liability under Title I of the ADA. Id. at 4–7 (Q&A 1), 8 FEP at 405:7554–55. Often, a staffing firm and its client will be joint employers of a staffing firm worker. For information on how to determine whether entities are joint employers, see Section 2: Threshold Issues, [Vol. I] EEOC Compl. Man. (BNA) 605:i (May 12, 2000).

12. Contingent Workers Guidance, supra note 6, at 19–22 (Q&A 8), 8 FEP at 405:7563–64.

13. ADA section 102(a) does not limit its protections to an employer's own employees, but rather protects an "individual" from discrimination. See 42 U.S.C. § 12112(a) (1994); 29 C.F.R. § 1630.4 (2000). Thus, an employer is prohibited from interfering with a person's employment opportunities with another employer, even if s/he is not its employee. Contingent Workers Guidance, supra note 6, at 11–13 (Q&A 3), 8 FEP at 405:7558–59. ADA section 503 also protects "an individual" and is not limited in its applicability to covered entities. See 42 U.S.C. § 12203 (1994); 29 C.F.R. § 1630.12 (2000). In contrast, a federal agency cannot be found liable for discrimination under a "third party interference" theory. Contingent Workers Guidance, supra note 6, at 13–14 (Q&A 4), 8 FEP at 405:7559.

14. The ADA prohibits employment agencies from engaging in all of the same types of discrimination as other covered entities. See 42 U.S.C. § 12111–12112 (1994); 29 C.F.R. § 1630.2(b), 1630.4 (2000). Therefore, the ADA requirements discussed in the following sections apply to staffing firms when they act as employment agencies.

15. See supra note 13.

16. See Pre-employment Questions and Examinations, supra note 7, at 6–7 (section entitled "The Pre-Offer Stage," sixth Q&A), 8 FEP at 405:7193–94.

17. Id.

18. 42 U.S.C. § 12112(d) (1994); 29 C.F.R. § 1630.14 (1998) (emphasis added). Generally, any medical information obtained must be kept confidential. 42 U.S.C. § 12112(d)(3) (1994); 29 C.F.R. § 1630.14(b)(1)–(2) (2000).

19. 42 U.S.C. § 12112(d)(4) (1994); 29 C.F.R. § 1630.14(c) (2000). For a more complete discussion of the circumstances under which employers may make disability-related inquiries or require medical examinations of employees, see Q&A 5 below.

20. For a discussion of the factors indicating an employment relationship, see Contingent Workers Guidance, supra note 6, at 4–7 (Q&A 1), 8 FEP at 405:7554–55.

21. See id. at 7–11 (Q&A 2); 8 FEP at 405:7555–58.

22. The Commission's position is consistent with Congress' reasons for prohibiting disability-related inquiries and medical examinations until after an offer of employment. Congress established this process so that individuals will know whether they have been denied employment because of a medical condition, and thus for the Commission to say otherwise would be to undermine Congressional intent. See S. Rep. No. 101–116, at 39 (1989); H.R. Rep. No. 101-485, pt. 2, at 72–73 (1990); H.R. Rep. No. 101-485, pt. 3, at 42–43 (1990); see also Pre-employment Questions and Examinations, supra note 7, at 1 ("Background"), 8 FEP at 405:7191.

23. A staffing firm may, but is not required to, ask the same disability-related questions or require the same medical examinations each time it sends a particular worker on an assignment in the same job category. Therefore, the staffing firm need only make disability-related inquiries and require medical examinations the first time it offers a worker an assignment in a particular job category. If the staffing firm chooses to administer the same questions or examinations each time it offers a position in a particular job category, however, that policy must be uniformly applied.

24. 42 U.S.C. § 12112(b)(6) (1994); 29 C.F.R. § 1630.10, 1630.14(b)(3) (2000); 29 C.F.R. pt. 1630 app. § 1630.14(b) (2000). Under current regulations applicable to federal sector employers, a federal agency must also demonstrate that there are no criteria available that would screen out fewer individuals with disabilities. 29 C.F.R. § 1614.203(d)(1)(ii) (2000). In March 2000, the Commission issued a Notice of Proposed Rulemaking regarding proposed revisions to 29 C.F.R. § 1614.203 to implement the ADA's nondiscrimination standards for federal sector employers. See 65 Fed. Reg. 11019, 2000 WL 226980 (3/1/00). As of the date of issuance of this Guidance, the Commission is proceeding with the rulemaking process.

25. 29 C.F.R. § 1630.15(b)(2), 1630.2(r) (2000).

26. Of course, for many types of temporary work assignments, a worker's medical condition is inconsequential.

27. 42 U.S.C. § 12112(d)(4) (1994); 29 C.F.R. § 1630.14(c) (2000).

28. "Direct threat" means a significant risk of substantial harm that cannot be eliminated or reduced by reasonable accommodation. 29 C.F.R. § 1630.2(r) (1998). Direct threat determinations must be based on an individualized assessment of the individual's present ability to safely perform the essential functions of the job, considering a reasonable medical judgment relying on the most current medical knowledge and/or best available objective evidence. Id. To determine whether an employee poses a direct threat, the following factors should be considered: (1) the duration of the risk; (2) the nature and severity of the potential harm; (3) the likelihood that potential harm will occur; and, (4) the imminence of the potential harm. Id.

29. The Commission explained this standard in its enforcement guidance, EEOC Enforcement Guidance on the Americans With Disabilities Act and Psychiatric Disabilities at 15, 8 FEP Manual (BNA) 405:7461, 7468–69 (1997) [hereinafter ADA and Psychiatric Disabilities]. This enforcement guidance can be found at EEOC's Web site, eeoc.gov.

30. See 29 C.F.R. § 1630.15(e) (2000) (It may be a defense to a charge of discrimination…that a challenged action is required or necessitated by another Federal law or regulation…).

31. See Disability-Related Inquiries and Medical Examinations of Employees, supra note 7, at 25–26 (Q&A 12), 8 FEP at 405:7714.

32. 29 C.F.R. pt. 1630 app. § 1630.9 (2000); see also Reasonable Accommodation Guidance, supra note 7, at 12–15 (Q&A 6), 8 FEP at 405:7607–08; Disability Related Inquiries and Medical Examinations of Employees, supra note 7, at 20–21 (Q&A 7), 8 FEP at 405:7711.

33. 42 U.S.C. § 12112(d)(3) (1994); 29 C.F.R. § 1630.14(b)(1)–(2) (2000).

34. The Commission has set forth the ADA principles on reasonable accommodation and undue hardship in the Reasonable Accommodation Guidance, supra note 7.

35. Id. at 2–7 (section entitled "General Principles"), 8 FEP at 405:7601–04; see also 42 U.S.C. § 12111(10) (1994); 29 C.F.R. § 1630.2(p) (2000); 29 C.F.R. pt. 1630 app. § 1630.2(p) (2000) (explaining term "undue hardship").

36. 42 U.S.C. § 12112(b)(5)(B) (1994); 29 C.F.R. § 1630.9(b) (2000).

37. A staffing firm is also obligated as an employment agency to provide reasonable accommodation for the application process. See supra note 14 and accompanying text.

38. See infra pp. 2–3 (stating this general principle of liability).

39. Where providing a reasonable accommodation is within the sole control of one entity that fails or refuses to provide it, the other can show undue hardship. See infra Q&A 9.

40. See Reasonable Accommodation Guidance, supra note 7, at 11–12 (Q&A 5), 8 FEP at 405:7606–07, for further information on the informal interactive process. As part of that process, the staffing firm and its client may share medical information about an individual submitted in connection with a request for reasonable accommodation where it is necessary to identify and provide needed accommodations. Generally, any medical information obtained by the staffing firm or client must be kept confidential. 42 U.S.C. § 12112(d)(3) (1994); 29 C.F.R. § 1630.14(b)(1)–(2) (2000). However, the ADA includes an exception for supervisors and managers who need to be told about necessary restrictions on the work or duties of the employee and about necessary reasonable accommodations. 42 U.S.C. § 12112(d)(3) (1994); 29 C.F.R. § 1630.14(b)(1)–(2) (2000). (Staffing firms and clients are subject to the ADA's confidentiality provisions if they qualify as a worker's employer. A staffing firm is subject to such provisions as an employ-

ment agency, as well. Even if a staffing firm or client does not qualify as a worker's employer, it is prohibited from interfering with the worker's exercise or enjoyment of ADA rights. See 42 U.S.C. § 12203(b) (1994); 29 C.F.R. § 1630.12(b) (2000)).

41. The ADA contains a specific provision which says that a covered entity cannot evade its obligations under the law through a contractual or other relationship. See 42 U.S.C. § 12112(b)(2) (1994); 29 C.F.R. § 1630.6 (2000). Thus, both the staffing firm and the client remain responsible under the ADA to ensure that the accommodation is provided. If either the staffing firm or client breaches a contractual obligation to provide a reasonable accommodation, the other entity may have a breach of contract action for the cost of providing the accommodation and for other costs. See 29 C.F.R. pt. 1630 app. § 1630.6 (2000).

42. See 42 U.S.C. § 12111(10) (1994) (defining "undue hardship" as significant difficulty or expense); 29 C.F.R. § 1630.2(p) (2000) (same).

43. Where a staffing firm and a client have both contributed to the cost of a reasonable accommodation, they may specify in a contract which one will keep it. If an entity breaches its contractual obligation, the other may have a breach of contract remedy.

44. See Contingent Workers Guidance, supra note 6, at 19–22 (Q&A 8), 8 FEP at 405:7563–64 (staffing firm is liable if it knew or should have known about a client's discrimination and failed to take prompt corrective measures within its control, such as affording the worker an opportunity to take a different job assignment).

45. Id.

46. Id.

47. If Clutter Corp. has a contract with X-perts according to which X-perts is required to pay all or part of the cost of reasonable accommodations, then Clutter Corp. may have a breach of contract claim against X-perts. See 29 C.F.R. pt. 1630 app. § 1630.6 (2000).

48. In such a situation, the EEOC might pursue injunctive relief against the entity that refuses to contribute to the cost of the accommodation.

49. For example, a staffing firm is not in a position to make structural changes to its client's premises and can establish undue hardship by demonstrating that it has made good faith, but unsuccessful, efforts to get the client to make the changes. See Reasonable Accommodation Guidance, supra note 7, at 60–61 (Q&A 46), 8 FEP at 405:7633–34.

50. See Contingent Workers Guidance, supra note 6, at 19–22 (Q&A 8), 8 FEP at 405:7563–64 (asserting that client may be liable if knows or has reason to know of staffing firm's discrimination and fails to take corrective action within its control).

51. 42 U.S.C. § 12112(b)(6) (1994); 29 C.F.R. § 1630.10 (2000). A qualification standard, employment test, or other selection criterion may be job-related and consistent with business necessity if it is related to a person's ability to perform the essential functions of a position. 29 C.F.R. pt. 1630 app. § 1630.10 (2000); 29 C.F.R. § 1630.15(b), 29 C.F.R. pt. 1630 app. § 1630.15(b) (2000).

52. 29 C.F.R. pt. 1630 app. § 1630.10 (2000). Under current federal sector regulations, a federal agency must also be able to demonstrate that there is no qualification standard available that would screen out fewer individuals with disabilities. 29 C.F.R. § 1614.203(d)(1)(ii) (2000). See supra note 24 (noting ongoing rulemaking process to revise 29 C.F.R. § 1614.203 to incorporate the ADA nondiscrimination standards).

53. See 29 C.F.R. § 1630.2(r) (2000).

54. 29 C.F.R. § 1630.11 (2000); 29 C.F.R. pt. 1630 app. § 1630.11 (2000).

55. Id.

56. See Contingent Workers Guidance, supra note 6, at 19–22 (Q&A 8), 8 FEP at 405:7563-64 (staffing firm is liable if it knew or should have known about a client's discrimination and failed to take prompt corrective measures within its control, such as affording the worker an opportunity to take a different job assignment).

Questions and Answers

Enforcement Guidance: Application of the ADA to Contingent Workers Placed by Temporary Agencies and Other Staffing Firms

Introduction

Why did the EEOC issue this Guidance?

▪ Contingent workers placed by staffing firms, including for example, temporary, contract, and leased workers, represent a growing segment of the labor force. Employment through staffing firms is particularly critical for individuals with disabilities who are seeking to move into the workforce.

▪ In 1997, the Commission issued an enforcement guidance titled, "Application of EEO Laws to Contingent Workers Placed by Temporary Employment Agencies and Other Staffing Firms" ("Contingent Workers Guidance") that dealt generally with the liability of staffing firms and their clients for violations of federal employment discrimination laws.

▪ This guidance addresses unanswered questions in the prior guidance and explains the responsibilities of staffing firms and their clients in complying with requirements unique to the ADA, including for example, reasonable accommodation and rules concerning disability-related questions and medical examinations.

What ADA issues does this Guidance address?

▪ This guidance focuses primarily on the allocation of responsibilities between employers and staffing firms.

▪ The most important issues covered in the guidance are:
 — the circumstances in which staffing firms and their clients may ask disability-related questions or require medical examinations of applicants and employees (Questions 1–5);
 — the extent to which a staffing firm and its clients are required to provide reasonable accommodations for staffing firm workers with disabilities (Questions 6–10); and
 — a staffing firm's and client's liability for using qualification standards and pre-employment tests that discriminate on the basis of disability (Questions 11 and 12).

▪ This guidance does not include a detailed discussion of when an entity is an employer or when a staffing firm and its client are joint employers. These concepts are fully discussed in the Contingent Workers Guidance.

For more information about the issues discussed in the Guidance, please consult the question numbers referenced throughout this document.

To whom does this Guidance apply?

■ The Guidance applies to private and to state and local government employers with fifteen or more employees. Federal sector employers also are covered by the Guidance, as the result of the 1992 amendments to the Rehabilitation Act.

■ The ADA's requirements generally apply to "qualified individuals with disabilities." However, the discussion of disability-related inquiries and medical examinations in the Guidance applies to all applicants and employees, whether they have disabilities or not.

Disability-Related Inquiries and Medical Examinations

The ADA sets forth rules about when covered entities may ask disability-related questions or require medical examinations of applicants and employees. This Guidance deals with these requirements in the unique setting of contingent work arrangements.

What constitutes an offer of employment to a staffing firm worker? (Questions 1 and 2)

■ Generally, the offer occurs when the worker receives an assignment with a specific client. A staffing firm's placement of someone on its roster for future consideration does not constitute an offer of employment because typically there is no employment relationship at that point.

What types of disability-related questions and medical examinations are permitted after an offer of employment has been made to a staffing firm worker? (Questions 3, 5)

■ After an offer has been made, a staffing firm or its client may ask any disability-related questions or require any medical examinations that it chooses, as long as it does so for all applicants for the same job. However, if the staffing firm or client wants to withdraw the offer from an applicant with a disability based on the answers to these questions or the results of medical examinations, it has to show that the applicant either: (1) cannot perform the essential functions of the job, even with a reasonable accommodation; or (2) would pose a direct threat (i.e., a significant risk of substantial harm).

■ During the work assignment, a staffing firm or its client generally may ask a staffing firm worker disability-related questions or require a medical examination only where it has a reasonable belief that a medical condition will make the worker unable to do the job or will result in a direct threat.

What if a job becomes available on very short notice and there isn't time for a staffing firm worker to provide needed medical information? (Question 4)

▪ The offer may be withdrawn. However, a staffing firm should consider telling an applicant what medical information will be needed before a particular assignment is made. That way, the applicant can obtain the needed information and provide it quickly if a particular assignment becomes available on short notice.

Reasonable Accommodation and Undue Hardship

Which entity—the staffing firm or its client—has to provide a reasonable accommodation for the application process? (Question 6)

▪ Typically, only the staffing firm will have to provide reasonable accommodations for the application process, since no particular client has been identified as a prospective employer.

▪ However, when a client sends an applicant to apply for work with it through the staffing firm, both the staffing firm and the client must provide reasonable accommodation for the application process.

▪ Even though a client does not usually have an obligation to provide a reasonable accommodation in the application process, it might still violate the ADA if it is a joint employer of staffing firm workers, and it knows or has reason to know that the staffing firm is not providing reasonable accommodations for the application process but fails to take corrective action within its control.

Where a staffing firm and its client are joint employers of a staffing firm worker with a disability, which one has to provide reasonable accommodations needed on the job? (Question 7)

▪ Both the staffing firm and the client are obligated to provide a reasonable accommodation needed on the job, absent undue hardship, if they have notice of the need for it. The staffing firm and client may wish to set out in their contracts how reasonable accommodations will be provided and who will pay for them.

What happens if a job becomes available on short notice and there is no time for the staffing firm or client to provide a reasonable accommodation? (Question 8)

▪ Some temporary work assignments become available on short notice and last only a brief period of time, during which certain tasks have to be completed. In these circumstances, the staffing firm or its client could establish undue hardship by showing that the job became available on short notice and the accommodation could not be provided quickly enough to enable the staffing firm worker to timely begin or complete a temporary assignment.

What does the Guidance say about how staffing firms and their clients should determine cost-related undue hardship? (Question 9)

▪ Where the resources of the staffing firm and its client together are insufficient to provide an accommodation without significant expense, both have an undue hardship defense.

▪ A staffing firm or client whose resources are insufficient to provide the accommodation also may have an undue hardship defense if it made good faith, but unsuccessful, efforts to have the other entity contribute to the accommodation's cost.

▪ Where a staffing firm and its client are both obligated to provide a reasonable accommodation, the entity that refuses to contribute to the accommodation's cost may be liable for failing to provide the accommodation. If the other entity is able to provide the accommodation without undue hardship, it must do so.

What should a staffing firm or client do if providing the accommodation is solely within the control of the other entity, e.g., where the accommodation requires changes to the client's workplace? (Question 10)

▪ Where a staffing firm and its client are joint employers of a staffing firm worker with a disability, one entity may claim undue hardship where providing the accommodation is solely within the other entity's control if it made good faith, but unsuccessful, efforts to obtain the other's cooperation in providing the reasonable accommodation.

Qualification Standards, Employment Tests, and Other Selection Criteria

What does the Guidance say about the liability of staffing firms and their clients for the use of discriminatory job standards? (Question 11)

▪ Job standards that staffing firms and their clients use that exclude an individual with a disability from employment have to be job-related and consistent with business necessity.

▪ If the qualification standard is not job-related and consistent with business necessity, the staffing firm is liable for violating the ADA if it is applying either its own standard or its client's standard. The client is liable if it requested the staffing firm to use the standard or if it used the standard directly.

■ A staffing firm also may be liable if it knows or has reason to know that a client is using a discriminatory qualification standard and fails to take corrective action within its control. The same is true of a client that knows or has reason to know that a staffing firm is using a discriminatory qualification standard.

■ If the qualification standard is job related and consistent with business necessity, the staffing firm and/or the client must consider whether there is a reasonable accommodation that will enable a staffing firm worker with a disability to meet the standard.

How does the ADA apply to the administration of pre-employment tests in the contingent work setting? (Question 12)

■ A staffing firm and a client must make reasonable accommodations so that individuals with disabilities can take any tests they administer directly or at the other entity's direction.

■ Also, a staffing firm and its client may not use tests results to screen out individuals from employment on the basis of disability, unless use of the test results is job-related and consistent with business necessity.

■ Finally, if the staffing firm or its client knows that the other entity is discriminating with respect to pre-employment testing, then it must take corrective action within its control in order to avoid liability under the ADA.

EEOC Instructions for Completing EEO-1 Report

The EEOC instructions set forth below are for the revised EEO-1 report which must be used beginning with the survey due by September 30, 2007.

The U.S. Equal Employment Opportunity Commission

EEO-1 JOINT REPORTING COMMITTEE
Equal Employment Opportunity Commission
Office of Federal Contract Compliance Programs
O.M.B. No. 3046-0007
Approval Expires 1/2009
EQUAL EMPLOYMENT
OPPORTUNITY COMMISSION
WASHINGTON, D.C. 20507

Equal Employment Opportunity

STANDARD FORM 100, REV. January 2006, EMPLOYER INFOR-
MATION REPORT EEO-1

Instruction Booklet

The Employer Information EEO-1 survey is conducted annually under the authority of Title VII of the Civil Rights Act of 1964, 42 U.S.C. 2000e, et. seq., as amended. All employers with 15 or more employees are covered by Title VII and are required to keep employment records as specified by Commission regulations. Based on the number of employees and federal contract activities, certain large employers are required to file an EEO-1 report on an annual basis.

See the Appendix for the applicable provisions of the law, Section 709(c) of Title VII, and the applicable regulations, Sections 1602.7-1602.14, Chapter XIV, Title 29 of the Code of Federal Regulations. State and local governments, school systems and educational institutions are covered by other employment surveys and are excluded from Standard Form 100, Employer Information Report EEO-1.

In the interests of consistency, uniformity and economy, Standard Form 100 has been jointly developed by the Equal Employment Opportunity Commission and the Office of Federal Contract Compliance Programs of the U. S. Department of Labor, as a single form which meets the statistical needs of both programs. In addition, this form should be a valuable tool for companies to use in evaluating their own internal programs for insuring equal employment opportunity.

As stated above, the filing of Standard Form 100 is required by law; it is not voluntary. Under section 709(c) of Title VII, the Equal Employment Opportunity Commission may compel an employer to file this form by obtaining an order from the United States District Court.

Under Section 209(a) of Executive Order 11246, the penalties for failure by a federal contractor or subcontractor to comply may include termination of the federal government contract and debarment from future federal contracts.

1. Who Must File

Standard Form 100 must be filed by —

(A) All private employers who are: (1) subject to Title VII of the Civil Rights Act of 1964, as amended, with 100 or more employees **EXCLUDING** State and local governments, primary and secondary school systems, institutions of higher education, Indian tribes and tax-exempt private membership clubs other than labor organizations; OR (2) subject to Title VII who have fewer than 100 employees if the company is owned or affiliated with another company, or there is centralized ownership, control or management (such as central control of personnel policies and labor relations) so that the group legally constitutes a single enterprise, and the entire enterprise employs a total of 100 or more employees.

(B) All federal contractors (private employers), who: (1) are not exempt as provided for by 41 CFR 60-1.5; (2) have 50 or more employees; **and** (a) are prime contractors or first-tier subcontractors, and have a contract, subcontract, or purchase order amounting to $50,000 or more; or (b) serve as a depository of government funds in any amount, or (c) is a financial institution which is an issuing and paying agent for U.S. Savings Bonds and Notes.

Only those establishments located in the District of Columbia and the 50 states are required to submit Standard Form 100. No reports should be filed for establishments in Puerto Rico, the Virgin Islands or other American Protectorates.

2. How To File

Note: Submission of EEO-1 data through the EEO-1 Online Filing System or as an electronically transmitted data file is strongly preferred. See paragraph 6, EEO-1 Alternate Reporting Formats.

Single-establishment employers, i.e., employers doing business at only one establishment in one location must complete a single EEO-1 online data record or submit a single EEO-1 paper report.

Multi-establishment employers, i.e., employers doing business at more than one establishment, must complete online: (1) a report covering the principal or headquarters office; (2) a separate report for **each** establishment employing 50 or more persons; and (3) a separate report (Type 8 record) for each establishment employing fewer than 50 employees, OR an Establishment List (Type 6 record), showing the name, address, and total employment for each establishment employing fewer than 50 persons, including a Type 6 employment data grid that combines all employees working at establishments employing fewer than 50 employees by race, sex, and job category. For the EEO-1 online application, keyed employment data automatically transfers to the overall Consolidated Report.

The total number of employees indicated on the headquarters report, **PLUS** the establishment reports, **PLUS** the list of establishments employing fewer than 50 employees, **MUST** equal the total number of employees shown on the Consolidated Report.

Employment data for multi-establishment companies, including parent corporations and their subsidiary holdings, must report all employees working at each company establishment or subsidiary establishment. For the purposes of this report, the term parent corporation refers to any corporation which owns all or the majority stock of another corporation so that the latter relates to it as a subsidiary.

3. When To File

This annual report must be filed not later than September 30. Employment figures from any pay period in July through September may be used.

4. Where To File [Paper EEO-1 form(s) Only]

Mail one copy to the address indicated in the annual survey mailout memorandum.

5. Requests for Information and Special Procedures

An employer who claims that preparation or the filing of Standard Form 100 would create undue hardship may apply to the Commission for a special reporting procedure. In such cases, the employer must submit **in writing** a detailed alternative proposal for compiling and reporting information to: **The EEO-1 Coordinator, EEOC-Survey Division, 1801 L Street, NW, Washington, D.C. 20507.**

Only those special procedures approved **in writing** by the Commission are authorized. Such authorizations remain in effect until notification of cancellation is given. All requests for information should be sent to the address above.

6. EEO-1 Alternate Reporting Formats

EEO-1 reporting is an electronic, online application. Pursuant to the Government Paperwork Elimination Act of 1998, we **strongly** recommend that EEO-1 reports be submitted via the *EEO-1 Online Filing System*, or as an electronically transmitted data file. A copy of the prescribed EEO-1 data file format is available at the Web site address in the survey mailout memorandum; or by calling the telephone number or writing to the address in the survey mailout memorandum. *Paper EEO-1 forms will be generated on request **only**, in extreme cases where Internet access is not available to the employer.* An EEO-1 report submitted on paper must be prepared following the directions in paragraph 2, HOW TO FILE.

7. Confidentiality

All reports and information from individual reports will be kept confidential, as required by Section 709(e) of Title VII. Only data aggregating information by industry or area, in such a way as not to reveal any particular employer's statistics, will be made public. The prohibition against disclosure mandated by Section 709(e) does not apply to the Office of Federal Contract Compliance Programs and contracting agencies of the federal government which require submission of SF 100 pursuant to Executive Order 11246. Reports from prime contractors and subcontractors doing business with the federal government may not be confidential under Executive Order 11246.

8. Estimate of Burden

Public reporting burden for this collection of information is estimated to average three and five tenths (3.5) hours per response, including the time for reviewing instructions, searching existing data sources, gathering and maintaining the data needed and completing and reviewing the collection of information. A response is defined as one survey form. Send comments regarding this burden estimate or any other aspect of this collection of information, including suggestions for reducing this burden to:

> The EEOC Clearance Officer
> Office of the Chief Financial Officer
> and Administrative Services—Room 2100
> 1801 L Street, N.W.
> Washington, D.C. 20507
>   AND
> Paperwork Reduction Project (3046-0007)
> Office of Management and Budget
> Washington, D.C. 20503

The full text of the OMB regulations may be found at 5 CFR Part 1320. **PLEASE DO NOT SEND YOUR COMPLETED REPORT TO EITHER OF THESE ADDRESSES.**

EEO-1 Terms Applicable to All Reporting Formats

Type of Report (Status Code)

1 Single-establishment company
   Multi-establishment company
2 Consolidated Report (Required)
3 Headquarters Report (Required)
4 Establishment Report (50 or more employees)
6 Establishment List (Option 1)
8 Establishment Report (less than 50 employees) (Option 2)

Company Identification

Refers to the company name and address of the headquarters office of the multi-establishment company (Report Types 2 and 3); or the establishment name and address.

Employers Who Are Required To File

Questions 1, 2 and 3 **MUST** be answered by all employers. If the answer to Question C-3 is Yes, please enter the company's Dun and Bradstreet identification number if the company has one. If the answer is Yes to Question 1, 2, or 3, complete the entire form. Otherwise skip to Section G.

Employment Data

Employment data must include **ALL** full-time and part-time employees who were employed during the selected payroll period, except those employees specifically excluded as indicated in the Appendix. Employees must be counted by sex and race or ethnic category for each of the ten occupational categories and subcategories. See Appendix for detailed explanation of job categories and race and ethnic identification.

Every employee must be accounted for in one and **ONLY** one of the categories in Columns A thru N.

Occupational Data—Employment data must be reported by job category. Report each employee in only one job category. In order to simplify and standardize the method of reporting, all jobs are considered as belonging in one of the broad occupations shown in the table. To assist you in determining where to place your jobs within the occupational categories, a description of job categories is in the *EEO-1 Job Classification Guide* or you may consult the EEO-1-Census Codes Cross Walk on the Commission's web site. For further clarification, you may wish to consult the Alphabetical and Classified Indices of Industries and Occupations (2000 Census) published by the U.S. Department of Commerce, Census Bureau.

Establishment Information

The major activity should be sufficiently descriptive to identify the industry and product produced or service provided. If an establishment is engaged in more than one activity, describe the activity at which the **greatest** number of employees work.

The description of the major activity indicated on the Headquarters Report (Type 3) must reflect the dominant economic activity of the company in which the greatest number of employees are engaged.

Remarks

Include in this section any remarks, explanations, or other pertinent information regarding this report.

Certification

If all reports have been completed at headquarters, the authorized official should check Item 1 and sign the Consolidated Report only. If the reports have been completed by the individual establishments, the authorized official should check Item 2 and sign the establishment report.

Appendix

1. Definitions Applicable to All Employers

a. "Commission" refers to the Equal Employment Opportunity Commission.

b. "OFCCP" refers to the Office of Federal Contract Compliance Programs, U.S. Department of Labor, established to implement Executive Order 11246, as amended.

c. "Joint Reporting Committee" is the committee representing the Commission and OFCCP for the purpose of administering this report system.

d. "Employer" under Section 701(b), Title VII of the Civil Rights Act of 1964, as amended, means a person engaged in an industry affecting commerce who has fifteen or more employees for each working day in each of twenty or more calendar weeks in the current or preceding calendar year, and any agent of such a person, but such term does not include the United States, a corporation wholly owned by the government of the United States, an Indian tribe, or any department or agency of the District of Columbia subject by statute to procedures of the competitive service (as defined in section 2102 of Title 5 of the United States Code), or a bona fide private membership club (other than a labor organization) which is exempt from taxation under Section 501(c) of the Internal Revenue Code of 1954; OR any person or entity subject to Executive Order 11246 who is a federal government prime contractor or subcontractor at any tier (including a bank or other establishment serving as a depository of federal government funds, or an issuing and paying agent of U.S. Savings Bonds and Notes, or a holder of a federal government bill of lading) or a federally-assisted construction prime contractor or subcontractor at any tier.

e. "Employee" means any individual on the payroll of an employer who is an employee for purposes of the employer's withholding of Social Security taxes except insurance sales agents who are considered to be employees for such purposes solely because of the provisions of 26 USC 3121(d)(3)(B) (the Internal Revenue Code). Leased employees are included in this definition. Leased Employee means a permanent employee provided by an employment agency for a fee to an outside company for which the employment agency handles all personnel tasks including payroll, staffing, benefit payments and compliance reporting. The employment agency shall, therefore, include leased employees in its EEO-1 report. The term employee SHALL NOT include persons who are hired on a casual basis for a specified time, or for the duration of a specified job (for example, persons at a construction site whose employment relationship is expected to terminate with the end of the employees' work at the site); persons temporarily employed in any industry other than construction, such as temporary office workers, mariners, stevedores, lumber yard workers, etc., who are hired through a hiring hall or other referral arrangement, through an employee contractor or agent, or by some individual hiring arrangement; or persons (**EXCEPT** leased employees) on the payroll of an employment agency who are referred by such agency for work to be performed on the premises of another employer under that employer's direction and control.

It is the opinion of the General Counsel of the Commission that Section 702, Title VII of the Civil Rights Act of 1964, as amended, does not authorize a complete exemption of religious organizations from the coverage of the Act or of the reporting requirements of the Commission. The exemption for religious organizations applies to discrimination on the basis of religion. Therefore, since the Standard Form 100 does not provide for information as to the religion of employees, religious organizations must report all information required by this form.

f. "Commerce" means trade, traffic, commerce, transportation, transmission, or communication among the several States; or between a State and any place outside thereof; or within the District of Columbia, or a possession of the United States; or between points in the same State but through a point outside thereof.

g. "Industry Affecting Commerce" means any activity, business or industry in commerce or in which a labor dispute would hinder or obstruct commerce or the free flow of commerce and includes any activity or industry affecting commerce within the meaning of the Labor Management Reporting and Disclosure Act of 1959. Any employer of 15 or more persons is presumed to be in an industry affecting commerce.

h. "Establishment" is an economic unit which produces goods or services, such as a factory, office, store, or mine. In most instances, the establishment is at a single physical location and is engaged in one, or predominantly one, type of economic activity (definition adapted from the *North American Industry Classification System, 2002*).

Units at different physical locations, even though engaged in the same kind of business operation, must be reported as separate establishments. For locations involving construction, transportation, communications, electric, gas, and sanitary services, oil and gas fields, and similar types of physically dispersed industrial activities, however, it is not necessary to list separately each individual site, project, field, line, etc., unless it is treated by you as a separate legal entity. For these types of activities, list as establishments only those relatively permanent main or branch offices, terminals, stations etc., which are either: (a) directly responsible for supervising such dispersed activities; or (b) the base from which personnel and equipment operate to carry out these activities. (Where these dispersed activities cross State lines, at least one such establishment should be listed for each State involved.)

i. "Major Activity" means the major product or group of products produced or handled, or services rendered by the reporting unit (e.g., manufacturing airplane parts, retail sales of office furniture) in terms of the activity at which the greatest number of all employees work. The description includes the type of product manufactured or sold or the type of service provided.

2. Definitions Applicable Only to Government Contractors Subject to Executive Order 11246

a. "Order" means Executive Order 11246, as amended.

b. "Contract" means any government contract or any federally-assisted construction contract.

c. "Prime Contractor" means any employer having a government contract or any federally-assisted construction contract, or any employer serving as a depository of federal government funds.

d. "Subcontractor" means any employer having a contract with a prime contractor or another subcontractor calling for supplies or services required for the performance of a government contract or federally-assisted construction contract.

e. "Contracting Agency" means any department, agency and establishment in the executive branch of the government, including any wholly-owned government corporation, which enters into contracts.

f. "Administering Agency" means any department, agency and establishment in the executive branch of the government, including any wholly-owned government corporation, which administers a program involving federally-assisted construction contracts.

3. Responsibilities of Prime Contractors

a. At the time of an award of a subcontract subject to these reporting requirements, the prime contractor shall inform the subcontractor of its responsibility to submit annual EEO-1 employment data in accordance with these instructions.

b. If prime contractors are required by their Contracting Officer or subcontractors by their prime contractors, to submit notification of filing, they shall do so by ordinary correspondence. However, such notification is not required by and should not be sent to the Joint Reporting Committee.

4. Race and Ethnic Identification

Self-identification is the preferred method of identifying the race and ethnic information necessary for the EEO-1 report. Employers are required to attempt to allow employees to use self-identification to complete the EEO-1 report. If an employee declines to self-identify, employment records or observer identification may be used.

Where records are maintained, it is recommended that they be kept separately from the employee's basic personnel file or other records available to those responsible for personnel decisions.

Race and ethnic designations as used by the Equal Employment Opportunity Commission do not denote scientific definitions of anthropological origins. Definitions of the race and ethnicity categories are as follows:

Hispanic or Latino—A person of Cuban, Mexican, Puerto Rican, South or Central American, or other Spanish culture or origin, regardless of race.

White (Not Hispanic or Latino)—A person having origins in any of the original peoples of Europe, the Middle East, or North Africa.

Black or African American (Not Hispanic or Latino)—A person having origins in any of the black racial groups of Africa.

Native Hawaiian or Other Pacific Islander (Not Hispanic or Latino)—A person having origins in any of the peoples of Hawaii, Guam, Samoa, or other Pacific Islands.

Asian (Not Hispanic or Latino)—A person having origins in any of the original peoples of the Far East, Southeast Asia, or the Indian Subcontinent, including, for example, Cambodia, China, India, Japan, Korea, Malaysia, Pakistan, the Philippine Islands, Thailand, and Vietnam.

American Indian or Alaska Native (Not Hispanic or Latino)—A person having origins in any of the original peoples of North and South America (including Central America), and who maintain tribal affiliation or community attachment.

Two or More Races (Not Hispanic or Latino)—All persons who identify with more than one of the above five races.

Instructions for assigning employees into the race/ethnic categories:

Hispanic or Latino—Include all employees who answer YES to the question, Are you Hispanic or Latino. Report all Hispanic males in Column A and Hispanic females in Column B.

White (Not Hispanic or Latino)—Include all employees who identify as White males in Column C and as White females in Column I.

Black or African American (Not Hispanic or Latino)—Include all employees who identify as Black males in Column D and as Black females in Column J.

Native Hawaiian or Other Pacific Islander (Not Hispanic or Latino)—Include all employees who identify as Native Hawaiian or Other Pacific Islander males in Column E and as Native Hawaiian or Other Pacific Islander females in Column K.

Asian (Not Hispanic or Latino)—Include all employees who identify as Asian males in Column F and as Asian females in Column L.

American Indian or Alaska Native (Not Hispanic or Latino)—Include all employees who identify as American Indian or Alaska Native males in Column G and as American Indian or Alaska Native females in Column M.

Two or More Races (Not Hispanic or Latino)—Report all male employees who identify with more than one of the above five races in Column H and all female employees who identify with more than one of the above five races in Column N.

As to the method of collecting data, the basic principles for ethnic and racial self-identification for purposes of the EEO-1 report are:

(1) Offer employees the opportunity to self-identify
(2) Provide a statement about the voluntary nature of this inquiry for employees. For example, language such as the following may be used (employers may adapt this language):

"The employer is subject to certain governmental recordkeeping and reporting requirements for the administration of civil rights laws and regulations. In order to comply with these laws, the employer invites employees to voluntarily self-identify their race or ethnicity. Submission of this information is voluntary and refusal to provide it will not subject you to any adverse treatment. The information obtained will be kept confidential and may only be used in accordance with the provisions of applicable laws, executive orders, and regulations, including those that require the information to be summarized and reported to the federal government for civil rights enforcement. When reported, data will not identify any specific individual."

5. Description of Job Categories

The major job categories are listed below, including a brief description of the skills and training required for occupations in that category and examples of the job titles that fit each category. The examples shown below are illustrative and not intended to be exhaustive of all job titles in a job category. These job categories are primarily based on the average skill level, knowledge, and responsibility involved in each occupation within the job category.

The Officials and Managers category as a whole is to be divided into the following two subcategories: Executive/Senior Level Officials and Managers and First/Mid Level Officials and Managers. These subcategories are intended to mirror the employer's own well established hierarchy of management positions. Small employers who may not have two well-defined hierarchical steps of management should report their management employees in the appropriate categories.

Executive/Senior Level Officials and Managers. Individuals who plan, direct and formulate policies, set strategy and provide the overall direction of enterprises/organizations for the development and delivery of products or services, within the parameters approved by boards of directors or other governing bodies. Residing in the highest levels of organizations, these executives plan, direct or coordinate activities with the support of subordinate executives and staff managers. They include, in larger organizations, those individuals within two reporting levels of the CEO, whose responsibilities require frequent interaction with the CEO. Examples of these kinds of managers are: chief executive officers, chief operating officers, chief financial officers, line of business heads, presidents or executive vice presidents of functional areas or operating groups, chief information officers, chief human resources officers, chief marketing officers, chief legal officers, management directors and managing partners.

First/Mid Level Officials and Managers. Individuals who serve as managers, other than those who serve as Executive/Senior Level Officials and Managers, including those who oversee and direct the delivery of products, services or functions at group, regional or divisional levels of organizations. These managers receive directions from the Executive/Senior Level management and typically lead major business units. They implement policies, programs and directives of executive/senior management through subordinate managers and within the parameters set by Executive/Senior Level management. Examples of these kinds of managers are: vice presidents and directors; group, regional or divisional controllers; treasurers; human resources, information systems, marketing, and operations managers. The First/Mid Level Officials and Managers subcategory also includes those who report directly to middle managers. These individuals serve at functional, line of business segment or branch levels and are responsible for directing and executing the day-to-day operational objectives of enterprises/organizations, conveying the directions of higher level officials and managers to subordinate personnel and, in some instances, directly supervising the activities of exempt and non-exempt personnel. Examples of these kinds of managers are: first-line managers, team managers, unit managers, operations and production managers, branch managers, administrative services managers, purchasing and transportation managers, storage and distribution managers, call center or customer service managers, technical support managers, and brand or product managers.

Professionals. Most jobs in this category require bachelor and graduate degrees and/or professional certification. In some instances, comparable experience may establish a person's qualifications. Examples of these kinds of positions include: accountants and auditors, airplane pilots and flight engineers, architects, artists, chemists, computer programmers, designers, dieticians, editors, engineers, lawyers, librarians, mathematical scientists, natural scientists, registered nurses, physical scientists, physicians and surgeons, social scientists, teachers, and surveyors.

Technicians. Jobs in this category include activities that require applied scientific skills, usually obtained by post secondary education of varying lengths, depending on the particular occupation, recognizing that in some instances additional training, certification, or comparable experience is required. Examples of these types of positions include: drafters, emergency medical technicians, chemical technicians, and broadcast and sound engineering technicians.

Sales Workers. These jobs include non-managerial activities that wholly and primarily involve direct sales. Examples of these types of positions include: advertising sales agents; insurance sales agents; real estate brokers and sales agents; wholesale sales representatives; securities, commodities, and financial services sales agents; telemarketers; demonstrators; retail salespersons; counter and rental clerks; and cashiers.

Administrative Support Workers. These jobs involve non-managerial tasks providing administrative and support assistance, primarily in office settings. Examples of these types of positions include: office and administrative support workers; bookkeeping, accounting and auditing clerks; cargo and freight agents; dispatchers; couriers; data entry keyers; computer operators; shipping, receiving and traffic clerks; word processors and typists; proofreaders; desktop publishers; and general office clerks.

Craft Workers (formerly Craft Workers (Skilled)). Most jobs in this category include higher skilled occupations in construction (building trades craft workers and their formal apprentices) and natural resource extraction workers. Examples of these types of positions include: boilermakers; brick and stone masons; carpenters; electricians; painters (both construction and maintenance); glaziers; pipelayers, plumbers, pipefitters and steamfitters; plasterers; roofers; elevator installers; earth drillers; derrick operators; oil and gas rotary drill operators; and blasters and explosive workers. This category also includes occupations related to the installation, maintenance and part replacement of equipment, machines and tools, such as: automotive mechanics, aircraft mechanics, and electric and electronic equipment repairers. This category also includes some production occupations that are distinguished by the high degree of skill and precision required to perform them, based on clearly defined task specifications, such as: millwrights, etchers and engravers, tool and die makers, and pattern makers.

Operatives (formerly Operatives (Semi-skilled)). Most jobs in this category include intermediate skilled occupations and include workers who operate machines or factory-related processing equipment. Most of these occupations do not usually require more than several months of training. Examples include: textile machine workers; laundry and dry cleaning workers; photographic process workers; weaving machine operators; electrical and electronic equipment assemblers; semiconductor processors; testers, graders, and sorters; bakers; and butchers and other meat, poultry, and fish processing workers. This category also includes occupations of generally intermediate skill levels that are concerned with operating and controlling equipment to facilitate the movement of people or materials, such as: bridge and lock tenders; truck, bus, or taxi drivers; industrial truck and tractor (forklift) operators; parking lot attendants; sailors; conveyor operators; and hand packers and packagers.

Laborers and Helpers (formerly Laborers (Unskilled)). Jobs in this category include workers with more limited skills who require only brief training to perform tasks that require little or no independent judgment. Examples include: production and construction worker helpers; vehicle and equipment cleaners; laborers; freight, stock, and material movers; service station attendants; construction laborers; refuse and recyclable materials collectors; septic tank servicers; and sewer pipe cleaners.

Service Workers. Jobs in this category include food service, cleaning service, personal service, and protective service activities. Skill may be acquired through formal training, job-related training or direct experience. Examples of food service positions include: cooks; bartenders; and other food service workers. Examples of personal service positions include: medical assistants and other healthcare support positions, hairdressers, ushers, and transportation attendants. Examples of cleaning service positions include: cleaners, janitors, and porters. Examples of protective service positions include: transit and railroad police and fire fighters, guards, private detectives, and investigators.

6. Legal Basis for Requirements

Section 709(c), Title VII, Civil Rights Act of 1964, as Amended

Recordkeeping; reports

Every employer, employment agency, and labor organization subject to this title shall (1) make and keep such records relevant to the determinations of whether unlawful employment practices have been or are being committed, (2) preserve such records for such periods, and (3) make such reports therefrom as the Commission shall prescribe by regulation or order, after public hearing, as reasonable, necessary, or appropriate for the enforcement of this title or the regulations or orders thereunder. The Commission shall, by regulation, require each employer, labor organization, and joint labor-management committee subject to this title which controls an apprenticeship or other training program to maintain such records as are reasonably necessary to carry out the purposes of this title, including, but not limited to, a list of applicants who wish to participate in such program, including the chronological order in which applications were received, and to furnish to the Commission upon request, a detailed description of the manner in which persons are selected to participate in the apprenticeship or other training program. Any employer, employment agency, labor organization, or joint labor-management committee which believes that the application to it of any regulation or order issued under this section would result in undue hardship may apply to the Commission for an exemption from the application of such regulation or order, and, if such application for an exemption is denied, bring a civil action in the United States District Court for the district where such records are kept. If the Commission or the court, as the case may be, finds that the application of the regulation or order to the employer, employment agency, or labor organization in question would impose an undue hardship, the Commission or the court, as the case may be, may grant appropriate relief. If any person required to comply with the provisions of this subsection fails or refuses to do so, the United States District Court for the district in which such person is found, resides, or transacts business, shall, upon application of the Commission, or the Attorney General in a case involving a government, governmental agency or political subdivision, have jurisdiction to issue to such person an order requiring him to comply.

Title 29, Chapter XIV Code of Federal Regulations

NOTE: A few aspects of the following regulations will need to be revised to conform with the EEO-1 Report to be used beginning with the 2007 reporting period.

Subpart B — Employer Information Report

§1602.7 Requirement for filing of report.

On or before September 30 of each year, every employer that is subject to Title VII of the Civil Rights Act of 1964, as amended, and that has 100 or more employees, shall file with the Commission or its delegate executed copies of Standard Form 100, as revised (otherwise known as "Employer Information Report EEO-1"), in conformity with the directions set forth in the form and accompanying instructions. Notwithstanding the provisions of §1602.14, every such employer shall retain at all times at each reporting unit, or at company or divisional headquarters, a copy of the most recent report filed for each such unit and shall make the same available if requested by an officer, agent, or employee of the Commission under the authority of section 710 of Title VII. Appropriate copies of Standard Form 100 in blank will be supplied to every employer known to the Commission to be subject to the reporting requirements, but it is the responsibility of all such employers to obtain necessary supplies of the form from the Commission or its delegate prior to the filing date.

§1602.8 Penalty for making of willfully false statements on report.

The making of willfully false statements on Report EEO-1 is a violation of the United States Code, Title 18, section 1001, and is punishable by fine or imprisonment as set forth therein.

§1602.9 Commission's remedy for employer's failure to file report.

Any employer failing or refusing to file Report EEO-1 when required to do so may be compelled to file by order of a U.S. District Court, upon application of the Commission.

§1602.10 Employer's exemption from reporting requirements.

If an employer claims that the preparation or filing of the report would create undue hardship, the employer may apply to the Commission for an exemption from the requirements set forth in this part, according to instruction 5. If an employer is engaged in activities for which the reporting unit criteria described in section 5 of the instructions are not readily adaptable, special reporting procedures may be required. If an employer seeks to change the date for filing its Standard Form 100 or seeks to change the period for which data are reported, an alternative reporting date or period may be permitted. In such instances, the employer should so advise the Commission by submitting to the Commission or its delegate a specific written proposal for an alternative reporting system prior to the date on which the report is due.

§1602.11 Additional reporting requirements.

The Commission reserves the right to require reports, other than that designated as the Employer Information Report EEO-1, about the employment practices of individual employers or groups of employers whenever, in its judgment, special or supplemental reports are necessary to accomplish the purposes of Title VII or the Americans with Disabilities Act (ADA). Any system for the requirement of such reports will be established in accordance with the procedures referred to in section 709(c) of Title VII or section 107 of the ADA and as otherwise prescribed by law.

Subpart C—Recordkeeping by Employers

§1602.12 Records to be made or kept.

The Commission has not adopted any requirement, generally applicable to employers, that records be made or kept. It reserves the right to impose record-keeping requirements upon individual employers or groups of employers subject to its jurisdiction whenever, in its judgment, such records (a) are necessary for the effective operation of the EEO-1 reporting system or of any special or supplemental reporting system as described above; or (b) are further required to accomplish the purposes of Title VII or the ADA. Such recordkeeping requirements will be adopted in accordance with the procedures referred to in section 709(c) of Title VII, or section 107 of the ADA, and otherwise prescribed by law.

§1602.13 Records as to racial or ethnic identity of employees.

Employers may acquire the information necessary for completion of items 5 and 6 of Report EEO-1 either by visual surveys of the work force, or at their option, by the maintenance of post-employment records as to the identity of employees where the same is permitted by State law. In the latter case, however, the Commission recommends the maintenance of a permanent record as to the racial or ethnic identity of an individual for purpose of completing the report form only where the employer keeps such records separately from the employees' basic personnel form or other records available to those responsible for personnel decisions, e.g., as part of an automatic data processing system in the payroll department.

§1602.14 Preservation of records made or kept.

Any personnel or employment record made or kept by an employer (including but not necessarily limited to requests for reasonable accommodation, application forms submitted by applicants and other records having to do with hiring, promotion, demotion, transfer, lay-off or termination, rates of pay or other terms of compensation, and selection for training or apprenticeship) shall be preserved by the employer for a period of one year from the date of the making of the record or the personnel action involved, whichever occurs later. In the case of involuntary termination of an employee, the personnel records of the individual terminated shall be kept for a period of one year from the date of termination. Where a charge of discrimination has been filed, or an action brought by the Commission or the Attorney General, against an employer under Title VII or the ADA, the respondent employer shall preserve all personnel records relevant to the charge or action until final disposition of the charge or the action. The term personnel records relevant to the charge, for example, would include personnel or employment records relating to the aggrieved person and to all other employees holding positions similar to that held or sought by the aggrieved person and application forms or test papers completed by an unsuccessful applicant and by all other candidates for the same position as that for which the aggrieved person applied and was rejected. The date of final disposition of the charge or the action means the date of expiration of the statutory period within which the aggrieved person may bring an action in a U.S. District Court or, where an action is brought against an employer either by the aggrieved person, the Commission, or by the Attorney General, the date on which such litigation is terminated.

Occupational Safety and Health Administration Record-Keeping Rules

Table of Contents

Excerpt from Department of Labor regulations relating to occupational injury and illness recording and reporting requirements (66 Fed. Reg. 6131, Jan. 19, 2001)

Section 1904.31 Covered employees.

(a) Basic requirement.

You must record on the OSHA 300 Log the recordable injuries and illnesses of all employees on your payroll, whether they are labor, executive, hourly, salary, part-time, seasonal, or migrant workers. You also must record the recordable injuries and illnesses that occur to employees who are not on your payroll if you supervise these employees on a day-to-day basis. If your business is organized as a sole proprietorship or partnership, the owner or partners are not considered employees for recordkeeping purposes.

(b) Implementation.

1. **If a self-employed person is injured or becomes ill while doing work at my business, do I need to record the injury or illness? No, self-employed individuals are not covered by the OSH Act or this regulation.**

2. **If I obtain employees from a temporary help service, employee leasing service, or personnel supply service, do I have to record an injury or illness**

occurring to one of those employees? You must record these injuries and ill-nesses if you supervise these employees on a day-to-day basis.

3. **If an employee in my establishment is a contractor's employee, must I record an injury or illness occurring to that employee?** If the contractor's employee is under the day-to-day supervision of the contractor, the con-tractor is responsible for recording the injury or illness. If you supervise the contractor employee's work on a day-to-day basis, you must record the injury or illness.

4. **Must the personnel supply service, temporary help service, employee leasing service, or contractor also record the injuries or illnesses occur-ring to temporary, leased or contract employees that I supervise on a day-to-day basis?** No, you and the temporary help service, employee leas-ing service, personnel supply service, or contractor should coordinate your efforts to make sure that each injury and illness is recorded only once: either on your OSHA 300 Log (if you provide day-to-day supervision) or on the other employer's OSHA 300 Log (if that company provides day-to-day supervision).

OSHA Recordkeeping Instruction— Frequently Asked Questions

U.S. Department of Labor
Occupational Safety and Health Administration

DIRECTIVE NUMBER: CPL 2-0.131
EFFECTIVE DATE: January 1, 2002
SUBJECT: Recordkeeping Policies and Procedures Manual (RKM)
PURPOSE: This instruction gives enforcement information on OSHA's new recordkeeping regulations
SCOPE: OSHA-wide

Executive Summary

This instruction is the Recordkeeping Policies and Procedures Manual (RKM) for the new recordkeeping rule that was published in the *Federal Reg-ister* on January 19, 2001. This manual is divided into five chapters:

Chapter 1—Background;
Chapter 2—Enforcement Policies and Procedures;
Chapter 3—Standard Alleged Violation Elements (SAVEs);

Chapter 4—Comparison of Old and New Rule;
Chapter 5—Frequently Asked Questions.

Chapter 5–Frequently Asked Questions

Paragraph X—Section 1904.31: Covered Employees

Question 31-1. How is the term "supervised" in section 1904.31 defined for the purpose of determining whether the host employer must record the work-related injuries and illnesses of employees obtained from a temporary help service?

The host employer must record the recordable injuries and illnesses of employees not on its payroll if it supervises them on a day-to-day basis. Day-to-day supervision occurs when "in addition to specifying the output, product or result to be accomplished by the person's work, the employer supervises the details, means, methods, and processes by which the work is to be accomplished."

Question 31-2. If a temporary personnel agency sends its employees to work in an establishment that is not required to keep OSHA records, does the agency have to record the recordable injuries and illnesses of these employees?

A temporary personnel agency need not record injuries and illnesses of those employees that are supervised on a day-to-day basis by another employer. The temporary personnel agency must record the recordable injuries and illnesses of those employees it supervises on a day-to-day basis, even if these employees perform work for an employer who is not covered by the recordkeeping rule.

Paragraph XI—Section 1904.32: Annual Summary

Question 32-1. How do I calculate the "total hours worked" on my annual summary when I have both hourly and temporary workers?

To calculate the total hours worked by all employees, include the hours worked by salaried, hourly, part-time and seasonal workers, as well as hours worked by other workers you supervise (e.g., workers supplied by a temporary help service). Do not include vacation, sick leave, holidays, or any other nonwork time even if employees were paid for it. If your establishment keeps records of only the hours paid or if you have employees who are not paid by the hour, you must estimate the hours that the employees actually worked.

Employers' Responsibilities Toward Temporary Employees

OSHA Standard Interpretations—Hazard Communication Standard
U.S. Department of Labor
Occupational Safety and Health Administration
February 3, 1994
Mr. Michael F. Moreau
National Employment Service Corporation
95 Albany Street Suite 3
Portsmouth, New Hampshire 03801

Dear Mr. Moreau:

This is in response to your inquiry of May 3, concerning the Occupational Safety and Health Administration's Hazard Communication Standard (HCS), 29 CFR 1910.1200.

Your question concerns clarification on employers' responsibilities towards temporary employees, particularly in regard to the HCS. Your questions will be answered in the order that you presented them:

1. Who is responsible for hazard communication training of the temporary employee. The [temp] agency or the client employer?

OSHA considers temporary employment agencies who send their own employees to work at other facilities to be employers whose employees may be exposed to hazards. Since it is your company, which maintains a continuing relationship with its employees, but another employer (the client) who creates and controls the hazards, there is a shared responsibility for assuring that your employees are protected from the workplace hazards. The client has the primary responsibility of such protection. The "lessor employer" likewise has a responsibility under the Occupational Safety and Health Act.

In meeting the requirements of OSHA's Hazard Communication standard the lessor employer would, for example, be expected to provide the training and information requirements specified by the HCS section (h)(1). Client employers would then be responsible for providing site-specific training and would have the primary responsibility to control potential exposure conditions. The client, of course, may specify what qualifications are required for supplied personnel, including training in specific chemicals or personal protective equipment (PPE). Contracts with your client employer and your employees should clearly describe the responsibilities of both parties in order to ensure that all requirements of the regulation are met.

2. **Who is responsible for the provision and assured use of appropriate personal protective equipment by the temporary employees?**

Client employers would be responsible for providing PPE for site-specific hazards to which employees may be exposed. However, again, the client may specify the services that it wants the lessor employer to supply, including provision of PPE for the placed employees. Contracts with the client employer should clearly describe the responsibilities of both parties in order to ensure that all requirements of OSHA's regulations are met.

3. **When medical surveillance or monitoring is indicated, who is responsible for conducting the monitoring and maintaining records?**

The client employer must offer and perform the required medical surveillance or evaluations. The lessor employer must ensure that the records of the required medical surveillance or evaluations are maintained in accordance with the appropriate OSHA standards.

4. **Is the temporary help service required to maintain cumulative exposure data (e.g., 30 day lead exposure, 6 months noise exposure, etc.) when the employee works for several different companies during the year?**

Yes, the temporary help service must maintain employee records in accordance with the appropriate OSHA standard (e.g. the Lead standard, the Occupational Noise Exposure standard, etc.). However, the client employer must perform the site characterization and monitoring of exposure to hazardous chemicals on the work site.

5. **If 29 CFR 1910.1200(h) requires training on hazardous chemicals in the work area at the time of the initial assignment and whenever a new hazard was introduced into their work place, when does the initial assignment begin and who is responsible for the initial training and the ongoing training?**

The lessor employer would be expected to provide some generic training and client employers would be responsible for providing site-specific training, or training to update employees on new hazards in the workplace. Please see the answer to question 1 for a further explanation.

6. **How does hazard communication training tie into the SIC code 7363?**

The current HCS final rule covers all Standard Industrial Classification (SIC) codes. In 1987 the Office of Management and Budget (OMB) prevented OSHA from enforcing HCS in the construction industry. On OMB's advice, OSHA published a statement of concurrence in the Federal Register on August 8, 1988 (Volume 53, page 29822). However, on August 19, 1988, the U.S. Court of Appeals for the Third Circuit invalidated OMB's actions as being outside OMB's authority under the Paperwork Reduction Act (see United

Steelworkers of America v. Pendergrass, 855 F.2d 108 (3rd Cir. 1988), Ex. 4-190). As ordered by the Court, OSHA published a notice in the Federal Register on February 15, 1989 (Volume 54, page 6886) to inform affected employers and employees that all provisions of the HCS would be in effect in all industries, and set March 17, 1989, as the date for initiation of programmed compliance inspections.

We hope this information is helpful. If you have any further questions please contact the Office of Health Compliance Assistance at (202) 219-8036.

Sincerely,

\s\

Roger A. Clark, Director
Directorate of Compliance Programs
National Employment Service Corporation
5 Albany Street, Suite 3
Portsmouth, New Hampshire 03801

May 3, 1993
OSHA
Attn: Roger Clark
Director of Compliance Programs
Room N3468
200 Constitution Ave. N.W.
Washington D.C. 22102

Subject: Temporary Help Supply Service

Dear Roger,

I am writing to you as requested by Tom Galassi of your office. I own a temporary service which provided industrial temporary employees to perform various tasks in different plants. There are several questions that I wish you could clarify for me.

1. Who is responsible for hazard communication training of the temporary employee. The agency or the client employer? 2. Who is responsible for the provision and assured use of appropriate personal protection equipment by the temporary employees? 3. When medical surveillance or monitoring is indicated, who is responsible for conducting the monitoring and maintaining records? 4. Is the temporary help service required to maintain cumulative exposure data (e.g., 30 day lead exposure, 6 months noise exposure, etc.) when the employee

works for several different companies during the year? 5. If 29 CFR 1910.1200(h) requires training on hazardous chemicals in the work area at the time of the initial assignment and whenever a new hazard was introduced into their work place. When does the initial assignment begin and who is responsible for the initial training and the ongoing training? 6. How does hazard communication training tie into the SIC Code 7363?

Your clarification of these questions would be appreciated.

Yours Truly,

\s\

Michael F. Moreau

President

OSHA Field Inspection Reference Manual
OSHA Instruction CPL 2.103

Sep. 26, 1994

Office of General Industry Compliance Assistance

Section 7—Chapter III: Inspection Documentation

C. Violations.

1. Basis of Violations.

a. Standards and Regulations.

Section 5(a)(2) of the Occupational Safety and Health Act states that each employer has a responsibility to comply with the occupational safety and health standards promulgated under the Act. The specific standards and regulations are found in Title 29 Code of Federal Regulations (CFR) 1900 series. Subparts A and B of 29 CFR 1910 specifically establish the source of all the standards which are the basis of violations.

NOTE: The most specific subdivision of the standard shall be used for citing violations.

(1) Definition and Application of Universal Standards (Horizontal) and Specific Industry Standards (Vertical).

Specific Industry standards are those standards which apply to a particular industry or to particular operations, practices, conditions, processes, means, methods, equipment or installations. Universal standards are those standards which apply when a condition is not covered by a specific industry standard. Within both universal and specific industry standards there are general standards and specific standards.

(a) When a hazard in a particular industry is covered by both a specific industry (e.g., 29 CFR Part 1915) standard and a universal (e.g., 29 CFR Part 1910) standard, the specific industry standard shall take precedence. **This is true even if the universal standard is more stringent.**

(b) When determining whether a universal or a specific industry standard is applicable to a work situation, the CSHO shall focus attention on the activity in which the employer is engaged at the establishment being inspected rather than the nature of the employer's general business.

(2) Variances.

The employer's requirement to comply with a standard may be modified through granting of a variance, as outlined in Section 6 of the Act.

(a) An employer will not be subject to citation if the observed condition is in compliance with either the variance or the standard.

(b) In the event that the employer is not in compliance with the requirements of the variance, a violation of the standard shall be cited with a reference in the citation to the variance provision that has not been met.

b. Employee Exposure.

(1) Definition of Employee.

Whether or not exposed persons are employees of an employer depends on several factors, the most important of which is who controls the manner in which the employees perform their assigned work. The question of who pays these employees may not be the determining factor. Determining the employer of an exposed person may be a very complex question, in which case the Area Director may seek the advice of the Regional Solicitor.

(2) Proximity to the Hazard.

The proximity of the workers to the point of danger of the operation shall be documented.

(3) Observed Exposure.

Employee exposure is established if the CSHO witnesses, observes, or monitors exposure of an employee to the hazardous or suspected hazardous condition during work or work-related activities. Where a standard requires engineering or administrative controls (including work practice controls), employee exposure shall be cited regardless of the use of personal protective equipment.

(4) Unobserved Exposure.

Where employee exposure is not observed, witnessed, or monitored by the CSHO, employee exposure is established if it is determined through witness statements or other evidence that exposure to a hazardous condition has occurred, continues to occur, or could recur.

(a) In fatality/catastrophe (or other "accident") investigations, employee exposure is established if the CSHO determines, through written statements or other evidence, that exposure to a hazardous condition occurred at the time of the accident.

(b) In other circumstances, based on the CSHO's professional judgment and determination, exposure to hazardous conditions has occurred in the past, and such exposure may serve as the basis for a violation when employee exposure has occurred in the previous six months.

(5) Potential Exposure.

A citation may be issued when the possibility exists that an employee could be exposed to a hazardous condition because of work patterns, past circumstances, or anticipated work requirements, and it is reasonably predictable that employee exposure could occur, such as:

(a) The hazardous condition is an integral part of an employer's recurring operations, but the employer has not established a policy or program to ensure that exposure to the hazardous condition will not recur; or

(b) The employer has not taken steps to prevent access to unsafe machinery or equipment which employees may have reason to use.

Case Index